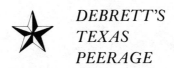

*DEBRETT'S
TEXAS
PEERAGE*

DEBRETT'S TEXAS PEERAGE

HUGH BEST

COWARD-McCANN, INC.
NEW YORK

PICTURE CREDITS

Acknowledgment is made to these photographers and friends for permission to include the following photographs:

Peter A. Silva: H.R.H. The Prince of Wales photograph. Reprinted by permission of Peter A. Silva. Copyright © 1976 by Peter A. Silva.

Mr. and Mrs. Hugo Neuhaus. Reprinted by permission of Mr. and Mrs. Hugo V. Neuhaus. Copyright © 1983 by Mr. and Mrs. Hugo V. Neuhaus.

The King Ranch photographs are reprinted by permission of King Ranch, Inc., from the Toni Frissell collection and by the Library of Congress' division of Photographic Collections.

The Hockaday Graduates photograph is reprinted by permission from the collections of the Dallas Historical Society.

Mrs. Lloyd H. Smith: Wiess family photographs. Reprinted by permission of Mrs. Lloyd H. Smith. Copyright © 1983 by Mrs. Lloyd H. Smith.

Ogden Robertson: Betty Ewing and Larry Hagman photograph. Reprinted by permission of Ogden Robertson. Copyright © 1983 by Hickey & Robertson.

Mr. Hugh Best: Minerva King Patch. Reprinted by permission of Mr. Hugh Best. Copyright © 1983 by Hugh Best.

The Lady Bird Johnson photographs are reprinted by permission of the LBJ Library. Copyright © 1983 by The LBJ Library.

Vogue: Electra Waggoner II (Mrs. John Biggs) photographed by Edward Steichen. Reprinted courtesy *Vogue.* Copyright © 1933 (renewed 1961) by The Condé Nast Publications, Inc.

Mrs. Kenneth Dave Owen: Sarah Campbell Blaffer photographs. Reprinted by permission of Mrs. Kenneth Dave Owen. Copyright © 1983 by Ms. Jane Blaffer Owen.

Robert Phillips: Margaret Tobin, Lawrence Woods photograph. Reprinted by permission of Robert Phillips, *Town & Country* magazine. Copyright © 1980 by Robert Phillips.

The photograph of Prince Carl of Braunfels is reprinted by permission of the Archives Division, Sophienburg Memorial Association, Inc., New Braunfels, Texas. Copyright © 1983 by the Sophienburg Memorial Association, Inc.

Electra Waggoner Biggs: The Biggs family photographs are reprinted by permission of Electra Waggoner Biggs. Copyright © 1983 by Electra Waggoner Biggs.

The Welder Memorial photograph is reprinted by permission of Mrs. Patrick H. Welder. Copyright © 1983 by Mrs. Patrick H. Welder.

Mr. George Tuley: Tobin and Ann Armstrong photograph. Reprinted by permission of George Tuley. Copyright © 1983 by George Tuley.

The Neiman-Marcus photographs are reprinted by permission of H. Keith Nix. Copyright © 1983 by Neiman-Marcus.

The Kleberg family photographs are reprinted by permission of Mrs. Belton K. Johnson. Copyright © 1983 by Mrs. Belton K. Johnson.

Charles Wrightsman's Meadowbrook Team, 1940, is reprinted by permission of Ms. Carolyn Naumer. Copyright © 1983 by the Retama Polo Center.

The photograph of Caroline Schoellkopf is reprinted by permission of Jeanette Korab. Copyright © 1983 by Jeanette Korab.

The photographs of the Yturria and Kleberg generations are reprinted by permission of Mr. Frank D. Yturria. Copyright © 1983 by Frank D. Yturria.

The photographs of Bayou Bend and of Miss Ima Hogg as a young woman are reprinted by permission of The Bayou Bend Collection. Copyright ©1983 by The Museum of Fine Arts, Houston.

LIBRARY OF CONGRESS CATALOGING IN PUBLICATION DATA

Best, Hugh.
Debrett's Texas peerage.
Includes index.
1. Texas—Biography. 2. Texas—Genealogy. I. Title.
II. Title: Texas peerage.
F385.B46 1983   976.4'009'92 [B]   83-2012
ISBN 0-698-11244-X

Designed by Helen Barrow
Printed in the United States of America

This book is dedicated
to my noble wife, Barbara Thornburgh Best,
and to our poodle without peer, Ms. Cici.

ACKNOWLEDGMENTS

This book would not have been possible without the generous help and hospitality of a network of friends, old and new. My special thanks to Jean and Lon Hill, Billie and Bill Carl, Patsy and B. K. Johnson, Madeleine Sandefur, Caroline Naumer, Mel Klein, Jane Owen, John Duncan, Isabel Wilson, Mary Sue and Henry Clay Koontz, Caroline Law, Elizabeth Smith, Gil Denman, Nancy Holmes, Mary Carter, Electra Biggs, Frank Zachary, Pete Kriendler, Spencer Samuels, Diane Lane, Stuart Hunt, Peggy Riddle, Jan Roberts, Jane and John Justin, Katie Welder, Electra Winston, Ed Harte, Betty Pillson, Jacques de Spoelberch, Robert Phillips, Clyde Newhouse.

Judith Skillings, Mrs. Albert Martin, Jr., Martha Hyder, Larry Sheerin, Titi von Furstenburg, Marshall Steves, Betty Ewing, Beverly Brannan, Wallace Litwin, Don Altmaier, Griffith Carnes, Bobo Parker, Frank Yturria, Tom Lea, Cecilia Steinfeldt, Ron Webb, Maury Maverick, Caroline Schoellkopf, Betty Moorman, Frank Miner, Hugo Neuhaus, Annette Strauss, Bobby Shelton, Brink Brinkman, James Boren, Mel Weingart, Margaret Outlaw Allen, Lauren Childress, Philip Scott, Margaret Fields, Martha Utterback, the staff of Houston's Inn on the Park, Helenita Groves, Walter Mathis and, especially, Ann Houston, the best typist in the world.

Contents

Foreword

DEBRETT'S HAS BEEN principally occupied for the last 214 years in producing *Debrett's Peerage and Baronetage,* a directory of the titled patricians of the United Kingdom, including in more recent years achievers ennobled for life only. The current edition, published in 1980, weighs 6.45 pounds and is more than 3 inches thick.

To those whose names are included within the listings the *Peerage* is known as "the Book." These not only number the actual Peers of the Realm and the all-hereditary category of Baronets, but embrace through the pedigrees of those so listed a vaster number of untitled issue, among whom upon elder sons without courtesy title, or all sons and daughters from certain high ranks of title, is conferred the right to use the prefix of "The Honorable" (as in "The Hon. John Smith"), which Nancy Mitford novel readers will immediately recognize as "the hons" of her childhood reminiscences.

"The Book," as such, can usually yield to a brief search for its location somewhere in the hall of their households, probably because the impending arrival there of unsuspecting guests can be furtively preceded by a search for them in its pages, especially when a daughter of the house is ripening into womanhood, for worries about the thickening of ancient lines can sometimes extend beyond such frets as the intrusion of unblue blood scaring the thoroughbred horses in their stables. In the most elevated households the absence of *Debrett's Peerage* from the hall can often be corrected with a discreet word in the ear of the butler, who will scurry off to his pantry and return briskly, laden with the heaving red-and-gold tome. There it tends to be stored with such other useful tools of his trade as the first-aid kit, the wine cellar inventory, the silver polish, a shoehorn, railway timetables, old used string, the spare scissors, *Debrett's Etiquette*, *Debrett's Correct Form*, and a clothesbrush. Top butlers tend to know their way around the pages as knowledgeably as the celebrity on the BBC's *Desert Island Discs* talk show, who chose the *Peerage* as the book of her selection if marooned on a desert island with only a single book to read.

Direct observation and the study of sales figures, however, suggest that most copies of our *Peerage* reside on the bookshelves of those not listed in it at all. There the inquisitive eye will spot it handsomely flanked by others of the more useful or decorative reference works and directories. No doubt, like them, it comes in handy now and again. After all, *Peerage* people tend to spread themselves around the world like moss from molting stones, which means they may never be far from shedding their coats to the care of the butler in one's hall. Partly for this reason, arrangements have been in effect for a number of years in this country to see to it that copies may be obtainable on application to Gale Research Company of Detroit.

In recent years Debrett has branched out from directories into publishing many series of books for the leisured, well-off and fashionable reader.

It was through this expansion of our publishing program that there emerged the idea of a sympathetic and progressive classification, both informal and formal, in various forms of books-to-be; of real American patricianhood and of its life-styles, particularly as little that has been comprehensively systematic seems to have been done to do justice to the fascinatingly varied social topography of the American aristocracy, its ecosystem and its behavioral peculiarities and occasional eccentricities. What Charles Darwin did in the last century when he set sail from Britain to classify and analyze the exotic fauna and flora of the hemisphere, Debrett became determined to finish before the onset of the next century in an all-weather range of roundups on the glittering star system of America's social leadership.

In order to be well guided we began to winkle out gifted American writers as Debrett trailblazers and moles. Hugh Best, here with *Debrett's Texas Peerage*, is the first to report back to the intelligence center in the Britannia Road headquarters of Debrett's. We did not ask for any clotted assemblage of unleavened fact, such as is so often assumed of social research in these mini-computered times. Instead we asked him to distill a digestible body of fact sufficient to enspirit the reader with insights into the flair, style, élan and special graces of the galaxies and constellations of Texan society leadership and its background in the history of the state.

Our American guides have been unanimous in reminding us (encouraged particularly by the welcome around the world for our other books), that this approach to society chronicling in the United States should be the correct Debrett path.

The sage advice of our American associates, The Putnam Publishing Group—around in America for relatively as long as Debrett's in Britain, with allowance for the special circumstances of American conditions—was to agree that full directories of the scope and detail of *Debrett's Peerage and Baronetage* would be too ambitious an overnight undertaking either for the whole country as one book or even region by region as a series. For a start, it is the old wisdom of the publishing trade that directories are subject to a rule of Rome in that they grow over the years, usually from edition to edition. The British *Peerage*, for instance, began in 1769 and it is a full-time operation merely updating it for our editions published about every five years. Secondly, our new genre of books, we have been told, shows how social histories and surveys of present-day patricianhood can act as the entertainment they should be. So, *Texas Peerage* in its inaugural edition is primarily intended as a jolly good read. Thanks to Hugh Best's antebellum style of bourbon and branch water talk, no doubt some of it also gleaned from gilded cracker barrels, the distinguished and vivid scene of Texas has come alive for us. In a secondary sense we intended that the book also begin to serve as a reference point on Texan peerage past and present, and on gentry of old stock descending from first Texas families. To that extent we already include around 3,000 names.

The approach in 1986 of the 150th anniversary of Texan Independence may well find us closer to a revised and more voluminous edition. We are happy to note that long before that glad event dawns we already include a virtual who was who of the Lone Star Republic (1836–1845) and its immediate origins, attaching to these luminaries of the Heroic age of Texas many descendant families of the twentieth century. This was a proposal suggested by writer Christopher Norwood, a descendant both of Marquis James, celebrated biographer of Sam Houston, and of James B. Woods, a signer of the Texas Declaration of Independence. For 1986 we would hope to list as much more genealogy as is possible. The nature of the growth of directories is a two-way flow of data between the publisher and the directory's universe. With this first edition, Debrett's is now at last in orbit over Texas and invites transmissions.

Whereas genealogy is the special nature of gentry, it is not necessarily always that of peerage people, as Hugh Best points out. For instance, it is not generally known that very little of Britain's ennobled version of peerage has titles going back before the beginnings of the Texan Revolution. It is, in fact, overwhelmingly "post-Texas" in that sense. Since the 1960s, most titles have been conferred for life and are uninheritable. There is nothing so very eccentric about this. The nature of aristocracy is to include the fellowship of leadership, because that's what it is principally with us to provide. Heredity and wealth are both factors acting to retain leadership through successive generations, particularly on the social scene. But without hereditary titles, the quality of aristocracy fluctuates in proportion either to loss of wealth or of social prominence, or in combination. In America, aristocracy's history has been more volatile in its ups and downs for those aspiring to the rarefied air around the sharp peaks of its social scale, and for those children and grandchildren seeking to cling, often precariously, to the motion of its shifts.

Hugh Best's technique in searching out peerage in Texas was to start with the idea of it as a star system, in which case why in Texas talk of "peerage"? The word suggested itself quite naturally. The hard meaning of peer is equal. It derives from pair, although Britain has invested its meaning with a gripping literal sway consolidated by the usage "Peers of the Realm" to denote those ennobled by the Monarchy. Elsewhere, from both the hard and special meaning, there has arisen a middle meaning equal to the task of describing a fellowship in aristocratic status. For Hugh Best researching who was peerage by American standards, Texas became a matter of consulting the keenest observers of Texas, in order to pick out who talk to each other as the Texas peer group.

Debrett's senior genealogist, Hugh Peskett, meantime was working on the period of the Lone Star Republic and before, using the criteria of heroism and notability to isolate the peerage of what that much loved historian of Texas, William Ransom Hogan, romantically called a "powder-stained, buck-skinned republic," in order to make a start in tracing today's Texas gentry as defined in the classic sense of distinguished historical pedigree. The parallel in Britain is the Baronetage, and also other landed gentry of ancient stock, whose lineages include some of the most ancient of British pedigrees. In fact, some British gentry combine a veritable broth of blue blood from the remote past, including even royal ancestry. Where a certain degree of wealth has been retained, they are content with a minor if stable degree of notability with no particular anxiety to lunge for the stars. They feel assured that the peerage is there to be mixed with freely when gentry is willing to make the effort and to push matters without going too far, this being easier for them than for most of us due to generations of breeding as gentlemen and the assurance and confidence instilled by that, even when in the most distressed circumstances. In the case of Texas, fate saw that much of the Republic's peerage were blasted out of their wealth during Reconstruction, whereas much of today's great wealth and power in Texas derives from the natural riches exploited after Reconstruction and during this century. Nonetheless, genealogy is as strong an interest in Texas, if not stronger, than in all parts of the world where gentry is established.

That leaves us with the question non-Texans will ask. Why should Debrett's start its American Society series of books with the Lone Star State? Perhaps part of the answer lies in the peculiarity of Debrett's that so many of us are Scots. Scotland shares something in common with

Texas in that it emerged as an independent country and joined a union of its own free will. Indeed, Texas has never been conquered. Even at the end of the War Between the States, Texas was still holding off the armies and fleets of the North. Another part of the answer lies in the romance so much of the world has for Texas and for Texans. And, logically, if one were to start with a peerage in one region of the United States, it would be natural to begin with its most independent and individualistic-minded people, a peerage people par excellence in an era when bureaucratization and suburbanization has so blunted the will to enjoy life. Beyond all that, and perhaps most important of all, we sensed quickly that Debrett's had stumbled on what may become the center of grace in world civilization by the beginning of the twenty-first century. The hard fact is that Texas has invested so much of its wealth in education. Among the sources behind such financing has been both oil riches and retention of ownership by Texas of its public lands, the only state to do so. If it is agreed that the standard of history has been to measure civilization by the gentility that learning bestows, then Texas may have ensured for itself a position in the future where more Texans will rise to peerage heights through the opportunities of education than almost anywhere else on the planet. Such a prospective vision of Texans at the beginning of the third millennium A.D. as the inheritors-to-be of the mantle of the Sumerians in Mesopotamia, who before the end of the third millennium B.C. from their then unrivaled learning invented much of what would prove useful to civilization until at least Renaissance times, may at first sight appear suspect as encouraging more Texas tall talk. Yet as a British lady visitor to the Lone Star Republic almost 150 years ago put it, imagination in Texas has been much assisted by "the bump of invention." Without it how can Prometheus unbind? And not to worry he may get burnt. As Hugh Best found, between the sexes, peerage Texans gently chide each other out of any accumulated belief in tall talk about themselves by asking as antidote, "But who *is* you, honey?" The astral charm of Texan eyes is knowing how to twinkle.

—MARTIN STANSFELD
Debrett's Peerage

Author's Note

Texas Peerage peers into the very private world of Texas noble families. A privileged few. People who have pioneered. And, produced. Creating a state that's almost a kingdom unto itself. The state of Texas.

It's big, this TEXAS. Larger than the country that spawned it—Spain.

If *Texas Peerage* based its content on wealthy families of Texas, this book would be encyclopedic. *Town & Country* magazine tried such a list and found it so long they had to limit it to families with fortunes over $30 million. At the top was the Hunt family of Dallas. Their combined wealth exceeded $8 *billion.*

Sometimes it takes a ruthless granddaddy robber baron, who makes it big and marries blueblood, to produce a dynasty of winners. Aristocrats. Born with natural administrative genius, iron will and the right gut-instinct. People who use privilege to enhance their communities and country. And sometimes, it just "runs in the family."

Mellons, Rockefellers . . . Astors, Vanderbilts . . . Cabots, Lodges . . . Houghtons, Harrimans—those families the world has heard about; we're proud to present Texas Peerage.

—HUGH BEST

Introduction

DEBRETT'S *Texas Peerage* does not pretend to cover all the luminaries in that big, big sky of Texas. Only those that shine the brightest. And some that twinkle-twinkle. For generations, Debrett's Peerage in England has been the acknowledged source for up-to-date information on the noble families of Europe. In the effete East, the *Social Register* keeps tab on Knickerbocker Nabobs, Boston Brahmins, First Families of Virginia and Perennial Philadelphians. However, on the international scene, the oil sheiks, couturiers, thoroughbred breeders and chemical czars could care less. They want to know who's who in TEXAS. That's where the action is. Where it's still possible to make millions. Texas isn't just a state, it's a fusion of America: Southern manners, Northern get-up-and-git, Eastern savvy.

They are not all necessarily monied. Some, like Mrs. Turner Williamson of Houston, and Miss Ela Hockaday of Dallas, had very modest incomes. In the twenties, Mrs. Williamson, socially prominent but widowed early, invested her small inheritance in fine English antiques. First she went to London's Victoria and Albert Museum and learned everything she could about sources for very best English antique furniture and porcelain. She returned with her treasures and opened The Shabby Shop. It was anything but shabby. Thanks to Mrs. Williamson, Houston mansions today preen with priceless Chippendale, Coalport and Adams.

Miss Hockaday made her mark as head of the most exclusive girls' school in the whole Southwest. Started in 1913, Miss Hockaday's School turned out "finished" young ladies with such polish and panache that they were rivaled only by Mrs. Turner's Hepplewhite heirlooms, which, by the way, Miss Hockaday collected, too. An invitation to Miss Hockaday's beautifully appointed private "cottage" was considered top-ticket in Dallas society.

Houston's touted hostess-with-the-mostest, Joanne Herring, claims that in Texas everything depends on what you are, rather than who you are. A lot depends, too, on where you are. In San Antonio, for instance, society clings closely to old established families. Dallas also keeps tight guard, seldom allowing newcomers into its inner circle. Mrs. Herring's Houston, on the other hand, is more Southern in its attitude. The elegant Mrs. Ted Law claims, "If you have something to offer, come with the right introductions and pass muster, there's a place for you in Houston. One reason why it's the fastest growing city in the United States."

When this writer was asked by Debrett's to pinpoint families or personalities who could be considered the nobles of Texas, it seemed like a David & Goliath project. King Ranch, I had heard, wouldn't let any writer inside its gates. Only Tom Lea and Charles Murphy for *Fortune* had been given their blessing. "It's like getting into China before they lifted the curtain," they said.

Fortunately, I have a few old friends who are Old Texas aristocrats, and I have relied on their suggestions for this book. "You must visit Jane Blaffer Owen," those who knew insisted. "She's a complete original. She's very religious, dramatic and delightful . . . has the happiest spirit afloat . . . you'll find her an angel, one gowned by Madame Grés and wearing a Garbo hat."

They were absolutely right. When she and her friend, designer Herbert Wells, pulled up in his new Mercedes 450SL to take us to Palm Sunday services at Christ Cathedral, the first thing we saw was the hat swooping almost the width of the windshield. "Mr. John always makes them for me," she laughs. "I've named this one for Howard Hughes' mega-plane, *Spruce Goose*. When the wind hits it—crash!"

It took quite a bit of doing to line up interviews for this book. You see, the nobles of Texas are nomadic. They jet from place to place, seemingly daily. When I called to set dates for interviews, I found that the Lloyd Smiths were at their place in Southampton. The Lawrence Woods in Acapulco. Patsy and B.K. Johnson were on an African safari with their children. Hugo Neuhaus wouldn't be back from Switzerland for weeks. Mr. and Mrs. Arthur Seeligson were in Paris with fellow Fellows of the Smithsonian Institution, and their glamorous daughter, Ramona, in California "on horse business." Isabel Wilson had gone with a group from Bayou Bend on a special trip to Winterthur. Will Farish was at his horse farm in Kentucky. Electra Biggs, in China. John Duncan, John Justin and Bobby Shelton were on a mission for their Cowboy Artists of America Museum project in Kerrville. Frank Yturria, playing polo in Palm Springs. Stuart Hunt was visiting his daughter who had married an Argentine. Margaret and Jim Elkins were in Europe. Gilbert Denman was working on a legal case in Austin. Helenita Kleberg Groves at her farm in Virginia. The Welders were in Palm Beach . . . and so it went. Then, miracle of miracles, the late Miss Ima Hogg came to the rescue. Everybody loved their "Aunt" Ima and wouldn't think of not attending the big benefit at Bayou Bend in honor of her 100th birthday. For that, the whole group flew home straight as swallows to Capistrano.

They didn't mind a bit talking about their dearly loved departed friends and relatives, but were absolutely mum about themselves. They would tell you choice tidbits such as "Well, you see, he married his roommate's mother. And, when she died, he married his roommate's wife. Then a widow, of course."

Everybody wanted me to check facts with Betty Ewing. "She's been keeping tab on us for her column in the *Houston Chronicle*, and she's a sketch," they said. "To keep her piano fingers nimble, instead of practicing at home, she moonlights, playing cocktail piano on Monday nights at the Rivoli Restaurant. Since she doesn't drive, her boss sends a chauffeur to pick her up and bring her home. Perhaps you can talk with her between gigs. It's where-to-be on Monday night."

Naturally, for someone who doesn't live in Texas, you assume that the Kings of King Ranch would be the place to start a book on Texas peerage. Start with the King. You soon find out that there are no Kings on King Ranch anymore. Richard King, direct descendant of the ranch founder, doesn't ranch, he runs the Corpus Christi National Bank. Friends refer to him as Richard The Third, though, actually, he is Richard V. Direct descendant and namesake of Captain Richard King, Dick King got such razzing at Princeton being The Fifth, that he had his name legally changed.

"Family" is very important in Texas. Texans are so proud of their progenitors that they keep naming their children after them. Helen Kleberg's daughter is Helenita and her daughter, Helencita.

Lon Carrington Hill III, whose granddaddy founded Harlingen, Texas, christened his son Lon IV. Granddad Hill named his town for Harlingen, Holland. But the natives didn't know that. They thought it was for his favorite booze, Holland gin.

"Of course, you'll want to cover, besides the Kings, the heirs of Sam Houston and Stephen Austin," it was suggested by those effete Easterners who didn't know.

What about Sam Houston?

After all, isn't he considered the "George Washington of Texas"? Of all Texas historic figures, Houston still looms the giant. And giant of a man he was. Literally. Some say he was six feet six. When he walked into a room, everyone knew it. No emperor ever had a more commanding presence. Yet there was nothing overbearing about General Houston.

He was a free spirit. Houston married an Indian woman while he was still legally hitched. In his mid-thirties, he took a teenage bride back in Nashville, Tennessee. Sam didn't pay much attention to such details in that stage of his life. He had always done it his way, and devil take the hindmost.

In his teens, he had run away from a refined Virginia family background to live with the Cherokee Indians. They adopted him and named him "The Raven."

Nothing seemed to stop Sam Houston. Even though he had only the equivalent of one-year's formal schooling, he left the Cherokees to teach school. His readin' and writin' were tolerable, but his 'rithmetic was deplorable. He made up for his deficiency by entertaining his rural scholars with tales of the wild frontier and soldiering.

Sam was a natural soldier. By the time he was twenty, he had become a hero in the Creek Indian War, showing such qualities of leadership that he became a protégé of the great General Andrew Jackson. After he had been severely wounded in the Battle of Horseshoe Bend, the General furloughed him to Nashville, Jackson's hometown, and appointed him subagent for the Cherokees. Houston, as part of the tribe, dressed in breechcloth and blanket when he took a delegation to Washington and called on the Secretary of War, John Calhoun. The prim and proper Calhoun was shocked.

In Tennessee, Houston also had a brief fling as a lawyer, an actor in Nashville's Dramatic Club, and was the state's adjutant general, with the rank of colonel—all before he was twenty-five. His fellow field officers elected him a major general at the age of twenty-eight. Within six years he had been elected governor of Tennessee, thanks to the firm backing of his old chief, Andrew Jackson. He was so popular at that time there was even talk of his running for president once Jackson had retired from office. But there was a hitch. The electorate liked a married president and Houston was still a bachelor. A thirty-four-year-old bachelor. A ladies' man, he was. He just hadn't met the right girl. That happened, however, during his second term as Tennessee's governor. Thirty-six, and a rising star in politics, he was considered the catch of the nation. And a beautiful blue-eyed, blond teenager caught him. But not for long. Their marriage lasted all of three months. No one ever knew what happened between them. Their breakup caused such a scandal that Houston was burned in effigy. His public turned against him. He resigned as governor, and went into self-imposed exile—back to his true friends, the Cherokees, now on a reservation in Arkansas.

Almost at once he fell in love with, and married, Tiana, daughter of Chief Ole-loo-te-ka, himself a descendant of a British soldier of the

American Revolution. Houston built her a log mansion and they lived in high style as upper-upper Cherokees. However, he was bitten by wanderlust within a year, and roamed off seeking new challenges.

His friend Andrew Jackson sent him to San Antonio to help make peace with the constantly attacking Comanches. Once in Texas, Houston never left. After his job with the Comanches had been successfully completed, he announced he was settling in Nacogdoches. The people there had urged him to stay and help protect them from menacing hordes of Mexicans, now on the warpath with their upstart province with all the foreigners settling there. Houston organized Texan forces to declare independence from Mexico. He won it, too, at San Jacinto, 25 miles east of present-day Houston. There, in an 18-minute battle, General Sam and his forces captured 730 and killed 630 Mexicans. He lost nine of his men, and 34 were wounded. Once again, Houston was a national hero.

The people of Texas made their hero of Independence their first president. The world had a new Republic, and Houston was head of it. He had dreams of stretching his Texas across Northern Mexico and up the Pacific Coast as far as Oregon. He had been governor, general, president, why not emperor? But Texas needed the United States, and in 1845, joined them—as the Lone Star State. Houston served it as a senator, and a violent opponent of secession. He felt the United States should stay united.

He became united, himself. In matrimony. In his first term as the Republic of Texas' first president, Houston married a twenty-year-old Alabama beauty, Margaret Lea. He was forty-seven. He dissolved his Indian marriage; had a private divorce from his Nashville wife. This third marriage was successful, and they lived happily ever after, until his death twenty-five years later. Their last granddaughter died at the age of one hundred and six, in 1977.

And what about the grandchildren of Stephen Austin? Alas, the "father of Texas" was a bachelor.

 # *PART ONE*

"If Texas hadn't joined the Union, we'd all be titled, anyway . . ."

> HER SERENE HIGHNESS
> **PRINCESS CECIL AMELIA VON FURSTENBERG**
> *of Monte Carlo, Paris, Salzburg and New York*
> (née Titi Blaffer of Houston)

Texas'
First First Families

María Curbelo and Descendants

T ODAY, descendants of Texas' first Spanish families hold their heads very high in the Texas social structure. None more so than the offspring of María de Jesús Curbelo (1813–1894).

Of all the San Antonio settlers who came over from the Canary Islands in 1731, the Curbelo clan is the one best remembered. Climb down María Curbelo's family tree and you'll find surprise after surprise on its branches. Here, the first lady ambassador to the Court of St. James's, Anne Legendre Armstrong. There, All-American athlete-sports commentator Kyle Rote. Names of San Antonio's elite inner circle abound—Tobin, Steves, Sheerin, Ray, Mathis.

Over the centuries, Maria's progeny has produced 16 San Antonio mayors, or alcaldes; 11 Queens and four Kings of Fiesta, San Antonio's version of Mardi Gras.

Until María Curbelo married John William Smith in 1830, the proud Canary Island colonists had never intermarried. They had been exiled to the Canaries for political reasons from Spain and came to San Antonio on a king's grant to escape. The king of Spain offered "families of pure Spanish blood, and high moral character" passage and a peerage to pull up stakes and settle in their new land. In addition to paying for their passage, the king granted each settler the honor of hidalgo, a title to be held by him and his heirs in perpetuity. Such a title automatically removed them from the nonaristocratic working class and put them in charge of all they surveyed.

Franciscan friars insisted that their colonists be married for they wanted a world of pure Spaniards, not any of that mixed blood stuff. But María broke away from that closed aristocratic Old World circle and mixed blood with abandon. After she became Mrs. Smith, the petite Spanish beauty gave birth to six daughters. All of them lived. And all of them "married well." Little mama saw to that. Each one married the crème of the Texas crop at that time—cattle baron, doctor, lawyer, banker, shipper, planter. Episcopalians all. And not a Latin among them.

Walk through the Gothic-towered Victorian villa of her great-great-grandson, Walter Mathis, on San Antonio's historic King William Street, and you get a collage of Curbelo-heirs' life-styles, generation after generation.

"They lived in great style," Mr. Mathis tells you. "They had their grand yachts on the Gulf and sailed away to New Orleans just to go shopping, with their valets and maids along to pick up the packages." He points to a room of French antiques. "That was bought during Napoleon's reign and furnished my great aunt's townhouse in Bayport.

"Those French-looking Belter chairs are all signed. They, too, came up from New Orleans."

A bachelor, Walter Mathis has been bequeathed family treasures, and they are all dramatically displayed in his private Texas version of London's Victoria and Albert Museum. Room after room, from basement to third floor, the marvelous mix that makes up Texas aristocracy is reflected in his furnishings and paintings.

Here are household treasures of Spanish dons; entablos and icons; Texas Shaker-simple cabinets, tables and chairs crafted by German cabinetmakers in Texas Hill Country; French furbelows imported from

New Orleans; Irish Waterford; Bohemian glass; a Bechstein player piano that automatically plays Bach, accompanied by a nearby mechanized string quartet. Here are family circus toys dating from 1850, chandeliers dripping from 15-foot ceilings; giant beds from giant ranches; a china service from a family yacht—all left behind by pioneers who whittled out their own elite in an environment so forbidding that the Spanish charted it on maps as "no man's land." Surviving are the Texas patricians . . . people of great strength . . . producers . . . yet provincial, proud, insular—and so publicity shy they are almost recluses to the outside world.

Some, however, move-and-shake so much that they just naturally emerge from their shell onto the world stage.

Dowagers like Margaret Batt Tobin.

Mrs. Tobin is doyenne of San Antonio society. Handsome, gently regal, she is an exquisite duchess in her eighties. Her name on lists as patron, chairman or sponsor is a must. If she's back of it, you can bet it's the thing to do. Age doesn't deter her from serving as board chairman of her late husband's Edgar A. Tobin Aerial Surveys. "Mag" Tobin is also one of America's most powerful patrons of the arts, from the Santa Fe Opera to the Spoleto Festival. She's president of San Antonio's museum of modern art, McNay Art Institute, and a board member of the Metropolitan Opera. She and her son, bachelor Robert L. B. Tobin, own, side by side, two of the last private residences on New York's Park Avenue. Her mansion walls in San Antonio glow with Impressionist masterpieces, including a pond-size Monet painting of water lilies. Her checks have kept many a cultural, medical and social institution alive and thriving.

Another nob on the Curbelo branch is Marshall Steves, Sr. A distinguished San Antonian, he and his wife, Patsy, carry on a family tradition of service to San Antonio started by his grandfather Albert Steves, Sr., over a century ago. Albert Steves was a major mover in preserving the city's past, evidenced by his collections and contributions that started the San Antonio Museum Association. A statue of Albert Steves, Sr., stands by the Witte Museum, which owes its existence to Steves' foresight and generosity.

Steves money came from lumber. The first Steves to come to America was Edward, a member of the German woodsmen colony who

*Patron of the arts Margaret Batt Tobin, grande dame of San Antonio,
with her pond-size painting, Monet's "Water Lilies." Her late husband,
Edgar Tobin, was a direct descendant of María Curbelo. (Photographed
for* Town & Country, *1980, by Robert Philips)*

had settled amongst the tall timber in Texas Hill Country before the
Civil War. After his sons Albert, Edward and Ernst were born, Edward
Steves moved his family to San Antonio to be near schools. Here he
started the Steves Lumber Yard, and the Steves lumber business is one
of the longest continuing companies owned and operated by one family
in the United States. The boys attended the city's German-English
School and St. Mary's College, which was equivalent to high school in
those days. In 1874, Albert, aged fourteen, and his two brothers traveled
by stagecoach, train and riverboat to attend Washington and Lee University in Lexington, Virginia. Ever since, Steves sons, grandsons and
great-grandsons have followed suit. The Steves family has the distinction of having more members represented as alumni than any in W&L
history—15 in all.

The Steves and Tobins are descended from María Curbelo Smith's
eldest daughter, Josephine Augusta Smith (1836–1908), who married
William Gerard Tobin. One of Josephine's granddaughters, Lucy Tobin

Carr, married Charles Armstrong, bringing another notable name into the family line. The Armstrongs had deep roots in Texas. Their fortune sprouted from reward money.

In 1877, grandfather John Armstrong, a Texas Ranger, received a $4,000 cash reward for capturing the most notorious bandit of his day, John Wesley Hardin. That windfall made it possible for him to marry his sweetheart, Mollie Durst, and buy a section of land adjoining the King Ranch. Here he founded Armstrong Ranch, which now encompasses 50,000 acres.

Armstrongs have been noted ranchers ever since. Today his grandchildren, John, Tobin and Lucie, Jr., are high in the saddle on separate spreads. John, the eldest, is executive vice-president of the King Ranch,

Rancher-polo player, Tobin Armstrong (left), another prominent Tobin descendant of María Curbelo. Wife Anne Legendre Armstrong (right) was first lady U.S. ambassador to Britain. They entertained H.R.H. The Prince of Wales in 1977 at an historic polo picnic on their 50,000-acre Armstrong Ranch near Kingsville.

THE CURBELO FAMILY

María de Jesús Curbelo *married* John William Smith

  John Miguel Smith

  Josephine Augusta Smith *married* William Gerard Tobin

    Zelime Susan Tobin

    Annie Cornelius Tobin

    Mary Ellen Tobin

    Agnes Lartigue Tobin *married* Samuel Cummings Bell

      Agnes Tobin Bell

      Jessie Bell *married* Arthur Mathis

        Arthur Mathis, Jr.

        Agnes Bell Mathis

        Mary Elizabeth Mathis

        Walter Nold Mathis

      Mary Ellen Bell

      Annie Tobin Bell *married* Albert Steves, Jr.

        Albert Steves III *married* Katherine Muir

          Albert Steves IV

          Katherine Anne Steves

        Sam Bell Steves

        David Pipes Steves

        Walter Steves II

        Marshall Terrell Steves

      Sam Tobin Bell

      Elizabeth Bell

      Josephine Tobin Bell

    Ella Bell Tobin *married* James Madison Carr

      Ella Josephine Carr

      Josephine Augusta Carr *married* Whitfield Scott Schreiner

      Josephine Tobin Schreiner

      Lucy Tobin Carr *married* Charles Mitchell Armstrong

        John Barclay Armstrong *married* Etta Kleberg Larkin

        Charles Mitchell Armstrong, Jr.

        Tobin Armstrong *married* Anne Legendre

        Lucie Carr Armstrong

    William Gerard Tobin, Jr. *married* Ethel Murphy

      William Gerard Tobin III

      Edgar Gardner Tobin

        married (1) Katherine Harrison

        married (2) Margaret Batts

          Katherine Tobin

          Robert Lynn Batts Tobin

      Ethel Murphy Tobin

      Janie Gardner Tobin

      Josephine Augusta Tobin

    John Wallace Tobin

    Josephine Augusta Tobin *married* William Pemberton Rote

      William Pemberton Rote, Jr.

      Tobin Cornelius Rote

      Josephine Augusta Rote

      Jack Tobin Rote *married* Emma Bell Owens

        Jack Tobin Rote, Jr.

        William Kyle Rote

      Gerard Tobin Rote

    Charles Milton Tobin

    Lucy Elizabeth Tobin

  Lucinda Isabel Smith

  Susan Elizabeth Smith

in charge of foreign operations and public affairs. A world-class polo player, he is married to a Kleberg granddaughter, Etta. Her sister, Illa, is the wife of James Clement, whose late father, Martin Clement, was president of the Pennsylvania Railroad when it was in its prime. Princeton-educated, Philadelphia Main Line-reared Jim Clement heads The King, with brother-in-law, John Armstrong, second in command.

John's younger brother, Tobin, runs the family's Armstrong Ranch. Their beautiful unmarried, red-haired "little sister," Lucie Armstrong, lives nearby on her own 5,000-acre ranch, San Rafael de la Partición.

Armstrongs have been much in the news since Anne Armstrong, Tobin's wife, became America's first lady Ambassador to the Court of St. James's. When England's future king, Prince Charles, stopped by Texas in 1977, he stayed with Anne and Tobin.

Exactly 100 years after John Armstrong the first started his ranch, the Prince of Wales was there playing polo with the great-great-great-grandson of María Curbelo.

If you're confused about who is related to whom, the facing family tree will show how some of María Curbelo descendants are kissin' cousins.

The Welder Family

The Welder family of Victoria may well be a Texas version of Tarkington's Magnificent Ambersons. Their family history encompasses the saga of Texas, combining Spanish land grant, Irish empresario and German settler. Welder ancestors are Texas legends:

—Don Felipe Roque de la Portilla, recognized as a forerunner of Stephen Austin, and sometimes called "Texas' First Empresario."

—James Power, the Irish empresario, soldier, signer of the Texas Constitution and senator, who founded the first Irish colony of Refugio County.

—John Welder, German colonist, rancher, developer of Texas' coastal plains area.

Felipe de la Portilla had come to Mexico from his home in Burgos,

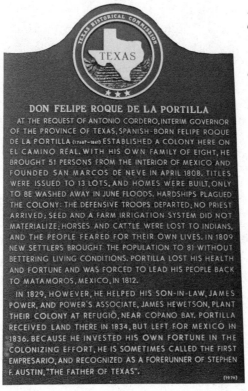

DON FELIPE ROQUE DE LA PORTILLA

AT THE REQUEST OF ANTONIO CORDERO, INTERIM GOVERNOR
OF THE PROVINCE OF TEXAS, SPANISH-BORN FELIPE ROQUE
DE LA PORTILLA (1767-1841) ESTABLISHED A COLONY HERE ON
EL CAMINO REAL. WITH HIS OWN FAMILY OF EIGHT, HE
BROUGHT 51 PERSONS FROM THE INTERIOR OF MEXICO AND
FOUNDED SAN MARCOS DE NEVE IN APRIL 1808. TITLES
WERE ISSUED TO 13 LOTS, AND HOMES WERE BUILT, ONLY
TO BE WASHED AWAY IN JUNE FLOODS. HARDSHIPS PLAGUED
THE COLONY: THE DEFENSIVE TROOPS DEPARTED; NO PRIEST
ARRIVED; SEED AND A FARM IRRIGATION SYSTEM DID NOT
MATERIALIZE; HORSES AND CATTLE WERE LOST TO INDIANS,
AND THE PEOPLE FEARED FOR THEIR OWN LIVES. IN 1809
NEW SETTLERS BROUGHT THE POPULATION TO 81 WITHOUT
BETTERING LIVING CONDITIONS. PORTILLA LOST HIS HEALTH
AND FORTUNE AND WAS FORCED TO LEAD HIS PEOPLE BACK
TO MATAMOROS, MEXICO, IN 1812.

IN 1829, HOWEVER, HE HELPED HIS SON-IN-LAW, JAMES
POWER, AND POWER'S ASSOCIATE, JAMES HEWETSON, PLANT
THEIR COLONY AT REFUGIO, NEAR COPANO BAY. PORTILLA
RECEIVED LAND THERE IN 1834, BUT LEFT FOR MEXICO IN
1836. BECAUSE HE INVESTED HIS OWN FORTUNE IN THE
COLONIZING EFFORT, HE IS SOMETIMES CALLED THE FIRST
EMPRESARIO, AND RECOGNIZED AS A FORERUNNER OF STEPHEN
F. AUSTIN, "THE FATHER OF TEXAS".

(1976)

Historical marker, one of several erected by the distinguished Welder family of Victoria, Texas. They also gave 7,800 acres of the original Portilla grant to establish Texas' famed Welder Wildlife Foundation.

Spain, in the latter part of the 1700s. He married the daughter of a wealthy landowner and became a leader of his area. It was a period of great expansion, not only by Spain, but also the new United States of America in the north. In 1803, Thomas Jefferson instigated the purchase of Louisiana. That hit very close to home, and the Spanish government of Mexico cast a fearful eye on their province of Texas abutting the Louisiana border. Hoping to avoid an occupation there by people from the Louisiana Territory, they sought to establish Spanish settlements from South Central to Northeast Texas. Don Felipe Portilla was chosen to head up the venture.

In December 1807, he led a group of 52 people across the Rio Grande. They settled on the San Marcos River, eight miles above the present town of Gonzales, and started a village, San Marcos de las Nieves. A month later, Portilla brought over ten more families, including his own wife and six children. Within a year the town was washed out by the flooding San Marcos. When it was rebuilt, Indians attacked it again and again. In 1812, jolted by the onslaught of the Mexican Revolution, these Spanish colonists went back to their homes across the Rio Grande. The Portilla family returned to Matamoros. It was there that he teamed up with the Irish empresario, James Power.

The year was 1829.

Having won its independence from Spain in 1821, Mexico was anxious to populate its frontier provinces—to develop the vast wastelands, cultivate the soil, raise stock, start towns. Mexico's provinces of Texas and Coahuila joined together to attract land agents, or "empresarios," to coordinate this colonization venture. In reward for their labors and expenses, each empresario received 23,000 acres of land for every 100 families he brought in as settlers. Each colonial family was granted 177 acres to farm, 4,251 acres to raise stock, or 4,428 acres to do both. Consequently, most colonists chose to raise cattle. Thus, Texas began as a cattle country.

Hoping to strengthen its citizenry against outside aggressors, Mexico also offered foreigners who married native Mexicans an extra bonus of one-fourth more land.

This promise of land, land and more land was particularly attractive to James Power and James Hewetson, natives of Ireland, who had come to Mexico to seek their fortunes. In 1826, they formed a partnership to act as agents in bringing colonists from Ireland to Texas. They succeeded in establishing the only colonies officially sanctioned to bring in settlers from abroad during the colonial period. Thus began their two Irish colonies of Refugio and San Patricio.

James Power, coming from an area lorded over by English lords and landowners, couldn't get enough acreage to sate his appetite for property of his own. He married Dolores de la Portilla, whose father and grandfather were important Mexican landowners. By marrying this "native American," the state rewarded him with an extra premium of land. Plus that, Dolores came with a large dowry. When she died four years, and two children later, he married her sister, Tamosa, thus doubling his property again. By this time, he had brought over boatloads of Irish colonists, and had been rewarded handsomely with more land.

When Power died in 1852, he had served under three flags, as empresario, soldier, signer of the Texas Constitution and senator. He had also acquired lots and lots of land, now the farms and ranches being lived on and cultivated today by the heirs of his daughter, Dolores Portilla, and the man she married in 1850, John Welder.

A century later, Robert H. Welder, their grandson, gave 7,800 acres of the original Portilla grant to establish the Welder Wildlife Foundation, "to further the education of the people of Texas and elsewhere in wildlife conservation . . . to develop scientifically methods of increasing the wildlife population of the state and nation for future generations. . . ."

 ★ *THE WELDER FAMILY OF VICTORIA* ★

Their Texas family history began with
Felipe Roque de la Portilla, who was born in Burgos, Spain, 1768.
He married María Ignacia de la Garza, of Mier, Mexico.
Her family owned much land there.
Their natural children were:
José Calixto
Juan
María Dolores
José Francisco
María Tomasa.
They adopted
Luciana and María Monica.
Dolores de la Portilla married (in 1832) James Power,
and after she died (in 1836) in childbirth,
Power married her sister, Tomasa (in 1837),
bringing the Portilla-Power lands together.
James Power, born in Ballygarrett, Ireland, 1788, fathered, in his first marriage,
James, Jr. (married Elizabeth Bower)
Dolores II (married John Welder).

His second-marriage offsprings were
    Tomasa (married Walter Lambert)
    Mary Agnes (married John Franklin)
    Eliza (married E. J. Wilson)
    Philip (married Mary Louise Luque).
Dolores Power II married John Welder
who came to America from Rhenish Bavaria with his father,
Franz, in 1830, becoming a leading rancher in the coastal bend counties.
John and Dolores Welder had ten children.

Today, descendants of Portilla-Power-Welder are among Texas'
most noted ranchers and bankers:

IN THE VICTORIA AREA
John J. Welder, IV
Leo J. Welder
Patrick Hughes Welder
Mrs. Lela Welder Cliburn

SAN PATRICIO COUNTY AREA
Mrs. Madaline Fleming O'Connor
Mrs. Nancy Fleming Shelton
Mrs. Patti Welder Edwards
Mrs. Diana Welder Hamilton
Mrs. Bobbie Welder Ford
Robert Hughes Welder, II

BEE COUNTY AREA
Amos Welder
Raymond Welder

REFUGIO COUNTY
Lawrence Wood
Wallace Shay

The Yturrias

Not all the old Spanish land-grant family names have disappeared from the Texas social scene. The Yturrias are still going strong. Among the most prominent, Leonora Yturria Wood and her cousins, the Frank Yturrias. Leonora and her husband, banker-planter-entrepreneur Lawrence Wood, live in palatial splendor in their Mexican-style manse on Corpus Christi's Ocean Drive. Created by San Antonio architect O'Neil Ford, the house is one of South Texas' handsomest. Here Leonora and Lawrence play hosts to visiting ambassadors and international social leaders, including friends and family from Mexico City and Acapulco.

Frank Yturria and his wife, Mary, divide their time between the original Yturria *rancho* in Rio Grande country and Brownsville. When their daughter Dorothy married George Farish of Houston, the wedding was one of the biggest Texas social events of the decade. Frank heads the family bank in Brownsville and plays the polo circuit from Palm Springs to Palm Beach.

Leonora is as Spanish as the Duchess of Alba.

Frank couldn't be less so.

And thereby hangs a tale.

Leonora's great-grandfather, who was from an old Basque family, came to the area in 1818 with a land grant from the king of Spain. A noted banker, Don Francisco Yturria first settled in Matamoros, across the Rio Grande from Brownsville. When Texas won its independence in 1836, he became a banking link between Texas and Mexico. Along the way, he accumulated railroads, shipping interests and lots of land in the South Texas valley.

An invitation to the Frank Yturrias' is a treat. Guests enter through a grape arbor covered with a striped canopy. By the lighted pool, amidst flaming torches, bartenders dispense margaritas. Gardens on two levels blaze with bloom—bougainvillea, frangipani, ginger blossoms, citrus trees and Hong Kong orchids. Candles glow on tables covered with colorful cloths and vibrant Mexican paper flowers. A mariachi band strolls from cluster to cluster. An outside staircase overlooking a small stream descends to a lower garden, and bountiful buffet. Costumed butlers and

*Lawrence Wood and his wife, the former Leonora Yturria, social leaders
of Corpus Christi. Wood's maternal grandfather, Irish empresario
Patrick Lambert, left his heirs a million acres, many in Refugio County,
home of Wood's ranch, bank, distillery and restored period Texas
country village, Sunshine Place.*

*Frank Yturria in hunting car with Bob Kleberg, Jr., at the
King Ranch.*

maids serve such Mexican-border specialties as *jalapeño* pie, guacamole,
enchiladas, roasted *cabrito*, cactus prepared with bell peppers, mango
mousse and *leche camada*, a frothy melt-in-the-mouth fudge.

Lordly, proud, of the land, the scions of the Spanish aristocrats still
bring an Old World elegance, a dash of color, north of the Rio Grande.

Don Francisco Yturria learned the banking business understudying
Charles Stillman in Brownsville, Texas. When the Don moved across the
Rio Grande from Matamoros to Brownsville in 1848, the Stillman family
owned almost half the town. Stillman's heir later became president of
New York's National City Bank (1891–1908), and he died in 1918,
leaving a fortune of $200 million.

Yturria didn't do too badly himself. By 1853, he had built the family bank, which is still thriving in Brownsville. He married a wealthy

land-grant heiress, Felicitas Trevino. And, during the Civil War, made a fortune.

It was a matter of the right man being in the right place at the right time. Since Southern ports were blockaded by the U.S. Navy, ships from foreign countries, if they wanted to trade with the South, had to sneak in the back door via Mexico along the Rio Grande border. As many as 300 vessels a day, from schooners to steamships, anchored off Matamoros at the mouth of the Rio Grande.

Not only did Yturria control banking in Matamoros, he was top government official there. Long a monarchist, believing only a powerful

Don Francisco Yturria.

European ruler could manage Mexico, he had sided with Catholic France and the man they placed as Emperor of Mexico, Maximilian. In appreciation, Maximilian appointed him Commandant of all the militias along the Mexican-American border. Yturria then made his older brother mayor of Matamoros and honorary British consul.

During the Civil War, Yturria would buy cotton coming down by the wagonload from huge Texas plantations. Even then, Texas was producing 250,000 bales annually. Don Francisco would buy it in Brownsville, transfer it to the Mexican side and sell it to the French and English waiting eagerly with their ships ready to sail. Onboard they had brought over guns, ammunition and medical supplies, which Yturria would bring back upstream and sell to the Confederate Army. As long as the War and Maximilian lasted, Yturria made a bundle, and shipped his gold off to foreign banks for safekeeping.

When both the South and Maximilian's reign collapsed, Yturria had to leave Texas and Mexico. He sailed for Cuba, and from there to France where he lived until things quieted down along the Rio Grande.

It didn't take long. Many of the Union soldiers were Texans beholden to him. Indeed, some of the state's largest ranches were bought thanks to money borrowed from Yturria. With well-placed friends in Washington, Don Francisco was able to secure a pardon for his participation in the Rebellion. Fortunately, too, his property was not confiscated. So within two years after the war, Yturria returned to Brownsville—and his banking. Since he was one of the few there with ready cash in the days of Reconstruction, land was his for a song. He wound up owning 140,000 acres, a hotel, a prosperous mercantile business and lots of livestock. To the outside world Señor and Señora Yturria had everything. One thing they wanted most, however, they couldn't produce: children.

Soon Don Francisco fixed that, too. One of his steamboat handlers, a Scottish gentleman named Louis McGraw, had a large family, including four sons. Yturria talked McGraw into letting him adopt one of his boys "to give him what you can't." Yturria convinced McGraw well, and that's how Daniel Yturria climbed on the branches of the Yturria family tree. So, the grandfather of all the present Yturria patriarchs was not Spanish at all. He was a Scot!

Son of Don Francisco Yturria, Daniel, as Mexican cadet during reign of Emperor Maximilian. (Note French soldier cap.)

 THE YTURRIA FAMILY

GENERATIONS
1st   2nd   3rd   4th   5th   6th

Captain Manuel Maria Yturria *married* Paula Navarro Ortosu

Francisco Yturria *married* Felicitas Trevino

Daniel Yturria *married* Leonor Espinosa

Fausto Yturria, Sr. *married* Marion Alexander

Frank Yturria *married* Mary Altman

Mary Elenor Yturria *married* Michael Irwin

Dorothy Yturria *married* George Farish

Fausto Yturria, Jr. *married* Sandra Longoria

Shelby Yturria

Casandra Yturria

Fausto Yturria III

Marion Yturria *married* Ray Smith

Ray Smith, Jr.

Casandra Smith

Leonor Smith

Herminio Yturria *married* Francisca Echazareta

Leonor Yturria *married* Lawrence Wood

Felicitas Yturria *married* Charles Downie

Leslie Downie

Lydia Yturria *married* Richard Butler

Daniel Butler

Richard Butler, Jr.

Daniel Yturria, Jr.

Pioneers
of the
German Prince

TEXAS HILL COUNTRY'S first settlers were German noblemen. Their leader, dashing Prince Carl of Solms-Braunfels, cut quite a figure on the raw Texas frontier of 1844. Errol Flynn-tall, dressed somewhat like Hamlet with a broadsword, wearing a slanted Musketeer-plumed hat, the Prince came to the new Republic of Texas looking for business. He and two dozen other nobles had formed a company to open markets for German products and spur trade between the promising new "country" of Texas and Germany. They called their enterprise "The Society for the Protection of German Immigration in Texas." For $240, each German immigrating family would get their transportation to the colony in Texas, a house, farm tools, 320 acres of land, and all expenses paid until their first crops came to harvest. Born woodsmen, horsemen, craftsmen and swineherds, many jumped at the chance to throw off the shackles holding them down in their Old World. Exactly 439 immigrants

Prince Carl of Solms-Braunfels, complete with plumes and sword, cut quite a swath in Texas hill country when he brought over German immigrants to establish a colony. By the mid-1850s, Germans were second in number to Anglos in the Lone Star State.

signed up for the first voyage, headed for "Germany-in-Texas." The Prince bought a 9,000-acre site 29 miles northeast of San Antonio for the colony. He named it New Braunfels, for his family estate in Germany.

In the next two years, 4,000 more colonists arrived from the Rhineland, then 3,000 more. They pushed farther north into Hill Country—to Castell, 50 miles away and 80 miles northwest to Fredericksburg. By the mid-1850s there were 35,000 Germans in Texas, making them second in number to Anglo-Americans.

The Schreiner family came over from Alsace in 1852. First they settled in San Antonio. The father died within a year, and his wife four years later, leaving five children.

The eldest son had headed for the gold fields of California. Two other boys found work in San Antonio. The only daughter married a pioneer Hill Country rancher, Caspar Real. Charles Schreiner (Charlie One) became a Texas Ranger. And range he did. He roamed the rugged ridges, plains and plateaus from the Colorado River north, to west of the Pecos on the extreme west. But the region that attracted him most was Texas' cool, inviting Hill Country. Instead of the sun-baked, bare-skeleton landscape he had been exposed to, here he had soft hills, refreshing streams, bountiful fish and game and almost perfect climate year round. In 1857, he and his brother-in-law, Caspar Real, joined forces and settled down to ranching on Turtle Creek, a tributary of the stream Spaniards had named for the Lady of Guadalupe. When the Civil War broke out, Charles joined forces with the South. He returned a captain to his ranch, where water and grass were free for the taking. Outposts of the U.S. Army in Texas were being reoccupied after the Civil War. One of them, south of the Schreiner Ranch, was Camp Verde.

Having a nose for business, Charles noted they needed beef and hay, which he had in abundance. He began to supply the garrison's needs, taking their pay in gold. On experiencing the world of commerce, he was hooked. He looked for bigger territory for trading and discovered it, down the road from his ranch. In Kerrville. German shingle-makers had been attracted to the area in the late 1840s thanks to its profuse groves of cypress trees along the Guadalupe River. Charlie One figured these manufacturers needed a general store. So he started one—in a cypress-board building 30x60 feet. Schreiner's Country Store was the

Texas German settlers made fortunes in livestock and lumber during the late 1800s. The longhorn breed of cattle, almost extinct, was rejuvenated recently by YO ranch owner Charles Schreiner III, great-grandson of a pioneer Bavarian settler, near Kerrville.

beginning of "civilization" for the Hill Country. Not only could you buy molasses, coffee, coal oil and calico, you could get whiskey for 50 cents a quart. And sit around a pot-bellied stove, spittin' and chawin' the fat. Since most citizens in those parts had ended up with worthless Confederate bills, they didn't trust paper money, so they paid in gold. Thanks to the area's great natural resources: water, grass, forage and land, lots of gold began to flow into Schreiner's Country Store. And there was nowhere to bank it. The closest bank was at Oppenheimer's in San Antonio, 60 miles away.

Also, no Wells Fargo or such was available to carry Schreiner's gold to the bank. Since the woods and paths were full of highwaymen, Charles entrusted his deposit to an old peg-legged Mexican cowboy from his ranch, Simon Azala. Old scroungy, one-legged Simon carried the gold in the horse's feed bag, dangling from the horn of his Mexican saddle. No bandit ever suspected it.

Later when Schreiner had more gold than that lunch-sack could hold, Captain Schreiner started the Schreiner Bank. And started to build the first Schreiner mansion in Kerrville.

The Captain's children all fared very well after daddy died. Aime Charles was given Charles Schreiner Company and a ranch. Gustave Fritz inherited a large ranch and the Schreiner Cattle Company. Louis Albert was left the Charles Schreiner Bank and a ranch. Charles Armand Schreiner was willed Wolff & Marx Mercantile Store in San Antonio, and a ranch. Emilie Louise, Frances Hellers and Caroline Marie were each given a large ranch. Walter Richard Schreiner got the most famous institution in Kerrville country—the YO Ranch. Run today by Charles Schreiner III and his sons, the YO spreads over 110 square miles, covering 50,000 acres. Mr. Schreiner, known locally as Charley Three, has single-handedly turned it into a Safari Club West. Notables from all over the world jet in to hunt exotic game. The late Shah of Iran was there. And Neil Armstrong. There are 10,000 animals on the YO. Native mountain lions, bobcats, javelina, deer, and zebra, giraffe, emu, ostrich, ibex, sika, black buck—over 30 different species in all. Charles Schreiner III has shown other ranchers over the years that just because an animal was born in Africa, Australia, South America or Asia, doesn't mean it can't thrive in Hill Country. But it is rather surprising for the uninitiated, when driving through the YO gates expecting to see longhorns roaming the range, to suddenly meet giraffe nibbling from tops of trees, a herd of zebra around the bend, and an ostrich or two running by the side of the road. If it gets too cold for the giraffe, they simply check in to the YO's "Giraffe Hilton," a high-ceilinged barn. (The YO has accommodations for paying guests, too.)

Exotic animals are not new to Texas. The King Ranch introduced the nilgai antelope way back in 1930. Two years later, The Kings' lawyer, Leroy Denman, imported rare fallow deer on his spread at Black Jack Peninsula, Texas. In 1951, Captain Eddie Rickenbacker's son, David, began the safari ranch idea, allowing paying guests to hunt exotic animals on his Bear Creek Ranch near Kerrville. It helped put the ranch on a paying basis. Many other ranchers followed suit. It added a dash of panache, and the game were compatible with their native livestock. Schreiner estimates that exotic animals roam today on 2,000 ranches in Texas.

Kerrville Country just seems to attract foreign fauna. Shortly before the Civil War, camels arrived from the Middle East. Herds of them, loping down the Hill Country roads, nostrils flared, with their bored, lorgnette-gazes surveying this strange new land. Jefferson Davis, then Confederate Secretary of War, thought camels would be ideal beasts of burden to transport army supplies over the arid Western plains. So he imported a boatload, with camel drivers, to boot, and headed them to headquarters at Camp Verde.

As it turned out, the camels' feet, used to soft sand, couldn't take the West's sharp rocks. Exit camels.

However, Glen Campbell came to Kerrville not long ago. With Country Western star Johnny Cash. They staged a TV special at the YO. (Dudes, hunters, photographers, filmmakers and tourists provide important additional income on the YO as well as on other ranches around Kerrville.) Earlier, ABC's *American Sportsman* series featured Governor John Connally hunting in Africa, with segments about exotic game shot on the YO. It looks like Tika.

"Once a Zulu chieftain visited here," recounts Charlie Three. "He couldn't believe it. Said if he had landed by parachute, he would swear he was back home in Africa."

Schreiner, like most Texas ranchers, is keenly aware of conserving wildlife. Every summer he holds a Conservation Camp for 1,500 high school students representing 35 schools from three states. Charlie Schreiner rejuvenated the almost extinct Texas longhorn breed of cattle. Longhorns, cattle that played such an important part in Texas history, had nearly gone the way of the buffalo until Charlie rescued them, registering the first Texas longhorn bull born on the YO in 1960. Now the ranch has more than 400 head of registered longhorns. Star of them all is Junior, a red and white bull that holds the world price record for its breed: $30,000. Thanks to Charlie Schreiner III, there's now a Texas Longhorn Breeders Association with more than 1,900 members, owners of 45,231 registered longhorns.

One of the YO's most popular attractions is its annual Longhorn Trail Drive every April. It's strictly for horseback riders who want to ex-

★ THE SCHREINER FAMILY ★

GENERATIONS					
1st	2nd	3rd	4th	5th	6th

Captain Charles Armand Schreiner *married* Mary Magdalena Enderle
Aime Charles Schreiner *married* Myrta Zoe Scott
Whitfield Scott Schreiner *married* Josephine Augusta Carr
Josephine Tobin Schreiner *married* Ernest Clyde Parker, Jr.
Scott Schreiner Parker
Ernest Clyde Parker III
Tobin Masterson Parker
Aime Charles Schreiner, Jr. *married* Nellie Elizabeth Ganter
Aime Charles Schreiner III
Nell Ganter Schreiner *married* Thomas Weir Labatt, Jr.
Thomas Weir Labatt III *married* Katherine Anne Steves
Charles Schreiner Labatt
Hester Palmer Schreiner *married* Harry Moss Harrison
Hester Schreiner Harrison *married* William Jarvis Dick, Jr.
William Jarvis Dick III *married* Mary Ellen Houston
Christina Dunbar Dick
Carolyn Lowry Dick
Philip Harrison Dick
Aime Schreiner Harrison *married* Helena Muir Hurst
Harry Moss Harrison III
Barrett Hurst Harrison
Kenneth Scott Harrison
Gustave Fritz Schreiner *married* Huldah Rummel
Louis Albert Schreiner
married (1) Emma Mae Shiner
Mae Louise (Billie) Schreiner *married* Edward Bennett Carruth, Jr.
Jane Schreiner Carruth *married* Robert Henry Flato
Mary Louise Flato
Edward Carruth Flato
married (2) Eveland Frances Brown
Caroline Marie (Lena) Schreiner *married* Hiram Partee
Alice Mary Partee *married* Robert Henry Stewart, Jr.
Alice Partee Stewart
married (1) Adrian Moore, Jr.
Adrian Moore III
married (2) Amos Eno
Amos Stewart Eno
Peter Eno
Jonathon Eno
Robert Henry Stewart III *married* Cynthia Gieseke
Alice Partee Stewart
Cynthia Caroline Stewart
Bessie Partee

Charles Armand Schreiner, Jr. *married* Kittie Elizabeth West

Kittie West Schreiner

  married (1) Jarrell E. Gross

  married (2) Strauder Goff Nelson

    Kittie West Nelson

      married (1) Charles Henry Coffield

      married (2) Henry Rugeley Ferguson

        Kittie West Ferguson

        Henry Rugeley Ferguson, Jr.

    Strauder Goff Nelson, Jr.

      married (1) Nancy Gail Jordan

        Nancy Katherine Nelson

        Anne Schreiner Nelson

        Strauder Goff Nelson III

      married (2) Carolyn Sue Moffitt

        Charles Schreiner Nelson *married* Shawn Adele Carpenter

          Charles Schreiner Nelson, Jr.

          Shawnee Carpenter Nelson

      married (3) Ronald H. Pugsby

Walter Richard Schreiner *married* Myrtle Barton

  Charles Schreiner III *married* Audrey Lee Phillips

    Charles Schreiner IV

    Walter Richard Schreiner

    Gus Louis Schreiner

    Louis Albert Schreiner

Frances Hellen (Fanny) Schreiner *married* Solomon Leroy Jeffers

  Charles Leroy Jeffers

    married (1) Mary Jane Kuntz

      Charles Leroy Jeffers, Jr.

      Carolyn Jeffers

    married (2) Mary Eleanor Nolte

      William Armand Jeffers *married* Alice Browne Combs

        Anne Frances Jeffers *married* James Marion Dunnan

          Alicia Anne Dunnan

          James Schreiner Dunnan

        William Armand Jeffers, Jr. *married* Billie Jeanette Street

          Virginia Gray Jeffers

    Frances Hellen Jeffers *married* James Walker Haymore

      Frances Hellen Haymore *married* Juan Monteroza Cagampong

        Constance Elizabeth Cagampong

        Juan Haymore Cagampong

      Charles Pittman Haymore *married* Candice Elizabeth Justin

        Constance Walker Haymore

perience what it might have been like bringing longhorns to market 100 years ago. Greenhorns find it rugged, but unforgettable. After a full day's loping along, they camp under the stars. A chuck wagon dispenses a Western feast of rattlesnake, calf fries, smoked salmon, fried red snapper and cold beer. Sitting on bales of hay, wranglers play local range songs, twanging banjos and gee-tar. Weary trail-riders curl into bedrolls and drift into dreamland.

Most of YO's guests, however, prefer bunking in one of the historic log houses Charlie restored in his "village." The Sam Houston Cabin, circa 1852, was once a schoolhouse. Its cypress walls were cut from the nearby Guadalupe River. The roof was made of cypress shakes, Kerrville's first industry. YO's old Boone Cabin was once a stagecoach stop. Perhaps the oldest is the Crockett Cabin, built on a land grant from Prince Solms-Braunfels, and moved to the YO from its original site near Fredericksburg. It's a reminder of how the Schreiners and other German families got to Texas in the first place.

III

The Royal Family
of Ranching

ROBERT JUSTUS KLEBERG, JR., was a god among Texas ranchers. They still talk about him today in reverent tones, not only on ranches around the world, but at "21," The Pierre, Saratoga, The Jockey Club and other exclusive enclaves which he used to frequent during racing season in the East.

Bob Kleberg was a cattle king with charisma.

And King he was. Head of the biggest family-owned and operated ranch in the world. During his reign, The King Ranch spread from Australia, Africa, Spain, South America and Pennsylvania, creating a cattle empire that encompassed over 13 million acres.

With his genius, the King Ranch originated the first American breed of cattle, Santa Gertrudis, created from the Indian Brahmin (zebu) and the English shorthorn. He also developed a virtually new line of quarter horse, Old Sorrel. Three King Ranch racehorses—Bold

The Klebergs of King Ranch, who owned more land than any other family in the world. (left to right) Henrietta (m. Major Thomas Armstrong); father Robert Kleberg, Sr.; Sarah (on lap), mother of today's B.K. Johnson and Robert Shelton; Alice (m. rancher Tom East); Richard M.; Robert, Jr.; and mother Alice King Kleberg, youngest daughter of King Ranch founder Captain Richard King. Alice, Texas, is named for her.

Venture, Assault and Middleground—won the Kentucky Derby. With Assault, the King Ranch stables captured the Triple Crown in 1946. Kleberg also purchased, for breeding, Canonero II, the Derby winner in 1971, at a cost of $1.25 million.

According to a *New York Times* piece about him in 1974: "The holdings that Mr. Kleberg directed were so vast as to beggar the imagination. The Texas ranch is roughly the same size as Rhode Island, the total of more than 13 million acres would be the equivalent to an area as large as 13 Rhode Islands. Almost 10 million of these acres are in Australia, with lesser amounts in Venezuela, Brazil, Argentina and Morocco. The Texas ranch which is in four divisions spreads over six counties between the Rio Grande and Corpus Christi, and is the country's largest. It contains valuable oil and gas fields, which are leased to the Humble Oil and Refining Company, now part of Exxon."

Indeed, it was due to Bob Kleberg's bringing oil onto the ranch that made it possible for its spectacular growth. At one time the King Ranch produced more oil than all of Saudi Arabia.

The King never had anything or anyone like Bob Kleberg and his beautiful wife, Helen. They were prototypes of the roles Rock Hudson and Elizabeth Taylor played in the movie *Giant*. But Bob and Helen were eons removed from Rock and Liz. Both were handsome and charming, yes. But while Rock was Rock, Bob was solid-rock. A hard-riding rancher, born and bred. The only King Ranch head, in fact, to be born and raised to ranch it.

Bob Kleberg's mother was the former Alice King, youngest daughter of Richard King, who had founded the King Ranch in 1853 with money made while a riverboat captain during the war with Mexico. Bob's father, a University of Virginia-educated lawyer, was handling the ranch's legal and business affairs when he married King's daughter. Then, King Ranch owned a half-million acres, stocked with cattle and horses. When Captain King died, Kleberg, Sr., not only inherited the job of running the ranch, he also fell heir to the longest-ruling mother-in-law since Queen Victoria. She ruled the roost, did Henrietta Chamberlain King, rooming just across the hall from daughter Alice and husband for forty years. The daughter of a New England Presbyterian minister, the first Protestant preacher in Rio Grande territory, she was prim, proper and Bible-pounding.

Despite a demanding mother-in-law in close proximity; despite starting at age thirty-one with no experience in ranching, Kleberg the First did remarkably well. A man of vision, culture and Germanic attention-to-detail, he introduced scientific methods into the cattle busi-

*Helen Campbell Kleberg (right), Rob's wife and mother of today's
Helenita Groves, entertained desert monarchs, English peers and
corporation presidents as the ranch's first lady. Shown here with a young
Kineno, the name given Spanish-Americans on the King Ranch.
(Photograph by Toni Frissell)*

ness. From 1886 to his death in 1932, he brought civilization to the South
Texas frontier. Mr. Kleberg saw South Texas as more than open range.
However, in order to create towns, farms, schools and cities, there was a
big missing link—water. In 1899, Kleberg heard about a new drill in the
Midwest that penetrated deeper than any. He put it to the test, and it
worked. With that definite source of water, he induced the Missouri Pa-

*Bob Kleberg sits in a King Ranch hunting car with his right-hand man,
nephew Richard Kleberg, Jr. Richard's son "Tio" is the ranch's senior
Kleberg today, vice-president in charge of ranching operations on his
family's 825,000 Texas acres.*

cific to run a rail line through the ranch, connecting it to the ports of Corpus Christi and Brownsville. King Ranch gave the land to provide a right of way. Before long, Kleberg had built the town of Kingsville. And he didn't stop there. He cultivated cotton, vegetables, citrus, palm and olive trees. He proved that oranges and grapefruit could bear prolifically there. Thus spawning the South Texas citrus industry. Robert Kleberg, Sr., used the land for more than harvesting cattle and horses. He brought in South African grasses to improve his pastures and increase his horse business. In the early 1900s, horses were the chief mode of transportation. The ranch sold as many as 12,000 horses a year, draft horses to the army, city governments, businesses and individuals throughout the United States.

Until the automobile took over, King Ranch had a booming horse business.

Kleberg constructed artesian wells with windmills serving each pasture around the ranch. He worked out ways to clear mesquite-choked pastures. He patiently accumulated evidence to solve what caused the Ranch's imported English breeds to die almost as soon as they arrived in South Texas. He found their killer—ticks—and single-handedly brought the disease under control by building the first cattle dipping vat, and initiating other programs to eradicate "Texas fever" in cattle.

When Robert Kleberg and Alice King went on their honeymoon in 1886, mama-in-law Henrietta King went along. Her bedroom at the Big House was directly across the hall from theirs for the rest of their married life. She presided at every meal, handing out advice to Robert, Alice and their five children right through dessert. For four decades, the King was known as "the widow's ranch." Mrs. King always dressed in black. Even covered her diamond drop earrings with black enamel, and toured the ranch in a mourning-black Rockaway stagecoach. Such was the tone she set. The widow King never allowed alcohol or dancing in her home. Hot as it was, she demanded that the men dine at her table in tie and jacket at all times. While Kleberg men suffered under stiff collars and wool coats, the women melted in corsets, chemises and heavy cloth down to their high-buttoned ankles. After a sweaty dinner, they would stage family entertainments, singing around the piano. They would close with Grandma King's favorite, "Rock of Ages," while she sat stiffly clutching the family Bible in her horsehair chair.

*Henrietta Chamberlain King as matriarch. Daughter of
a Presbyterian missionary, she frowned on flamboyance;
coated her diamond earrings, gift of Captain King, with
black enamel rather than look "showy."*

Robert Kleberg, Sr., who died one year after his mother-in-law, never had a life of his own. Nor did his wife, Alice. Robert Justus Kleberg, Jr., however, made up for it.

Bob was the younger son, with three sisters, and an older brother, Washington congressman Richard Mifflin Kleberg, apple of his mother's eye. Richard had Captain King's flair. He personified all the fun and gaiety Alice King had lacked living side-by-side her strict, straitlaced mama. Dick was a natural athlete, linguist and musician. Tall, graceful and dashing, Richard Kleberg could charm any assemblage, whether making speeches in German, Spanish or English, playing his guitar or singing songs.

Bob, on the other hand, couldn't carry a tune. He was shorter than his brother. He had a low, squeaky voice. Bob enjoyed books, but loathed study and stricture of school. Ranching was his thing. He learned to ride, cut, rope and shoot before he entered first grade. Since there were no schools within 45 miles, all five Kleberg children spent the school year in Corpus Christi. Returning home on weekends, they were met at the depot 20 miles away and brought back to the ranch ceremoniously in a stagecoach drawn by dashing white horses. When Kingsville finally did get railroad service, a special engine and caboose were dispatched every Friday to tow the Kleberg children back for a joyous reunion on the Ranch. Bob could hardly wait each week to be back in the saddle again.

His closest companions were Kinenos, the name given King Ranch cowboy families. He lived with ranch foreman Sam Ragland in the foreman's cottage next to the ranch's Big House. He rode with his cousin Caesar Kleberg, poker-playing family bachelor who instituted Texas' first game laws. Caesar headed the ranch's southern division and lived in a railroad section-house right on the private track. There was no indoor plumbing or electricity and his bathtub sat on the porch. Caesar's bird dog kennels came right up to the back door, so close that his cook Willie Flores could throw bones to them.

Kleberg, Sr. and the ranchmen taught Bob all they knew. Fortunately, Bob learned well, for before he could finish college, his father became an invalid. In 1916, he had to return from the University of Wisconsin to run the ranch.

In 1925, at the age of ninety-two, Henrietta King died. Ostensibly, young Bob had been running the ranch for the past ten years. Still in his twenties, he now could put all he had learned into effect and run the ranch his way. As total boss.

Things began to change rapidly on the King Ranch, especially after Bob brought home a bride. In the middle of February, less than a year after Bob Kleberg had been appointed manager of the ranch, he went to San Antonio on business. He planned to spend a day. But that night, he met a beautiful young visitor: Helen Campbell, daughter of a Kansas Congressman, the Honorable Philip Pitt Campbell. Smooth, sylphlike, sophisticated, with bronze hair and sparkling brown eyes, Helen swept Bob off his feet. She had grown up in Washington society; been active in the Junior League and had lived a life very far removed from ranching.

It was love at first sight for both of them. Not only did Bob Kleberg ride like the wind, he courted Helen with the speed of a whirlwind. Seventeen days later, they married.

Helen brought to the ranch gaiety and charm. The two moved from the Big House to a cottage of their own nearby. Helen converted it into a charming country lodge. Rambling and private, she glassed in a ranch-style porch and furnished it with plants, chintzes and comfortable sofas and chairs to make a handsome living room. Helen provided an articulate calm to Bob's driving force. For "Mister Bob" was a hard taskmaster. Into everything. On top of every facet of the ranch operation. When he wasn't riding the range, he holed up in a tiny office in Kingsville and conducted business on the telephone. Though soft-spoken with no put-on whatsoever, he sometimes would let it be known in no uncertain terms, who was boss, indeed, *King* of King Ranch country.

"There's a trace of Charles de Gaulle in him, and even more of Captain Bligh," Charles J. V. Murphy said about him in a 1969 *Fortune* profile. "He does not make things easier for his lieutenants."

Helen made things easier for him, though. She was a delightful hostess, and entertained the powerful often and well. Bob served as advisor to five U.S. presidents and scores of corporation presidents. "I've negotiated with seven successive presidents of Humble Oil," he once told a friend. "We've never had a serious disagreement."

Humble brought to King Ranch much of the money for Kleberg's future enterprises. In 1969, it was estimated the revenues from the King fields were bringing in $18 million annually to the ranch's treasury.

Oil money enabled him to continue his breeding operations, and expand his ranching to tropical countries. It financed forest-felling, land-clearing inventions, machines that made it possible to convert vast wasteland into pastures.

With all his wealth, Kleberg was as active as any Kineno. He would rise at 6 A.M., drink a cup of coffee, and by 7 A.M. have telephoned the foremen of all the ranch's main sections. By 9 A.M., pulling his upswept Stetson over his cool, piercing eyes, he would hop into a stripped-down hunting car (built especially by Buick) and speed over the grasslands to help round up a herd. There, he would put on white leather chaps, climb on a horse and pitch in.

"The Little House on the Prairie"—King Ranch's 25-room Big House. A marble-and-bronze stairway in its great hall leads to second-floor apartments set aside for various branches of the family, as well as visiting potentates, presidents and polo-playing ranchers.

Before oil, and Helen Kleberg, the King Ranch had been known as "The Walled Kingdom." She introduced her provincial husband to what lay on the other side of those King Ranch fences. Thanks to Helen, Bob became fascinated with thoroughbred racing, which led to frequent trips to New York and lifelong friendships with the Whitneys, Vanderbilts and other horsey families of the East. Helen made sure that their daughter, and only child, Helenita, saw more of the world than the ranch. Helenita attended Foxcroft and Vassar, bringing back schoolmates on gala visits. One of them, Anne Legendre from New Orleans, met her future husband, Tobin Armstrong, here. Anne Armstrong became America's first lady ambassador to the Court of St. James's, as well as chatelaine of the Armstrong Ranch next door.

Bob and his brother Richard were superb shots and entertained

Richard M. Kleberg, King Ranch chairman, taking a siesta in the shade of the ranch's trees. A dashing figure of the plains and politics, he served his area as congressman in Washington for 13 years. His grandson, Tio, is the Kleberg tall-in-the-saddle at King Ranch today.

with select hunting parties at Christmastime. During racing season, Bob enjoyed New York—and playing the prince from the plains. He kept a suite at the Pierre, where he was once photographed in white tie and tails, with a serape draped over one shoulder.

Always in motion, he equipped his telephones with 30-foot cords so he could talk and walk at the same time. He did a lot of talking as he walked, and never stopped expounding and expanding. In addition to the ranch, he supervised a bank, newspaper, store, dairy, lumberyard and a highly successful racing stable. Aside from Assault, Middleground, Stymie and Bold Venture, his most successful horses were High Gun, Dawn Play, Gallant Bloom, Bridal Flower and Better Self. His racing colors, designed by Helen, were brown and white with the King Ranch running W brand.

The epitaph on his simple grave reads: Robert J. Kleberg, Jr., "Your life is an expression of what you are."

Next to his, his wife Helen's tombstone is enchiseled: Helen Campbell Kleberg, "An inspiration to us all."

The King's Men

King Ranch cowboys and their families are called Kinenos, the King people. Some have served the Kings and Klebergs for four or five generations. Men, working on the range. Their women, in King-Kleberg households or offices. Houses of King Ranch families are furnished free, along with electricity, water and milk. Some sections have their own schools. Many workers are descendants of the vaqueros recruited from Mexico by Captain King as early as 1850. They say he persuaded an entire Mexican village to cross the Rio Grande and work for him.

Kinenos are fiercely loyal to their patrons. Ignacio Alvarado, for instance. Dependable as night following day, he never missed a roundup. Then one day, as Bob Kleberg was checking men heading out to round up cattle, he saw Ignacio's son galloping furiously across the plain. The boy leaped off his horse, ran to Kleberg, took off his hat respectfully, saying breathlessly: "Señor, my father says to bring you his apologies. He cannot be at the roundup today, since he has to die."

Ignacio Alvarado died that day. Always true to his word.

Descendants of the King

Growing up on the King Ranch, Belton Kleberg Johnson was considered the crown prince. He was the oldest male in the King-Kleberg bloodline. He had worked side by side with King Ranch genius Bob Kleberg, who raised him as his own son. Bob Kleberg had taken B.K. and his half-brother, Robert Richard Shelton, when their parents died and left them orphans as very young boys. Their mother was Bob's younger sister, Sarah.

Matriarch of the King-Kleberg clan, Minerva King Patch. In her nineties, Corpus Christi's grand lady. Daughter of Captain King's only surviving son, she married World War I's noted General Joseph Dorst Patch. They met when he was sent to protect her family's ranch from raiding Mexican bandidos.

B.K. and Bobby grew up in the Captain's House with the Klebergs' only child, Helenita. In the ranch world, this was the castle. The children were raised like ranch royalty. They each had their own Kineno companion to look after them. Everyone knew the significance of who they were. Yet despite their wealth, they lived very simple lives. Young King Ranch cowboys were their playmates. They worked the roundups right along with them. They spent all of their youth growing up on the ranch—the largest playground in the world.

Besides knowing everything about ranching and the ranch itself, B.K. had great family pride. When he went off to boarding school at exclusive Deerfield, in Massachusetts, the school's motto, "Honor Thy Heritage," became his own personal credo. A young man of great inner strength and drive, he determined to prepare himself to be the strongest possible King's man. After Deerfield, he studied agricultural economics at Cornell, served in the Korean War, and returned to attend Stanford business school. Raised at his uncle's knee, he knew every facet of the King Ranch's gigantic operations. Bob Kleberg took him along with him on his initial trip to buy millions of ranchland acres in the Australian outback, then to South America and Africa.

When the King Ranch board of directors was formed in 1954, B.K. Johnson, at twenty-five, was by far the youngest member, just as his uncle, Bob Kleberg, had been the youngest trustee following Mrs. Richard King I's death 30 years before. Then, too, B.K. was put in charge of the King Ranch showplace, its Santa Gertrudis Division. Casually sophisticated, uniquely well educated for the ranch baronetcy, he seemed destined to fill his uncle's boots.

But B.K. wanted to be his own man.

If he couldn't have complete command, absolute authority in the family ranch operations, he didn't see how he could do the job. So he left the King-dom, and started his own.

At twenty-seven, he took his financial statement to the bank and borrowed to buy the 70,000-acre Chaparrosa Ranch, 160 miles northwest of the King. Starting from scratch, he bred a string of animals that won the top prizes at major cattle shows. His bulls won grand champion at the Houston Show five years in a row. Everything he learned from his uncle, Bob Kleberg, the genius who developed North America's only original breed, Santa Gertrudis, B.K. put into practice at the Chaparrosa. His annual cattle sales there rivaled the King's, attracting breeders from all over the world. His 1982 sale auctioned an unprecedented 106 Santa Gertrudis bulls.

B.K. Johnson's scope is international. The age of the jet (he has his own) has made it possible for him to devote his considerable talents on top boards across the nation. They include AT&T, Campbell Soup, Tenneco, U.S. Trust and First City Bancorporation. In the winter of 1982, B.K. opened a world-class Hyatt-Hilton in San Antonio, where he and his wife, Patsy, also have a home.

"Honor Thy Heritage," B.K.'s motto from Deerfield days, plays a big part in all that he does. From the King side of the family, he acquired historic La Puerta de Agua Dulce, the ranch Captain King gave to his son, Richard II, as a wedding present. B.K. and his wife have transformed it into a charming turn-of-the-century-style ranch mansion.

They use it as their "other ranch," and entertain visiting guests there at the "best bird shooting in America." Since 1964, he and Patsy have run an annual summer camp to bring King-Kleberg cousins together and keep the King family and their traditions alive, and to introduce children of their friends to the self-discipline and glories of ranch life.

With La Puerta, also, came the original King Ranch brand, H-K—for his grandmother, Henrietta King. The crown prince in exile still bears his royal crest proudly.

B.K. Johnson's younger half-brother also opted to sell his interest in the King Ranch after his Uncle Robert Kleberg died. With his King Ranch millions, Bobby Shelton moved to Kerrville, the new Texas "Palm Springs." A natural rancher with enormous imagination, drive and organizational genius, he started an empire of his own—Shelton Ranches Enterprises.

"In two years, Robert Shelton and his wife, Froney, built what it takes anyone else a lifetime to do," says a Kerrville neighbor, Lloyd Brinkman. "Bobby Shelton hit Kerrville, and no cyclone ever left a greater impact so fast. He and Froney have given employment to about 800 locals, transformed the landscape, and built a quarter-horse breeding farm that's downright mind-boggling. It's what a pharaoh might do

★ THE KING RANCH FAMILY ★

GENERATIONS

1st 2nd 3rd 4th 5th 6th

Captain Richard King *married* Henrietta Maria Morse Chamberlain
Richard King, Jr. *married* Pearl Ashbrook
Richard King II *married* Pierpont Heaney
Richard King, Jr.
married (1) Marie Sullivan
Richard King III
married (1) Jimmie Rose Harrison
Richard King IV
James Harrison King
Kathryn Marie King
married (2) Florence Johnson Shinkle
married (2) Dean Hodges Kuykendall
Alfred Ashbrook King *married* Ellen Earl Umphres
Alfred Gilbert King *married* Marcella Kay Citty
Ellen Pierpont King
Gordon Ashbrook King *married* Alma Gene Sollinger
Minerva King *married* Joseph Dorst Patch
Joseph Dorst Patch, Jr. *married* Patricia Corbett
Joseph Dorst Patch III
Richard King Patch *married* Ginette Villaret
Cheri Patch
married (1) Richard Conrad Lutgen
married (2) Ray Edward Courtemanche
Richard King Patch, Jr. *married* Lucille Sirianni
Richard King Patch III
Andrea Leone Patch
Ginette Marie Louise Patch
married (1) Philip Hoytt Childers
married (2) Charles Hield Davis
William Ashbrook Patch *married* Helena Fletcher
William Ashbrook Patch, Jr. *married* Linda Ann Thompson
Alexander McCarrell Patch
Robert Douglas Patch
Mary King *married* Richard Gentry Estill
Richard Gentry Estill, Jr.
married (1) Edna Easley
married (2) Mary Susan Moberly
Alice King Estill *married* Floyd Myron Johnson, Jr.
Gentry Estill Johnson
Mary Virginia Estill *married* Porter Feary
Mary King Estill Feary *married* James McEwen Dewar
Leah Marie Dewar

Robert Lee King
Alice Gertrudis King *married* Robert Justus Kleberg
Richard Mifflin Kleberg *married* Mamie Searcy
Richard Mifflin Kleberg, Jr. *married* Mary Lewis Scott
Richard Mifflin Kleberg III *married* Olive Anne Musgrave
Oliveanne Marie Kleberg
Christina Lee Kleberg
Richard Mifflin Kleberg IV
Sally Searcy Kleberg *married* Kip McKinney Espy
Benjamin McKinney Espy
Thomas Kleberg Espy
Stephen Justus Kleberg *married* Janelle Gerald
Christopher Chamberlain Kleberg
Adrian Gerald Kleberg
Robert Justus Kleberg

Scott Masterson Kleberg

Mary Etta Kleberg
married (1) Forrest Lee Andrews
married (2) Greer Wentworth Sugden
Richard Greer Sugden *married* Susan Mack
Glenn Edward Sugden
Katherine Lynne Sugden

Katherine Searcy Kleberg *married* William Blake Yarborough
James Leonard Yarborough
William Blake Yarborough, Jr.
Linda Berkeley Yarborough *married* Mark Leonard Crawford

Alice Gertrudis King Kleberg
married (1) Richard Wells Reynolds
Richard Wells Reynolds, Jr.
Katherine Berkeley Reynolds
Michael Mifflin Reynolds
Alice Kleberg Reynolds
married (2) Vaughan Benjamin Meyer
Beverly Vaughan Meyer
Catherine Howard Meyer *married* Richard Abbott Lange
Casey Abbott Lange

Robert Justus Kleberg, Jr. *married* Helen Mary Campbell
Helen King Kleberg *married* John Deaver Alexander
Helen Campbell Alexander
Emory Graham Alexander
John Deaver Alexander, Jr.
Caroline Randall Alexander
Henrietta Kleberg Alexander
Dorothy Deaver Alexander

(*continued overleaf*)

THE KING RANCH FAMILY (continued)

G E N E R A T I O N S
1st   2nd   3rd   4th   5th   6th

Sarah Spohn Kleberg
married (1) Henry Belton Johnson, Jr.
Belton Kleberg Johnson married Patricia Lewis Zoch
Belton Kleberg Johnson, Jr.
Sarah Spohn Kleberg Johnson
Cecilia Lewis Johnson
married (2) Joseph Harrison Shelton
Sarita Kleberg Shelton
Robert Richard Shelton
married (1) Mary Bell Reagan
married (2) Deborah Ann Dembski
married (3) Fronie Ann Kempe
Helen Anice Shelton
Deborah Noel Shelton
Sarita Michelle Shelton
Robert Richard Shelton, Jr.
Katherine Renée Shelton
Susan Alicia Shelton
Sarah Saphronia Shelton

Alice King Kleberg married Tom Timmons East
Alice Hattie East
Tom Timmons East, Jr. married Evelyn Kuenstler
Mike East married Kathryn Irene Hatmaker
Thomas Allen East
Lica Elena Kenedy East
Alice Gertrudis King Kleberg East

Henrietta Rosa Kleberg
married (1) John Adrian Larkin
Henrietta Alice Larkin married John Barclay Armstrong
Charles Mitchell Armstrong
Henrietta Julia Armstrong married Andrew Jitkoff
John Nicholas Jitkoff
Thomas Tobin Armstrong
Stewart Larkin Armstrong married Catharine Coble Whittenburg
Catharine Coble Armstrong

Peter Alexander Larkin
married (1) Jean Motley Morehead
married (2) Catherine Manning Hannon
John Adrian Larkin III
Peter Alexander Larkin, Jr.
Louise Lindsay Larkin
Jean Morehead Larkin

Ida Louise Larkin married James Higbie Clement
Leslie Larkin Clement married Perry Herman Finger
Henrietta Chamberlain Finger
Perry Clement Finger
Henrietta Pruyn Clement married Ira Polk Hildebrand III
Marshall Shiner Hildebrand

James Higbie Clement, Jr. *married* Judy Capera Beggs
Alice Kleberg Clement
John Adrian Larkin, Jr.
married (2) Thomas Reeves Armstrong
Ella Morse King *married* Louis Morris Welton
Henrietta Mary Welton *married* Nathaniel Burwell Page
Henrietta King Page *married* John Henderson Farrar
John Henderson Farrar, Jr.
married (1) Dorothy Virginia Genau
married (2) Tami Agmon
John Henderson Farrar III
Frederick Lyons Farrar
Douglas Patch Farrar
Virginia Lee Farrar
Ilan William Farrar
Sharon Mabel Farrar
Nathaniel Burwell Page, Jr. *married* Mary Virginia Gordon
Mary Catherine Page *married* Frederick McOwen Middleton, Jr.
Frederick McOwen Middleton III
Frances Byrne Page *married* Morris J. Ambrose
Gordon J. Ambrose
Andrew Kane Ambrose
Adam Morris Ambrose
Henrietta King Page *married* Michael David Aguda
Henrietta Maria King *married* Edwin Byron Atwood
Edwin King Atwood
Alice Byron Atwood
Elise Henrietta Atwood *married* James Playfair Baldwin
Virginia Atwood Baldwin *married* Harry Bertram Fike
Thomas James Fike *married* Beth Ann Hardwick
Darci Christine Fike
Cari Elizabeth Fike
Elisa Anne Fike
James Playfair Baldwin, Jr. *married* Julia Ellen Lane
Richard Scott Baldwin
Mary Elise Baldwin
Bruce James Baldwin
Lane Ellen Baldwin
Elise Ashbrook Baldwin *married* William Virgil Vasu
Henrietta King Baldwin *married* Hugo Sterling Miller
Susan Elise Miller
married (1) James Robert Whitley III
married (2) Richard L. Loveless
Elizabeth Baldwin Miller

Boys of the range, brothers B.K. Johnson and Bobby Shelton, with a Kineno. Sons of star-crossed Sarah Kleberg, who was widowed twice and killed in an auto accident when the boys were tots. Raised by their Uncle Bob Kleberg, they learned ranching early and well. Both are prominent independent ranchers today. (Photograph by Toni Frissell)

today if he had Bobby's money—and talents."

Even James Bond would be awed by Shelton's quarter-horse breeding farm, Comanche Trace. Here a staff of veterinarians, biologists, computer experts, mechanics, wranglers and trainers are on the premises at all times. Often, as many as 200 mares are in foal at Comanche Trace's "Mare Hotel," their stalls monitored by closed-circuit television.

Comanche Trace in Kerrville is just one of Shelton Ranches Enterprises' booming operations. Its luxurious, IBM-computerized offices, however, serve as central headquarters for interests encompassing ranch, fruit and timberlands in large hunks of Florida, Louisiana and Montana.

Obviously, Bob Kleberg taught his sister Sarah's orphaned boys well. B.K. and Bobby are becoming ranching legends in their own time, too.

At King Ranch, the senior Kleberg today is Stephen Kleberg, mustachioed son of Bob Kleberg's right-hand man, the late Richard Kleberg, Jr. Called "Tio" (Spanish for uncle), he's vice-president of four King Ranch home divisions: Encino, Laureles, Norias and Santa Gertrudis. While his Uncle Jim Clement handles the business side, and Uncle John Armstrong the international, Tio runs the ranching operations. He's Mr. Fixit, the man cowboys and Kinenos turn to with their problems. Growing up on the ranch, Tio's whole life has been centered around horses and cattle. Like his father before him, he works the ranch's 825,-000 acres as if he were the only cowboy on the place. To improve the King's quarter-horse program, Tio invested $125,000 to buy the breed's all-time champion stud, Mr. Sam Peppy. Adding his blood to the line has made King Ranch quarter horses, once again, the best in the business. Today, Mr. Sam Peppy, with Tio in the saddle, is still cutting calves. Even though he's now worth $4 million, Mr. Sam still works like a cow pony, pride of his master, Tio Kleberg, the King's king cowboy.

Jesse Jones, kingpin of Texas politics, lumber and real estate, ruled the roost in East Texas for decades. Helped FDR weather the Great Depression. In 1902, he presided as King Notsuoh (Houston spelled backwards) at "his" city's premier social event, Carnival.

Jesse Jones

W HEN THAT ROOSTER CROWS," said a knowing shoeshine man in explaining Jesse Jones' clout, "it's daylight in East Texas."

Jones, a Tennessee-born, multimillionaire lumberman, held the title "Mister Houston," entrepreneur absoluta. He amassed a fortune in downtown real estate, building over 50 mid-city buildings in Houston, Fort Worth and New York.

"Jesse Jones liked to own things he could see and touch," recalled the Texas-born columnist Stanley Walker. "Rather than oil wells that lie far underground . . . and smell . . . and stain your clothes."

Mr. Jesse preferred to own banks, hotels, lumber, newspapers— things like that.

Jones grew up in Tennessee, where his father, William Hasque Jones, farmed and exported tobacco. Jesse's mother died young, so the five Jones children were raised by Will Jones' widowed sister, Nancy

Hurt, along with her own two. (Harry Hurt II, the *Texas Monthly* writer, is a descendant.)

All of Jesse's uncles left Tennessee before the Civil War, settling in Illinois. His father, who remained behind, ended up fighting for the Confederacy. Jesse's uncle Martin Tilford served in the Union Army, and after the war came to Terell, Texas, in 1875. There he opened a small lumberyard. It thrived, spreading statewide with 30 retail yards and two sawmills. Jesse came to Texas when he was twenty to work in his Uncle Martin's Dallas lumberyard. Not only couldn't you keep young Jesse down on the farm, you couldn't hold him back in the lumberyard, either. To further his education he went to Texarkana, graduating from Dr. Draughan's Business College, peddling outlines of the bookkeeping course on the side, for ten cents a copy. He was a cowboy briefly, peddled cigars, and after his uncle died, he moved to Houston, taking over management of MTF's entire lumber interests. Jesse operated the company so successfully that by the time he closed it in 1906, he had made a fortune. And married his Uncle Martin's son's widow, Mary Gibbs (Mrs. William Jones).

Jones would do anything to boost Houston. His personal deposits kept a number of Houston banks afloat during the panic of 1907. As chairman of the Houston Harbor Board, he headed a drive in the U.S. Legislature that opened the Ship Channel, guiding its development into a world port. Jones is given credit for the fact that no Houston bank closed during the Depression. In 1928, to lure the Democratic Convention to Houston, he built a hall to house it and tossed in a $200,000 contribution to the Party. A smooth dealer, he managed to move Gulf Oil headquarters from Beaumont to Houston by building a skyscraper, to their specifications, and naming it the Gulf Building.

Uncle Sam sent for Mr. Jesse when he needed help. During the First World War, Jesse Jones was director general of Military Relief for the American Red Cross. FDR called on him to serve as director and, later, chairman of the Reconstruction Finance Corporation during the Great Depression. Here he exerted the pow that pushed the passage of federal deposit insurance and increased capital reserves legislation, strengthening, greatly, America's banking system.

During World War II, President Roosevelt appointed Jones Secretary of Commerce.

Jesse and his wife, Mary Gibbs Jones, had no children of their own. However, her children by her first husband, William Jones, benefited mightily from Jesse's will. One of them, John T. Jones, Jr., took over as the most prominent Jones. He became president of the *Houston Chronicle*, his Uncle Jesse's newspaper (from 1949 to 1966). He was also a banker, restaurateur, radio station owner, cattle rancher and head of the Houston Endowment, the largest foundation in Texas, with assets of more than $209,000,000. Founded in 1937 by Jesse and Mary Jones, one of its announced intentions was to build a library for the Houston Academy of Medicine. This library, the Jones Pavilion at Houston's Hermann Hospital, and another Pavilion at the Neurosensory Center, are major Jesse Jones-inspired donations to Houston's mighty Medical Center. Jesse Jones' stepdaughter, Audrey, Mrs. John Beck, is donor of a priceless collection of Impressionist paintings to the Houston Museum of Fine Arts.

Scions
of Spindletop

ON JANUARY 10, 1901, the age of liquid fuel was born when the well of wildcatters Captain Anthony F. Lucas and Patillo Higgins gushed in, roaring 100 feet into the air, at Spindletop, Texas. It changed the history of the earth and the social strata of Texas. Fortunes were made here. Thanks to the salt dome at Spindletop and its trillion-dollar-plus reserve, America was to surpass Russia as the leading oil country of the time. It led to breaking the Rockefeller oil monopoly, producing twice as much as the fields of Pennsylvania where Rockefeller's Standard Oil of New Jersey reigned rampant.

Oil had been drilled in Texas since 1866, but until Spindletop, production had never come close to equaling the output of Pennsylvania's big boomers. Spindletop might never have been discovered, either, if Patillo "Bud" Higgins hadn't been "born again." Bud was a Beaumont boy who had been a real hell-raiser until "he saw the light." He'd even lost an arm fighting with the local cops. But once he became a born-again Baptist, Bud didn't drink, smoke, gamble, chew or go with wild girls who did.

Instead, he devoted his off hours to teaching Sunday school. He'd take his Sunday school class on picnics at Spindletop Springs, a park on the outskirts of Beaumont. He'd amuse the boys and girls by sticking his finger into the moist ground near the springs, then, light the gas that spurted out. It didn't take genius to figure that he had discovered something important.

His neighbor, Captain Lucas, an experienced driller, concurred. Lucas lassoed some backing for drilling and they went to work. When they struck oil, a stream spouted so high it could be seen plainly in Beaumont four miles away.

Up to that time, if an oil well produced 50 barrels a day, it was considered spectacular. Spindletop blew out a barrel of oil every second. So many wells sprang up around it, you could step from one rig floor to the other and walk clear across the field of derricks without getting your feet muddy. So much oil rained down that 40 four-horse teams were put to work building levees to hold the emerging lake.

Men from every corner of the earth descended. Special trains chugged into Beaumont, packed with people looking for quick riches. Pittsburgh Mellons, John D. Rockefeller and Howard Hughes, Sr., all had a piece of the action. Houston's Howard Hughes, Sr., snapped up leases on credit and developed the rock-bit that revolutionized drilling and gave him an oil-tool industry second to none. Mellon, with Laurence Phipps and James Galey, loaned the money to start Gulf Oil. With a $50,000 investment, Joseph S. Cullinan and friends founded the Texas Fuel Company, which became Texaco. (A world leader in oil and natural gas, Texaco's daily crude oil production exceeded more than three million barrels a day.)

From New Orleans came a young financial genius, Robert E. Lee Blaffer. From Natchez, a brilliant lawyer, William S. Farish. They would later found Humble Oil Company with Harry C. Wiess and Walter W. Fondren. Humble would become the largest oil producer in America, emerging into Exxon.

By 1920, the oil discovery at Spindletop had transformed Houston's small-town society into a cultivated milieu predicated directly or indirectly on oil.

The city's oil millionaires were divided into two social factions: New-Oil-Money, the wildcatters; and Old-Oil-Money, composed mostly of the scions of Spindletop.

Glenn McCarthy, of Shamrock Hotel fame, and "Silver Dollar" Jim West, who wore his Stetson and passed out silver dollars wherever he traveled, belonged to the New-Oil-Money group. The media of the day gave them such attention that the general public got the idea that Houston was populated with rough-and-ready, wildly eccentric oil kings. Actually the real social, financial and political power of Houston was consolidated with the Old-Oil-Money monarchs—men like Texaco's J. S. Cullinan, Will Hogg, Will Farish, Lee Blaffer and Harry Wiess.

Three decades after Spindletop, Old-*Houston*-Money—the pre-established lumber, cotton, real estate and banking families (Rice, Baker, Neuhaus, Carter, et al)—had their fortunes augmented by the oil bonanza. Old-*Houston*-Money began to merge and marry with Old-*Oil*-Money, forming one big, happy, very rich Houston establishment. Unlike the widely publicized Wildcatter Rich, their taste was restrained. Simple, yet sophisticated. Never vulgar.

Crème de la crème topping Houston's new social parfait was "The Stables Set," centered around Humble Oil's Harry Wiess and his elegant wife, the former Olga Keith.

"The Stables" was the name of her country place, on Post Oak Road eight miles out of Houston. Here the oil elite gathered for their polo, backgammon, horseback riding and tennis, rather than ultra-exclusive Houston Country Club and River Oaks. On any given weekend, you'd find a Farish, Rice or a Neuhaus at "The Stables" pool or on its tennis court. Informal luncheons and drinks were served by Olga Wiess' retinue of grooms and the Wiess' faithful retainers, Willie and Tommy.

Hostess and horsewoman supreme, Mrs. Wiess had architect John Staub build her a combination lodge for entertaining fine friends and a stable to house her fine horses. The results were quite splendid indeed. Staub modeled the lodge-stable on buildings he had seen in the Beguinage section of Bruges—stately, gabled, exuding a Medieval ambience. Lodge, stables and pool house were built of tiny specially molded brick.

Olga Keith Wiess' private country place, The Stables, designed by architect John Staub, was scene of Houston's haut monde and horsey-set weekend soirees.

Ceiling beams in sitting room and tack room were salvaged from an old weathered wooden oil derrick. Guests would come out for noon drinks, lunch and a swim, as well as participate in the action-packed polo or tennis tournaments.

In the era that England's Lady Astor was presiding at Cliveden, Houston high society had "Olga Keith's Stables Set." Even though she had been Mrs. Harry Wiess for decades, her intimates still referred to her by her maiden name, Olga Keith. It was much the same for Barbara Hutton and Doris Duke. They were called by their natal, not married, names also.

As Olga Keith, daughter to lumber baron J. Frank Keith, she had grown up in one of Beaumont's grandest mansions, Arbol Grande. A newspaper account in 1913 called it "undeniably one of the most beautiful homes in Texas." As a young girl, Olga entertained her friends during hot Beaumont summers in one of Arbol Grande's two swimming pools. One, indoors. You didn't find many other private outdoor and indoor pools in 1913.

Her father had given Beaumont its flora-abundant plaza, named Keith Park in his honor. Inspired by town squares he had seen on travels to Mexico and Central America, Mr. Keith, at his own expense, converted a bare square in the middle of Beaumont into a tree-laden oasis with lawn seats, bandstand, pond and fountain.

Olga's mother, daughter of lumber king Frank L. Carroll, was considered about as top-top in Beaumont as you could get. Only Bess Kirby, wife of an even richer lumber mogul, John Henry Kirby, rivaled Mrs. Keith as a hostess. As early as 1902, Bess Kirby was sending her chef to New York's posh Marguery Restaurant to learn haute-French cooking.

On Beaumont's "millionaire's row," Calder Avenue, Olga Keith's beau-next-door was the dashing Harry C. Wiess. His family seemed to have "invented" money, first in cotton buying, then lumber, merchandising and real estate. All started by Simon Wiess who was born in Lublin, Poland, on January 1, 1800. At age sixteen, Simon left home to see the world, and nobody in his day saw it better. Simon lived in Turkey, Asia Minor, the West Indies, Mexico, Central and South America. In between, he was quite well traveled, as representative of the Masonic

Hosts of "The Stables Set," Houston's Mr. and Mrs. Harry Wiess. She was Olga Keith, heiress to the Beaumont lumber fortune; he a founder of Humble Oil. (Photograph by Toni Frissell, 1940)

The Stables in the year 1940. Watching tennis (left to right), Palmer Bradley, Fred Asche, Leslie Luftin, Harry Wiess and Hugo "Baron" Neuhaus.

Mrs. Wiess' girlhood home, Arbor Bend, in Beaumont, had both outdoor and indoor swimming pools.

Lodge in Europe and the United States. By the time he arrived in Texas in 1833, he could read, write and speak, fluently, seven languages.

Representing the Masonic Lodge, he first visited the United States in 1826, and in that capacity he came to Texas, then part of Mexico, seven years later. The Mexican Government appointed him Deputy Collector of Customs at Galveston from 1833 to 1835. Here he became well acquainted with Sam Houston and others who were to make Texas history. When Sam Houston became president of the new Republic of Texas in 1836, he made Simon Wiess his Deputy Collector of Customs at the Texas-Louisiana bordertown of Camp Sabine. At this post, he met, fell in love and married Miss Margaret Sturrock. Shortly after their marriage, he went into a business of his own. The young Wiesses moved to Natchitoches, Louisiana, and opened a merchandising business, using as its building the historic stone fort there. He became a cotton broker, and in 1838 loaded up his entire household on a keelboat to take the first load of cotton ever transported down the Neches River to market in New Orleans. After selling his boatload of cotton, he and his family bought land on the Neches River about 15 miles north of Beaumont, where tall pines rimmed the riverbanks. It came to be known as Wiess Bluff.

Simon was a wheeler-dealer and man of action. He operated a flourishing merchandising business, as well as a formidable receiving and forwarding enterprise. Since there was no railroad for transporting cotton, he was most concerned about developing steamboating on the Neches River. In his twenties, he had owned several vessels in the English–West Indies trade, so he knew something about shipping. To clear the Sabine and Neches rivers for riverboat traffic, he personally supervised scooping out mud and removing snags and silt from the river bottoms.

Cotton and shipping were not Simon's only interests. Not by a long shot. He dabbled in land speculation, cattle and horses, too. By 1842, Wiess Bluff was a thriving river port and trade center. It later became an important log transportation depot and lumber site. But by that time, he had died, leaving his sons to run the Wiess business interests. All the sons, including twins Mark and William, had their business acumen keenly honed in their early teens. William, like his father, followed many pursuits and was successful at all of them—mercantile, cattle, lumber, real estate and banking. He had fought in the Civil War, enlisting with the Confederate Army when he was only eighteen years old. During Reconstruction years, the Wiess brothers found that supplying lumber for rebuilding cities destroyed by the war became even more profitable than cotton. In 1876, William helped organize the Reliance Lumber Company, joining forces with his brothers Mark and Valentine, and with Harry Potter. A decade before that, William was master of two Neches River steamboats, the *Alamo* and the *Adrianne*. During the 1870s, too, William and his brother Valentine joined Dr. O. M. Kyle and the McFaddins in founding the Beaumont Pasture Company, which ran a herd of 10,000 cattle on the open prairie. McFaddin, Wiess, Kyle Trust Company also owned a large ranch in Greer County nearby, and it was on their land that Spindletop, the greatest oil geyser in the history of the world, erupted.

At first, the Wiess brothers, although part-owners of the gusher site, weren't terribly enthused about the oil discovery on their property. They looked with a certain disdain on the roughnecks and boomers who were piling into their city, disrupting their refined life in their mansions along "Lumbermen's Row." William was so aloof that he and his family spent the first week after Spindletop aboard his yacht on the Neches River. Son Harry Wiess was thirteen at the time, soon to embark for Lawrenceville, New Jersey, to attend boarding school.

Harry's father may not have been enthusiastic about "oil" in the beginning, but he made up for it in the ensuing years. He was a heavy investor in the just-formed Texas Company, now Texaco. In 1903 he organized the Paraffine Oil Company and brought in the Batson Prairie field, pumping 10 million barrels of oil from it in 1904, alone. He later became sole owner of Paraffine Oil and Reliance Oil companies, and owned a half-interest in the Ardmore Oil Company of Oklahoma. All the while, Harry was away at Lawrenceville, then Princeton University, where he graduated in the class of 1909 with a civil engineering degree. Olga and he were very much in love, and after graduation they were married, sailing away to Europe on their honeymoon. When Harry returned to Beaumont, he started a printing business which was thriving when he had to cut it short. His ailing father needed him to take over the booming Wiess oil interests. At the age of twenty-three, Harry Wiess was made a director and secretary of Reliance Oil Company. In 1914, after his father died, he became president of both Paraffine Oil and Reliance Oil companies. He was then twenty-seven years old. During this period, Harry Wiess came in close contact with other independent oil operators. Ross Sterling, William Farish, Robert E. Lee Blaffer, W. W. Fondren and other Spindletop veterans all shared the same problems in marketing and pricing. Refiners and pipeline operators could charge them whatever they felt the traffic would bear. To free themselves of these headaches, they joined together and organized Humble Oil and Refining Company.

Harry, then twenty-nine, was elected a director and vice-president of marketing. He brought much to the company: youth, a Lawrenceville-Princeton education and his family's considerable oil-producing properties. He was also the only Humble founder whose family had been "in oil" previously. Harry, with eight years of oil production and management under his belt, was given full responsibility for developing Humble's refining operation. Under his guidance, Humble's Baytown refinery was built. One of his finest days occurred in 1944, when he was Humble's president, and Baytown had turned out its *billionth* gallon of gasoline.

After the Wiesses had moved to Houston in 1917, they became leaders in society and community affairs. With three charming daughters, Elizabeth, Caroline and Margaret, their art-filled, antiques-laden estate at 2 Sunset Road was the scene of gala debuts and dinners. Young men from the East, down to learn the oil business, were frequent guests. Winthrop Rockefeller and Bob Wood, Sears Roebuck-head General Robert Wood's son, were among them. At a Wiess debut party, Bob Wood was having such a good time that he almost forgot his dawn shift on an oil rig. He rushed, still in his white tie and tails, to report for duty among the derricks. He wasn't there long, however. His foreman looked at him with great disdain and said, "Wood, you don't come to this roughneck job in an outfit like that. And you don't get here late. Besides,

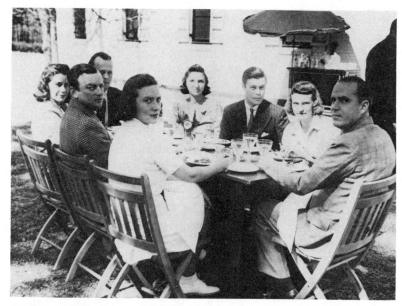

Dining (left to right), Elizabeth Wiess; her future
husband, Lloyd Smith; John Burnett; Mary Wood Farish;
Martha Farish Gerry; Will Farish II; Betty Crotty and
Victor Carter.

you ain't even supposed to be here. It's your day off!"

Phil Harris and his orchestra were trained in from Hollywood to play at Elizabeth Weiss' coming-out party in 1936. For the occasion, her father had a ballroom constructed over the swimming pool. It looked like part of the house, complete with heating and plumbing. After the party it was dismantled and stored until Caroline's debut in 1938. Due to World War II, Margaret missed having a debutante party. However, when she married banker James Elkins, Jr., right after the war, the ballroom went up again for her wedding reception.

Like most of their school chums, the Wiess girls had gone to Houston's exclusive Kincaid School until the ninth grade, and then "gone away." Elizabeth to Miss Porter's in Farmington, Connecticut; Caroline and Margaret to Ethel Walker, also in Connecticut. Elizabeth later was schooled abroad, learning language and art history while living on-the-scene, in Florentine palazzos and Parisian palaces. Today, as Mrs. Lloyd

Smith, she has exquisite châteaux of her own in both Houston and Southampton, Long Island.

Caroline, who married Theodore Law, scion of a prominent Oklahoma oil family, is a powerhouse behind Houston's Museum of Art. At home, her glass and terrazzo rooms are bedecked with a wall-filling Picasso, a colossal Franz Kline and sculpture by Jean Arp. Over the mantelpiece is her multi-paneled portrait by Andy Warhol.

Margaret and her husband, James A. Elkins, Jr., chairman of First City Bancorporation, live in one of the few contemporary mansions designed by Houston's "court architect," the late John Staub. And all three sisters entertain, on very special occasions, in that other John Staub triumph, their mama's "The Stables." Their own "Stables Set" is still tout-Houston.

★ *THE WIESS FAMILY* ★

GENERATIONS

1st	2nd	3rd
Harry Carothers Wiess *married* Olga Keith		
	Elizabeth Wiess *married* Lloyd L. Smith	
		Sandra Keith Smith *married* Robert Mosbacher
		Sharon Lloyd Smith *married* David Keller
		Sydney Carothers Smith
	Caroline Wiess *married* Theodore N. Law	
	Margaret Wiess *married* James A. Elkins, Jr.	
		James A. Elkins III
		Leslie Keith Elkins
		Elise Elkins

Portrait of
Sarah Campbell Blaffer
by Waymand Adams.

MON·DIEU·EST·MA·ROCHE

VI

The Queen Mother

ACCORDING TO MANY of Houston's old guard, Sarah Campbell Blaffer was the nearest equivalent of Texas royalty.

Her husband was Robert E. Lee Blaffer, a founder of Humble Oil. Her father, William Thomas Campbell, signed the original charter of the Texas Company, which became Texaco. The Blaffer-Campbell marriage combined two of the world's great oil fortunes. Governor James Hogg, a partner of Campbell's, later called it "the conglomerate of the century."

When they exchanged vows in the little town of Lampasas, April 22, 1909, it was indeed the royal wedding of Texas. A private railroad car brought out Houston's highest of the high in society, including Governor Hogg, the J. S. Cullinans, W. B. Sharps, Turner Williamsons, M. S. Farish, Dr. F. B. King and the Right Reverend George Herbert Kinsolving. The governor's daughter, Ima Hogg, was maid of honor. The ceremony was held by candlelight in St. Mary's Episcopal Church, built of Texas limestone, with choir stalls imported from an ancient English chapel. The church was a gift to the community from the bride's father. Mr. Campbell was a Scottish aristocrat, a member of the Campbell Clan of Argyle. Descended from a family of stockbrokers, he had genes of financial genius. (His great friend and fellow Briton-turned-oil-prospector, Burke Roche, was the younger twin brother of the 3rd Baron of Fermoy, a direct ancestor of Britain's present Princess Di. Since Roche and Campbell were both "second sons," they came to America to seek their fortunes.) At age twenty, Campbell was working as a cub reporter for the *Cincinnati Enquirer.* He and a fellow cub, Henry Vuillard, had their first scoop interviewing William Howard Taft. Vuillard went on to found the Great Northern Railroad. His Madison Avenue mansion in New York is now the Palace Hotel. Campbell later named his third son, Henry Vuillard Campbell, for his old friend and fellow journalist.

Campbell's "palace" in Lampasas was called Argyle Heights. A white colonial mansion, high on a hill, it was surrounded by walls and guarded by an English gateman, Mr. Ross. Daughter Sarah, called "Sodie," was a Garbo-ish beauty, with a coltish glamour that attracted suitors in swarms. One was eccentric genius Howard Hughes, Sr., who courted her with violets while she attended a convent school in Houston.

"Howard and Sodie would not be a good match," Mr. Campbell had remarked. "She's poetic and he's eccentric and their children would undoubtedly turn out to be degenerates."

However, Mr. Campbell did seek out bright young men for his daughter to meet. One of the brightest, Robert E. Lee Blaffer, was instantly smitten. Lee Blaffer had struck it big at Spindletop. Plus that, he was from a distinguished German family of bankers and steel magnates who had settled early in the century in New Orleans. His father, John August Blaffer, the first Blaffer born in New Orleans (in 1835), had established himself by building up a successful brick and lumber business after the Civil War. During the war, John Blaffer had served as an officer under General Robert E. Lee. When his son was born, he named him Robert E. Lee Blaffer. The boy, Lee Blaffer, grew up in New Orleans surrounded by a family of bankers. (His mother's father, Christian

Schneider, founded the Canal Bank of New Orleans. After studying at Heidelberg University in Germany, he worked for one of his uncles, Adolf Blaffer, president of the Germania Bank of New Orleans.)

Courtly, cosmopolitan and big, Lee Blaffer stood out from the crowd pouring into Beaumont after Spindletop gushed in 1901. In appearance he was every bit the German aristocrat. Tall, weighing nearly 300 pounds, with curly brown hair and pale blue eyes, he was impeccably groomed at all times. He would emphasize his coloring by wearing a pearl-gray hat and a violet in his buttonhole. In Beaumont, near Spindletop and its trillion-dollar-plus reserve, he first met his lifelong partner and friend, William S. Farish, a young lawyer from Natchez, Mississippi. Lee Blaffer was a financial whiz. Farish had technical knowledge of the field. After their chance meeting, in the middle of the street, they later lodged together at "Mrs. Chicken's Boarding House," forming their future partnership while there. By the time of the Campbell-Blaffer wedding, the groom, bride's family and most of the guests were big-rich, thanks to the big Spindletop oil strike eight years before.

A top Lone Star cast was there. The bridal couple left for their three-month European honeymoon in a private railroad car. People greeted them at station stops, pelting them with flower petals. All along the tracks, pranksters had tied wedding bells. They were given a beautiful cow as a wedding present, which they promptly named "Wedding Bell." She was the forebear of many Blaffer cows to come, ranging from Wedding Bell I to Wedding Bell VIII. Later, when the Blaffers had built their mansion in Houston's exclusive Shadyside section, theirs was the only house with a cow in the yard. First hint that "the Blaffers are a bit eccentric."

Sarah definitely was a bit different from the other Spindletop millionaires' wives. While at school in Boston, she had visited Isabella Stewart Gardner's Fenway Court and been enthralled by her exquisite art collection. As a young girl in Lampasas, she had often dreamed of having fine paintings, even to the extent of making shadow images on her bedroom walls by lighted candle. But it was on her wedding trip to Paris, dutifully visiting the Louvre, that she had her first mature contact with great works of art. Here the art bug struck her like a lightning bolt and completely changed her life. Her children were raised by a French governess, Mlle. Suzanne Glemet, and spent every summer on her farm in the wine district of Charente in order for them to perfect their French, and their mother to visit the studios and galleries in Paris. Her daughter, Titi, born in Houston, now Her Serene Highness Princess Cecil Amelia von Furstenberg of Monte Carlo, Paris, Salzburg and New York, recalls that her mother began to collect Soutine and Munch long before they were big names in art.

"Mother was always collecting . . . and so was I, right along with her. I bought my first painting when I was sixteen. A Dufy. For two hundred dollars. Mother adored Dufy for she had his kind of spirit. She could be bowled over by color. That's why she loved the Impressionists so. Her favorite painting, I'm sure, was Dufy's 'Pink Lady.'

"She had a great 'eye,' a gut instinct of what was great. She became an early collector and lifelong friend of Milton Avery. Paintings of his, bought in the 1940s and 1950s at about two hundred dollars each, have appreciated to forty to fifty thousand."

Art became her passion, and one she wanted to share with her fellow Texans. Her influence played an important part in Texas cultural history. She got the Houston Museum of Fine Arts off to a fine start by donating to the Museum paintings by Renoir, Cézanne, Soutine, Vlaminck and Frans Hals. In 1971, she gave 12 paintings, then valued at $900,000, to the University of Houston, and financed a series of exhibitions there. She preferred to share her paintings rather than hang them on her mansion walls, and started her own traveling art exhibitions.

Says Princess von Furstenberg: "Mother wanted a museum without walls because she herself lived in a small town once and never forgot the hunger of intelligent people in such places for excellent things."

Sarah Blaffer once said, "It is an experience I want everyone to share: poor, rich, townfolk and country. I'm not interested in bricks and mortar, I want to bring fine art to far-flung Texas areas where there are no art treasures."

Fortunately for Texas, Sarah Blaffer had the money, urge and expertise to collect at a time when truly fine art was available to buy. With the help of New York's Knoedler Gallery and New York art dealer Spencer Samuels of the French & Company family, she gathered a phe-

*Sarah Campbell Blaffer (right) on her
three-month European honeymoon. Fellow
passengers and bride pose as groom takes
snapshot.*

*Sarah Campbell Blaffer as young belle
at boarding school.*

nomenal collection of Old Masters, Impressionists, American Abstract Expressionists—all with her "moveable art feast" in mind.

Most of her buying took place before World War II. Her friend and trustee, San Antonio lawyer Gilbert M. Denman, Jr., recalled: "She became an important connoisseur and collector at a time when almost no one else in Texas shared her understanding. Her ample philanthropies were largely devoted to encouraging a similar appreciation among her fellow citizens, an appreciation she devoutly believed would bring them greater happiness and moral strength."

In making Mr. Denman a trustee of her Foundation a few years before her death at age ninety-one, she told him: "I believe that love of art is closely associated with love of God. It has been true all through Christian history. Man's art is God's gift to him. It is His signature across the Face of Creation. Every experience of man's art is an experience of God . . . in the creation of art we are fellow workers of God, whether we recognize it or not."

Her "exhibition" was alive and running before she died in 1975. The first of the Sarah Campbell Blaffer Foundation's traveling shows was one featuring American Abstract Expressionists. "When we started collecting those paintings," says Mr. Denman, "she was quite an old lady, and a very beautiful one. To the end, she was still very avant-garde. When we suggested such a collection be put together while the masterpieces of the genre were still obtainable, it was she who said the core of the collection should be Jackson Pollock. Actually, our first purchase was a Clyfford Still. A Pollock came later. When Mrs. Blaffer was no longer able to visit galleries, we would bring color slides of suitable paintings to her room and project them on the wall. Many superb pieces were acquired this way. She knew instinctively what to buy."

The paintings were loaned free to Texas schools, colleges and many museums without big collections of great art. The Houston-based foundation provided $600,000 a year for art purchases, and additional money to pay for circulating the exhibitions, and for publications expenses.

In the Golden Age of Paintings exhibition, 41 masterworks by such sixteenth- and seventeenth-century masters as Hieronymus Bosch, Brueghel, Rubens and Van Dyck traveled to all parts of the state. Included in the show was a film series about each of the artists, an introductory videotape gives a crash course in art appreciation, all gratis, thanks to the Foundation. The Blaffer daughters feel it is the perfect memorial to their mother—a catalyst to culture all their lives. Sarah not only was an art connoisseur, she also collected philosophers, musicians, poets and visiting English nobility. It was not unusual at all in the Blaffer household in exclusive suburban Shadyside to walk the block with Irish writer A. E. Russell spouting his poetry, or to host the British ambassador of the moment.

Growing up in the Blaffer family was more "constant nymph" than Texan, even though each member was fiercely Texas-proud. While other Houston girls were off at summer camp near Kerrville, or on the beach at Bayport, the Blaffer girls were soaking up beauty and culture in the great galleries and concert halls of Europe. Or, simply doing their thing—writing poetry, reading philosophy or whatever—at their Mademoiselle's country place in the South of France. No one else in Houston was quite like the Blaffer entourage. Instead of Tex-Mex, they were Tex-French—and full of beans. They were all very properly brought up. Jane, for instance, attended Kincaid, the private school her father founded in Houston; then to boarding school at chic Ethel Walker in Simsbury, Connecticut . . . and on to several years at Bryn Mawr, alma mater of a similar free spirit, Kate Hepburn. In between family visits, she made pilgrimages to schools for the deprived with her close school chum, another Jane, daughter of IBM's Tom Watson. She was particularly impressed by Martha Berry and her college for mountaineer boys and girls near Rome, Georgia. Later she married oilman-geologist-rancher Kenneth Dale Owen and brought enlightenment, herself, by restoring the utopian community of New Harmony, Indiana, one of the most unique accomplishments in America. Here her husband's ancestor, the idealist and Scottish textile magnate Robert Owen, had started a utopian colony and introduced to America equal rights for women and Medicare, as well as boatloads of distinguished educators, naturalists and scientists. From 1830 to 1860, New Harmony had been a center for the study of geology. When the Owens were married in 1941, they visited his ancestral town, then very much bypassed by time and care. Jane Blaffer Owen felt the entire village had been just waiting for her to adopt it. She took it under her wing. Instead of restoring the Harmonist buildings, she renovated many, and added such inspirational contemporary architectural innovations as the Roofless Church, designed by Philip Johnson; a dazzling-white library, product of Richard Meier's architectural genius, and a handsome inn by Indianapolis architect Evans Woollen. Jacques Lipchitz sculpted the town's Ceremonial Gates.

Second sister Titi's mate is His Serene Highness Prince Tassilo von Furstenberg, former husband of Fiat-king Gianni Agnelli's sister, Clara. The designer Diane von Furstenberg was married to his son, Egon. An internationally recognized art expert, with her father's financial savvy, Princess Titi makes the Foundation wheels go 'round. An astute collector herself, she, with New York art dealer Spencer Samuels and San Antonio attorney Gil Denman keep it going . . . and growing.

Youngest daughter is Joyce Blaffer von Bothmer, wife of Dietrich von Bothmer, chairman of Greek and Roman Art at the Metropolitan Museum. She was formerly married to the Marquis de la Begassière and her three daughters by that marriage were brought up at the Marquis' ancestral castle in Brittany.

One of the most remarkable art coups assembled by the Sarah Campbell Blaffer Foundation was one that brought the oeuvre of Edvard Munch to the United States. Outside of his native Norway, the opportunities to view the work of this remarkable Norwegian artist had been few. Over the years, Munch had found it difficult to part with his pictures, even when extremely hard up. When he became in demand, he couldn't have cared less about painting more. When he died, he left the city of Oslo most of his life's work, so the clamor for the remaining body of his paintings, prints and drawings was great among connoisseurs. When a painting of Munch's comes up at auction or for sale, it was, and still is, an event.

Sarah Campbell Blaffer acquired six rare Munch paintings, and her Foundation brought together the largest concentration of Munch's work ever assembled in this country; some on loan from the Munch Museum in Oslo.

In a foreword to the catalog for that exhibition, Jane Owen revealed much about the very private personality of her mother. She wrote: "Although my mother and the celebrated Norwegian never met during their lifetimes, and only one of them had a painter's training, both possessed a painter's eye. Long before Mother brought this eye to the serious collecting of art, she designed and furnished the rooms of her house as though she was painting on canvas. She created her uncluttered rooms in subtle planes of color and with the sure touch of a master who does not make an unnecessary brush stroke, and with the economy of a poet who does not settle with two words while the apt one can be found. I can hear her say: 'It is better to live with an empty space than with the wrong piece or the inaccurate word.' She was the first woman of her generation to uncurtain her windows, to strip her floors, and to exile embroidered centerpieces from her dining table, to flood her house with candlelight. Her philosophy of interiors can be best understood in the answer she invariably gave her friends when they sought her counsel: 'It's not so much what you put in a room as what you leave out.' Her approach was painterly in the Munch sense.

"Painter and patron were again alike in their need for privacy. I was permitted a glimpse into this side of the painter's personality by Eva Arneberg, the charming mother of my Norwegian son-in-law. Her husband, who had been the king's architect, asked Munch to paint a ceiling for a room in Oslo's Town Hall for which he was the architect. Also I was taken to the great Munch Museum which houses as complete a pictorial biography of an artist's emotions as I have seen assembled in one place. I recall my wonder over the portrait of a frail, unmilitary figure pointing a rifle out of a window. There was no visible target, and I asked: 'Who is the enemy?' 'That is another portrait of his feelings,' Frau Arneberg explained wistfully. 'Poor Edvard, he felt like shooting anyone who invaded his privacy.'

"Mother's passion for privacy never reached these paranoid extremes. But she had no time for those who brought small talk or people who bought art as a status symbol or purely as an investment. For those who understood her most quoted dictum: 'Art Is What It Creates in You,' for those who could appreciate her flights of fantasy, and who viewed the world widely, a visit was possible and would remain an unforgettable experience.

"Her faithful steward of a lifetime, 'Old Jim,' knew when to say 'Mrs. Blaffer is resting,' and when to gently say she was not.

"Imagination," I once heard her say, "is a paper key, until steel makes it a fact." Like most of Mother's thoughts, this one was expressed uniquely and is open to various interpretations. For me, Mother may have been contrasting the art of conversation, the poetic phrase, the assemblage of a room, with the more tangible, permanent legacy of the painter. To Mother, it was always the artist who unlocked the great mysteries, who wove the finest nets with which to catch and hold the inexpressible.

"But Sarah Blaffer need not have underestimated the importance and quality of her own key. Art is a long corridor, with door after door. The first must be opened by the student, and his or her key must be fashioned of a deep desire, or it shall never turn the lock. The art school, the university, and those who teach or administer must each bring his own right fitting keys of steel. But how is any door to open without the master key of those who endow and collect? Mother's keen perception of art and an uncommon business acumen placed such a key in her hand, but she never knew it. She was aware that the Creator had given her a seeing eye, a sense of poetry, and good business judgment, and she had no false humility about these gifts. But she never envisioned how far the combination of these gifts (all rarely found in one individual) could be conveyed through her Foundation, or how deeply her descendants would feel about realizing her wishes.

"Let us then, as we stand on the threshold of this major retrospective, look upon patron and artist in a new and close relationship. Let us enjoy the paradox of two people who often closed their private doors and are opening the portals so generously for us on this occasion! While alive, their sensitivities were too near the surface for frequent visitors or public encounters. Their awareness of this tragic century caused them a pain which could not be healed with quick or purely social panaceas. Art alone for them offered the diagnosis, the purification, and, in the last analysis, the resurrection. It would be their wish that the works in this exhibit offer each visitor a greater acceptance of their own lives and their times, and, if possible, bring them a greater joy. For how can the creator of "The Kiss" and the lady who brought it to Houston (preferring it to any other painting in her collection) not believe that life could be joyous and worth living? How can we not call these two, one a great master of modern times and the other a native Texan with vision, celebrators of a world that was, even in its anguish, always hauntingly beautiful?" Signed:

JANE BLAFFER OWEN for the Sarah Campbell Blaffer Foundation

When Mrs. Blaffer died at the age of ninety-one, her lifelong desire for a "museum without walls" had been achieved with enormous success. Always private, her tendency to keep aloof kept her name from the social columns and limelight. It was part of her upbringing. Her father had even forbidden that she be photographed at her wedding in 1909 "in case some of the boys in the bars and barbershops bandy it around."

Sarah's funeral, like her life, was very private. Held in the drawing room of her Houston home, only her closest family and friends were there. Her favorite paintings from five generations of collecting were removed from the walls. In their place were hung portraits of her beloved family—the Blaffer dynasty.

A poem, penned by Sarah herself, was read.

It is reprinted here:

RELEASE

When I am set free from this mortality
Apart from all but mind
May my spirit be like the mist of the sea
Leaving the brine behind
And—like the mist as it floats and drifts,
Refreshing turf and leaf—
Let the spark of me serve eternity
In nature's kind relief.

Included in the Collection of the Sarah Campbell Blaffer Foundation:

- *28 Abstract Expressionist Paintings* (de Kooning, Kline, Still, Gorky, Gottlieb/Hofmann, Motherwell, Pollock, Rothko)
- *42 Dutch, Flemish and German Paintings* (Cranach, Van Dyck, Cuyp, Quentin Massys, Rubens, Van Goyen, circle of Hieronymus Bosch, Steen, Ruisdael)
- *89 Francisco Goyas* ("*Los Desastres de la Guerra,*" complete set—83 plates—of the first edition; six other etchings)
- *30 Italian and Spanish Paintings* (Bernardo Daddi, Giulio Romano, Jacopo Tintoretto, Pietro Longhi, Claudio Coello, Francisco de Zurbarán)
- *Twentieth-Century Paintings* (three by Munch, two by Feininger, Beckmann, Bonnard, Dufy, Léger, Nolde, Sisley, de Staël)

★ THE BLAFFER FAMILY ★

The Children and Grandchildren of Sarah Campbell Blaffer

GENERATIONS

1st	2nd	3rd	4th

Robert Lee Blaffer *married* Sarah Campbell

John Hepburn Blaffer *married* Camilla Davis

Camilla (Coco) Blaffer *married* John Royall

Catherine (Trinka) Blaffer *married* Nicholas Taylor

Sarah Blaffer *married* Dan Hrdy

Joan Blaffer *married* Luke Johnson

Robert Lee Blaffer III

Jane Blaffer *married* Kenneth Dale Owen

Jane Blaffer Owen

married (1) Per Arneberg

married (2) Peter Jarvis

Carolyn Owen *married* James Coleman

Anne Dale Owen

Cecil Amelia (Titi) Blaffer

married (1) Edward Joseph Hudson

Edward Joseph Hudson, Jr.

married (1) Hope Lockwood

married (2) Christine Gerard

Robert Lee Blaffer Hudson *married* Betty Lou Drewes

married (2) Richard Sheridan

married (3) Prince Tassilo von Furstenberg

Joyce Blaffer

married (1) Jacques de la Begassiere

Marisal de la Begassiere

Jacqueline de la Begassiere

Diane de la Begassiere

married (2) Dietrich von Bothmer

Bernard von Bothmer

Maria von Bothmer

First Ladies

LADY BIRD, IMA AND ELECTRA.
Three First Ladies. In every sense of the word.

Lady Bird Johnson, 36th First Lady of the United States.

The late Ima Hogg, legendary "First Lady of Texas," the daughter of Texas' first Texas-born governor, Will Hogg.

Electra Waggoner Biggs, proprietor of the ½-million-acre Waggoner Ranch, "First Lady of Ranching."

All outstanding personages. On their own.

Then there are those who ride on the coattails of their family's accomplishments.

They tell the story of a cattle baron's darling daughter. She couldn't understand why she was treated like all the other girls when she first arrived at an exclusive Eastern boarding school.

"Daddy," she cried over the telephone. "This place won't do. I don't think anyone knows just exactly who I am."

Her father, whose name is one of Texas' biggest, thought for a moment and answered softly, "Who *is* you, honey?"

Lady Bird Johnson

When a case of self-importance seems to be setting in, "Who *is* you, honey?" is quoted by many of Texas' most prominent families. Of course, when you're the daughters of Lyndon Baines Johnson, President of the United States, it's hardly necessary to ask "Who is you?"

Nevertheless, their mother let them know, early in the game, that it was not they who were being honored with special attention, it was the Office of the Presidency, which they represented.

"Destiny has thrust this responsibility on you. It's a privilege few have. Do it honor. Use it to help others, not yourself, and it can work miracles."

Lady Bird Johnson practiced what she preached. When she became First Lady, ugliness had gripped the land. She was determined to wipe it out. She had a deep, roaring faith in, and love for, her country. She wanted its citizens to see it, treasure it, keep it beautiful.

As wife of the President, she stood in a unique position to do something, and "Beautify America" became her personal crusade.

Mrs. Lyndon Baines Johnson's role as First Lady began on Friday, November 22, 1963. In Dallas. It had started to be a beautiful day. The Johnsons and Texas Senator Ralph Yarborough were riding in a motorcade, heading for a campaign luncheon. Leading the parade was President John F. Kennedy, his wife, Jacqueline; Texas Governor John and Nellie Connally; and their Secret Service men. Streets were lined with people . . . smiling, throwing confetti, waving from curbs and windows. The Johnsons were in the third car, when suddenly a shot rang out, then two more—and the next thing they knew their Secret Service bodyguard was leaping over the front seat throwing himself on top of her husband, shouting "Get down . . . on the floor . . ."

Those shots not only interrupted the parade, but drastically changed her life.

Within the space of a morning, John F. Kennedy was dead and her husband, Lyndon Baines Johnson, had been sworn in as 36th President of the United States.

When Mrs. Johnson moved into the White House, someone heard her remark: "I feel as if I'm onstage for a part I never rehearsed."

It was a natural reaction, however. No other First Lady ever had

*LBJ and his Lady Bird. President and Mrs. Lyndon Baines Johnson were
first Texans to occupy White House.*

better training for the role. Most of her married life had been devoted to serving her country in the nation's capital—starting in 1937 as a congressman's wife. In 1948, LBJ moved to the Senate. In between those years, during World War II, she had served as a Navy wife when her husband served on active duty. As wife of the Vice-President, she had on occasion taken over for Jacqueline Kennedy in the White House.

Her background was directly opposite from Mrs. Kennedy's. Instead of Miss Porter's in Farmington, Connecticut, she had attended Saint Mary's Episcopal School for Girls in Dallas. Mrs. Kennedy was married in a Catholic church in Newport. Mrs. Johnson at St. Mark's Episcopal church in San Antonio. Kennedy walls bloomed with Impressionist paintings. Lady Bird Johnson's Monet was her meadow of wild flowers at the LBJ Ranch near Stonewall in the Texas Hill Country.

Of all First Ladies, Lady Bird Johnson seemed most naturally approachable to all America. She combined Western pioneer with Southern graciousness; traditional mother with modern businesswoman. She had worked hard to back her husband's career. She knew the necessity of making ends meet . . . and the nitty-gritty of moving, mothering, entertaining, packing, renting houses and saving for one of their own, bringing up daughters late in life. Along the way, too, she had emerged as a very canny businesswoman.

Consequently, it was easy for her to find things in common with people wherever she went—grass-roots, big-business, Washington-power or the Garden Club of America. Her crusade to beautify America sprang from her natural interest in the latter.

When she went to the White House, upon being asked what role she would play—doyenne of the castle, social worker, or friendly companion—she had no answer other than, "My role must emerge in deeds, not words." It probably never occurred to her that she would be filling a role. She had always been herself, and saw no reason to change. So it was only natural that with love of flowers so close to her heart, she set her course in the area she knew something about.

Her beautification idea evolved when Secretary of the Interior Stewart Udall visited the LBJ Ranch late in 1964. It was a bleak wintry day, and during a chat before a roaring fire, they talked about how she might help the cause of conservation. Once they had decided on a course, it didn't take long for her to spring into action. By February 1965, the

Lady Bird Johnson touring National Park with Secretary of Interior Stewart Udall (right).

First Lady and Secretary Udall had formed a Committee for a More Beautiful Capital. Mrs. Johnson spearheaded the committee as its chairman, bringing together the country's foremost preservationists, landscape designers and philanthropists. Borrowing a slogan from her close friend and committee member Mary Lasker, she promoted "planting masses of flowers where the masses pass."

By Eastertime, Pennsylvania Avenue was abloom with 10,000 azalea bushes. Masses of tulips and daffodils were planted around hundreds of small traffic circles. Parks appeared in grimy downtown Washington areas. Schoolgrounds and walks took on a bright new hue with colorful playground equipment and plantings.

The effect was magical. Next came The Society for a More Beautiful National Capital. This still-continuing supplemental committee served as a clearinghouse to receive private donations for projects that might be more widespread than the Park Service would undertake.

In 1969, when she left the White House and returned to the ranch, Mrs. Johnson didn't let the momentum of her beautification crusade falter one whit. There she focused on her neighboring "hometowns in the Texas Hill Country." With her love of wild flowers, she set out to make Texas roads and highways "gardenways" for tourists and travelers to enjoy all seasons of the year. In 1970, the Lady Bird Johnson Award was established. Every year, at a barbecue luncheon at LBJ State Park, she gives the award to the Highway Department foreman who does the best job that year in helping beautify his section of highway or road.

Seeing how her Beautification Committee had enhanced the nation's capital, she honed in on her state's capital of Austin. She formed the Citizens' Committee for a More Beautiful Town Lake, creating "people places" with flowering trees, benches, and hike-and-bike trails.

No one in the White House since Theodore Roosevelt had taken such personal interest in America's national parks, and all facets of "environment." She became a valued member of the National Park Service Advisory Board. She was also honored to be the first woman on the Board of Trustees of The National Geographic Society.

As a private citizen, Lady Bird Johnson has to flee to her ranch or a holiday spot to be really private. Her every move is watched. She is constantly contacted to make a public appearance or a statement. Her secretary, Mrs. Betty Tilson, says, "At first, she was just a girl-who-can't-

---

★ *THE FAMILY OF LADY BIRD JOHNSON* ★

GENERATIONS

1st	2nd	3rd	4th
Thomas Jefferson Taylor, Jr. *married* Minnie Lee Patillo			
	Thomas Jefferson Taylor III		
	Antonio J. Taylor		
	Claudia Alta (Lady Bird) Taylor *married* Lyndon Baines Johnson (37th President of USA)		
		Lynda Bird Johnson *married* Charles Robb	
			Lucinda Desha Robb
			Catherine Lewis Robb
			Jennifer Wickliffe Robb
		Luci Baines Johnson *married* Patrick Nugent	
			Patrick Lyn Nugent
			Nicole Marie Nugent
			Rebekah Johnson Nugent

say-no. The demands on her time were enormous. Now she can say no. The Carter Administration wanted her to be U.S. Ambassador to Mexico. Magazines constantly call her. She's quite an eloquent writer, as she proved in her best-seller, *A White House Diary,* but she has turned down publishing offers. Even American Express wanted her to do one of those 'Do you know who I am?' commercials. But she explains that she just doesn't have the time. She concentrates her energies on things close to home and close to her heart—like raising money for the LBJ Library, her highway wild flowers, meals on wheels, and, of course, her radio stations and cable TV interests. She sees an endless stream of visitors and entertains, lavishly, visiting famous friends. But she's the most unpretentious person you ever saw. Everybody just loves her. She's always *Herself.*"

When Mrs. Johnson became First Lady of the land, Anne Morrow Lindbergh said of her: "She has the strength to stand up for what she believes—in the home or on the platform. She has the courage to be herself. Living in the glare of publicity is like walking constantly down halls of mirrors; it is almost impossible not to pose—just a little. One must make an heroic effort to be oneself. Mrs. Johnson resolutely walks those halls without looking in the mirrors. I have seen her."

Ima Hogg

"There's a lady in Houston, Texas, whose name is Ima Hogg. No kidding. She has three brothers and, you know what their names are? Heza, Sheza, and Ura!"

Such were the wild tales told about Texas in the first part of the twentieth century. Like most of them, it was only partly true.

There *was* a lady in Houston named Ima Hogg. She *did* have three brothers. However, their names were Will, Tom and Mike. And she was a lady—a grand lady. To this day, "Miss Ima" is still revered as "The First Lady of Texas," an honor usually reserved for the wife of an acting governor.

Born July 10, 1882, Ima was named for a character in an uncle's poem. As the daughter of Texas' first native-born governor, James Stephen Hogg, she grew up in an atmosphere of privilege, right from the

*Miss Ima when her father, James Hogg, was
governor of Texas.*

beginning. Pretty, charming, talented, and the only daughter, she was idolized by her father and brothers. The governor's mansion in Austin played host to a constant flow of famous people in politics, business and the arts, and the Hogg children were usually included at the dinners for dignitaries. Before she was twelve, little Miss Ima Hogg was noted as a delightful, poised young hostess, at ease and interested in people from all walks of life. She and her older brother, Will, often went along with the governor on political trips. Their father's concern for the citizens of Texas became their concern. And when her mother died, Ima took over as lady of the house—at age thirteen.

The Hogg household was very similar to another First Family of that era—the Theodore Roosevelts. Ima was of the same mold as Alice, but a Southern-belle version. The sons were as active as Teddy's boys, too. The governor's mansion echoed with sounds of children chasing pets and sliding down banisters. The family's menagerie included a bear, two ostriches, a fawn, dogs, a horse, and a parrot named Jane that cawked: "Papa, Papa" whenever Governor Hogg entered the room.

Ima not only had perfect poise, she had perfect pitch, too. For as long as she could remember, she could play the piano. In the third grade, her piano teacher thought she had a child prodigy on her hands. At Misses Carrington's Preparatory School in Austin, Ima began to pursue her interests in music seriously, and she eventually studied at New York's National Conservatory of Music, and later, in Munich. Her expertise and financial influence led to her founding the Houston Symphony Society in 1913. She served as its president from 1917 to 1921. During this formation period of the Houston Symphony another of her great attributes surfaced: her power of persuasion.

"Miss Ima has an enormous facility for getting people to work for her," said her secretary, Mrs. Prym Specht. "Her friends would tell you that in the early days she would pound the pavements up and down Main Street getting ads for the Symphony programs. Miss Ima's father, who had been attorney general then governor and a founder of Texaco, had a long list of powerful friends. Miss Ima saw to it that they not only joined the Symphony Society, she had them working many hours getting their friends to get their friends to do so."

She served as president of the Houston Symphony after both World Wars. Betty Ewing, the *Houston Chronicle* social reporter, said she was a wonder-in-action. Also: "Remember how all eyes would be on Mrs. Cornelius Vanderbilt at the Metropolitan Opera. Well, for decades Miss Ima's settling in her seat at the Symphony had the same effect in Houston."

Music was only one of Ima Hogg's many loves. As a student at the University of Texas, her favorite courses were German, Old English and psychology. Thanks to Dr. Caswell Ellis, her psychology professor and lifetime friend, she honed in on mental health. Later on, her Hogg Foundation contributed to the positive approach of maintaining mental health, in contrast to treating mental illness and insanity. It pioneered a broad-based program in schools throughout Texas.

The Hoggs firmly believed that their wealth never really belonged to them. Since it came from Texas land, as if it had been handed to them in trust, they felt responsible to use it wisely for the people of the state.

Ima's father, who had one of the great legal minds of his time, was fortunate in being at the right place at the right time. For instance, he bought land, and lots of it, prior to the big Spindletop oil strike of 1901. You would have thought he was clairvoyant, in the acres he picked to buy. It came about almost by accident. The widowed ex-Governor was a devoted family man. He wanted a home where his children could always return from school, work or travel and share as a family. "An ark of safety . . . a haven of rest in old age." He found his sanctuary, The Varner Plantation, outside of West Columbia, Texas. Situated between Houston and Victoria, near Lake Jackson and the Gulf of Mexico, it was an ideal place for Ima, Will, Mike, Tom and the Governor to entertain their friends. The house itself was a classic white-columned Southern colonial mansion, with a widow's walk on top. He bought Varner for the charm of the house, not the property around it. However, once settled in West Columbia, he and his partner purchased property nearby for land development. From these tracts, the Hogg family fortune soared. For nearby, oil was discovered at Spindletop, in greater quantities than the world had ever seen. Hogg had a hunch that there was oil on his property, too. You could drop a lighted match on his ground and it would send up a spurt of flame. At times, his artesian well would spew a geyser of water 20 feet high. So, Mr. Hogg turned his attention to the burgeoning petroleum industry. His close proximity, legal genius and political clout served him well. He didn't live to see an oil strike on his plantation, however. But with the same intuition that had guided him throughout his life, and that Ima seemed to have inherited from him, he stipulated in his will that Varner Plantation should not be sold for at least 15 years after his death. Thirteen years after his death, in 1919, a rich new oil-bearing sand was discovered on the property. Two years later, the West Columbia oil field was producing 12 million barrels a year.

With all that money gushing in, it was Hogg Heaven. Now the family had ample resources for all their pursuits.

Will assumed primary responsibility to the clan. Ima became the matriarch. Together, Will and Ima developed a lifelong love for antiques, and it was as a collector that she achieved her greatest glory.

Hallway in Ima Hogg's antiques-laden Houston home, Bayou Bend, now a museum. (Photograph by Ezra Stoller)

A family friend, Mrs. Turner Williamson, first introduced them to English antiques. A member of the Houston elite herself, she had a great influence in furnishing some of the finest mansions in Texas. After her husband died, Mrs. Williamson had invested her inheritance in an antique business. First she went to London's Victoria and Albert Museum to learn everything she could about English furniture. With her Shabby Shop, she brought exquisite antiques into the oil-financed collections of Houston.

Ima had been fascinated with "old things" since childhood. First at her grandfather Stinson's antebellum homestead with its elaborately baroque Victorian furnishings. Then, as a resident of the Governor's Mansion in Austin, she had the thrill of sleeping in Sam Houston's four-poster bed.

Mrs. Williamson and her English antiques started Ima collecting truly fine furniture. Then, after the West Columbia oil strike gave her ample capital, Ima began to collect seriously. In 1920 she bought her first important American piece, a maple Queen Anne New England armchair with rush seat. With her strong interest in history, she studied its provenance carefully. Ima excited her brother Will about assembling an American collection. "We have a rare opportunity," she told him in 1920, "to collect American antiques for a museum in Texas." It had never been done before.

Certainly the time was right. American antiques were not considered fashionable before the 1920s, so were in ample supply. She and Will together combed the country for the choicest early American furniture, with America's leading dealers to help them. Ginsburg & Levy, a foremost New York dealer in early American furniture, found them an important Connecticut high chest and tea table. Ima attended auctions, house sales and antique shops herself. By the time her brother Will died in 1930, they had an enormous collection. And a very important one.

By 1927, their collection had become so vast that the Hoggs needed an appropriate home for it. They commissioned Houston's fashionable architect John Staub to design it. The result is Bayou Bend, Staub's and Houston's most famous house.

Staub's design was inspired by an early nineteenth-century country house, Homewood, in Baltimore. The floor plans were drawn by Miss Ima, with ample instructions, also, as to the style of the exterior. "In this

Exterior, Bayou Bend, considered Houston architect John Staub's masterpiece.

climate, New Orleans architecture works very well," she said. "I think it would look very pretty here. Also, I remember those buildings in Greece. Like Houston, Greece has brilliant sunlight, and they use pale pink."

Miss Ima got her pink. To achieve just the right shade, one of Will's companies provided crushed minerals to mix with wet cement. To weather and harmonize with the copper roof, shutters and doors were painted brown, glazed a pale-green.

Not forgetting Miss Ima's suggestion about New Orleans architecture, Staub included a front balcony with iron grillwork, and Louisiana plantation-house triple-sash windows on the first floor.

Bayou Bend's main-entry doorway was inspired by one in Charleston's Nathaniel Russell House.

The interior, too, had a bit from here, a bit from there. Scrolled pediments above the living-room doorways were copied from Virginia's famed eighteenth-century plantation mansion, Shirley. Floorboards in Miss Ima's sitting room came from an ancient house that had been dismantled in Massachusetts.

Since Ima, Will and Mike were to reside there, Bayou Bend was built in three sections. The men had bachelor apartments with their own sitting room, taproom, kitchen and two bedrooms. Miss Ima's domain was the center section, over the major living rooms and dining areas. Servants and guest rooms occupied the west wing.

Tom had married and moved to San Antonio, so Will, Mike and Ima settled down in solid splendor, surrounded by priceless early American furniture and decorative arts. Bit by bit Ima had disposed of her handsome English pieces, selling them to close friends for the same prices she had paid for them before World War I.

Will and Mike, who was called Mickey by his hosts of friends, were inseparable. They were in the oil business with Texaco co-founder J. S. Cullinan, and others from time to time. They also dealt in Houston real estate and were developers of exclusive River Oaks. Then, Mike fell in love with Alice Nicholson Frazer, of Dallas. "When Mike married Alice, it nearly killed Will," Miss Ima told a friend. "Almost immediately after the wedding, Will left for Europe. He never came back, and died in Baden-Baden after an emergency operation for gallstones."

Mike and Alice had a happy marriage. When he died in 1941, she married one of their closest friends, Harry Hanszen, who had recently lost his mate, too. Widow and widower merged.

Bayou Bend and everything in it had belonged to Will and Ima. After his death in 1930, she inherited it all. As doyenne of the most noted domicile in Texas, Miss Ima became the Perle Mesta of Houston. Hostess with the mostest. At Miss Ima's you could expect powerful people, potent potables, graciousness and wit.

"I just like to bring people together to make things happen," she explained.

There were so many parties and meetings held at Bayou Bend that some of the River Oaks neighbors complained—until Miss Ima called on them personally and invited them to join in the fun. Then, once there, she persuaded them to help carry out one of her projects of the moment. You just couldn't say "no" to Ima.

She did say "no," charmingly, herself. Many years before, a French nobleman, Prince du Prés, ardently pursued her. But Miss Ima was just too busy . . . besides, Paris, France, just wasn't Paris, Texas, was it?

Not that she didn't adore visiting there. On one visit to the City of Light, she brought back a number of works on paper, including some by Matisse and Picasso. However, during the Depression, the Hogg family's cash flow began to trickle just a bit. Will had died leaving several business ventures in need of substantial financing. So Miss Ima economized and concentrated almost exclusively on gardening and collecting more affordable treasures, such as Indian art. Especially native American pottery, kachina dolls and silver jewelry.

In developing the grounds at Bayou Bend, Miss Ima became an expert on horticulture. Her grounds supervisor, Kenneth Burkhardt, was amazed that she knew as much about agriculture and gardening as he did. "She was quite a taskmaster, too," he recalled. "Miss Ima would survey the estate from an upstairs window, and if she saw you doing something she didn't like, she'd call you in with her whistle. She had a different toot for key people. Mine was three short blasts."

Demanding perfection in herself, Miss Ima expected it in others. She never did anything halfway. Before attempting a project, she'd first do her homework. Then knowing how it should be done, she would supervise.

When she turned sixty, Miss Ima began to restrict her collecting almost entirely to early American furnishings. She gave most of her Russian avant-garde, post-Impressionist and Southwestern Indian art to the Houston art museum. After World War II, her attention focused once again on furniture. She turned for advice to Joseph Downs, curator of the Metropolitan Museum's American wing. Prior to the Metropolitan, Downs had assisted Henry Francis duPont at his private museum of American furniture, Winterthur, near Wilmington, Delaware. She told him her desire to convert Bayou Bend into a similar museum of period rooms. At his suggestion, she began attending the Antiques Forum each year in Colonial Williamsburg. Here she met for the first time other collectors. They became her friends and advisors. Among them were Mr. and Mrs. duPont of Winterthur; Electra Havemeyer Webb, of Shelburne; Henry N. Flynt, of Deerfield Village, Michigan; and Katherine

Prentis Murphy, of New York. Mrs. Murphy became her closest friend. In 1954, Ima invited them all to Houston to see her collection. Impressed, Ruth and Henry duPont urged her to do what they had done. Inspired and encouraged by them, she began to follow the path they had set in Winterthur. Charles F. Montgomery, its curator at that time, became her resource for technical advice.

During this period, she bought some of her finest pieces. Seeing the scarcity of American antiques and their steadily rising prices, she took her shopping list to America's best dealers—Israel Sack; Ginsburg & Levy; John Walton and David Stockwell among them. They, too, became her close friends. And she, one of their best customers.

Not only did she amass a formidable collection of American furnishings, her large collection of friends was perhaps unequaled anywhere. Old and young. Rich and poor. She and collector Katherine Prentis Murphy became so chummy that they telephoned each other every Sunday, laughing, chatting, passing on tips about "finds" and upcoming auctions.

In June of 1957, then age seventy-five, Miss Hogg donated Bayou Bend and its contents to the Houston Museum of Fine Art. At the dedication she told a friend, "Now I am free to pursue my other projects . . . and to watch sunsets from a high-rise apartment."

She retained the right to live in the house as long as she wished, and to draw upon income from her endowment for Bayou Bend's improvements and upkeep. She moved into that high-rise apartment, alright, and took her exercise pedaling down the halls on a giant tricycle.

The first period room completed in Bayou Bend was based on an early eighteenth-century Connecticut tavern common room. Katherine Prentis Murphy's specialty was William and Mary, and the two friends created the room together, furnished entirely with pieces from that and the Pilgrim period. Ima dedicated "The Katherine Prentis Murphy Room" in November 1959.

Creating complete period rooms made it necessary to gather the accessories—rugs, paintings, pewter, glass, silver and ceramics. She went to Norman Hirschl of New York's Hirschl & Adler Gallery for help in acquiring eighteenth-century art. In one year she bought nine works of John Singleton Copley; Edward Hicks' "Peaceable Kingdom," two Wollaston portraits and a painting by Badger.

In the pursuit of antiques for her museum's Texas Room, she became waylaid by a wayside inn. In the Stagecoach Inn of Winedale, Texas, built in 1834, she found primitive German decorations painted on the walls. German culture had always fascinated her since studying music in Munich as a girl. Now in her eighties, she delved into learning everything she could about the great influence of German settlers on Texas architecture and customs. Since she couldn't move the inn to Bayou Bend, she bought it and started another museum right there.

Nothing was spared to assure its authenticity. Square nails were shipped from Massachusetts; only timber from the Winedale farm itself was used, cut and shaved with tools used when the Inn was built. A sample of the parlor's original wallpaper was duplicated. Hang the expense. No matter if special rollers had to be produced for it, and that just a tad would be used for one small living room. It had to be authentic!

Miss Ima became so engrossed in restoring the Inn that she took a cottage nearby to make sure the work met her standards. She would spend her weekends there, supervising, pointing with her walking cane to something that might be out of order.

On one occasion she saw that the roofline had been straightened. She immediately telephoned the architect, Wayne Bell.

"What happened to the sag in the roof?" she asked.

Upon investigation, Mr. Bell found that the carpenter had taken it upon himself to put up supports and straighten it.

Miss Ima had the sag put back, just the way it was.

While restoring, she began exploring. In the tiny community of Round Top, near Winedale, she found an old German organ in the quaint church there. She saw that it was restored. When the organ was in shape to play again, she showed that she was in shape enough to climb up to the steeple and play it. The townspeople gathered below and cheered.

On her treasure hunts for antiques, her driver and "right-hand man" for 30 years, Lucius Broadnax, would bring along a big picnic basket containing her famous Fish House Cocktails for her guests. "It just made the occasions more festive in those small-town cafés without a liquor license," she explained.

When the Winedale restoration was completed, she had other early Texas-German buildings moved to the grounds. It became the Center of

Texas Cultural History, which she presented to the University of Texas in 1967, with an endowment for its support. She was then eighty-five.

Prior to Winedale, Miss Ima had restored Varner, the 1834 Greek-revival plantation house where she had moved when a young lady of nineteen. She furnished it with rococo revival and Empire furnishings. In 1958, on her father's birthday, she turned it over to the state as a museum and park. A decade later, at Bayou Bend, she furnished the Chillman Room entirely with Empire. She named it The Chillman Room in honor of her friend, James Chillman, Emeritus Director of the Houston Museum of Fine Arts.

Varner's Victoriana led her to rounding up Belter-style furniture for a "Gone With the Wind" parlor at Bayou Bend. Through her network of collector-friends, she heard that Brown University in Portsmouth, Rhode Island, was auctioning off all contents of the George Corliss 1860 mansion. She bought a truckload.

When her Chippendale–Queen Anne cronies sneered at her purchase, thinking the style a bit too exuberant, she laughed, and told them, "Better get with it. It's the coming thing."

She was right, too. Market and auction prices a decade later proved she was several hundred percent correct.

By the time she was ninety, Ima Hogg had presented her state with four house-museums, the most recent being her parents' "Honeymoon Cottage" in Quitman, Texas.

With her four museums in mind, she brought along shopping lists wherever she went. Seeking German antique porcelain for Winedale Inn, in 1974 she returned to Munich, scene of her student years.

There she joined "young friends whose parents had been old friends of her family's": lawyer Gilbert Denman and the Marshall Steves of San Antonio. Before the trip, upon hearing they were going to the Wagner Festival at Bayreuth, she had called Mr. Denman at home. "Gil," she said. "Do you remember when you were a young boy and we were in Munich with your family? And all those little German boys were marching along with swastikas on their armbands? Well, I haven't been back since. I'd like to hear Wagner at Bayreuth again . . . and tackle those antique shops in Munich. May I join you?" He was delighted. Mr. Denman and Miss Ima had a close bond. In the late 1800s, his lawyer-grandfather had backed her lawyer-father for governor. Later, when Hogg was governor, he talked Denman's grandfather into serving on the Texas Supreme Court. Although they were generations apart in age, family ties in Texas stay tightly bound . . . and Mr. Denman and Miss Ima went antiquing in Munich together.

Surprisingly, the antique shops had survived the bombings of World War II. Only the prices had changed. When Denman discovered the cost of the complete set of Nymphenburg porcelain on her list, he was stunned.

"Miss Ima," he told her. "You'd better revise your shopping list. The price of that porcelain is eighty thousand."

"I knew it would be something like that," she laughed. "Buy it."

With Miss Ima, quality counted. Not cost.

That night at supper, ninety-two-year-old Miss Ima raised her wineglass in a toast. "We've had such a delightful time. I propose that we return here next year—and do Bayreuth again together."

Return she did. At age ninety-three. But that was the last time. A week later in London, alighting from a taxi, she fell and broke her hip. Taken to an English hospital, she lingered only a short time. Miss Ima died happy, however, for when she fell, she had been on her way to Harrod's—with her shopping list in hand.

 THE HOGG FAMILY OF HOUSTON

James Stephen Hogg *married* Sarah Ann Stinson
     Ima Hogg
     William C. Hogg*
     Mike Hogg† *married* Alice Nicholson
     Thomas E. Hogg

---

*Except for minor bequests to Miss Ima and his brothers, the bulk of Will Hogg's estate went to the University of Texas.

†Mike Hogg's estate went to his widow, and at her death, to the University of Texas to establish a department of municipal government.

Electra Waggoner Biggs

Tallulah.

Salome.

Electra.

Names become legends. Especially if they belong to fascinating ladies.

Electra Waggoner Biggs was bequeathed the name made famous by her glamorous aunt, Electra Waggoner Wharton Bailey Gilmore. Electra the First. Prototype of Texas extrava-gals.

Extravagant she was.

When Electra married Philadelphia blueblood A. B. Wharton in 1900, everything in her trousseau, from tip to toe and underneath, had a Paris label.

In the history of Dallas' super-luxurious Neiman-Marcus store, she was the first to buy $20,000 worth of clothes in one visit. And, to come back the following day for $20,000 more goodies that she had forgotten. That would total about $140,000 in today's dollars. Electra could afford it, of course.

She was the only daughter of William Thomas Waggoner, who owned one of the biggest ranches on earth. He and his dad, Dan Waggoner, had first started ranching in Oklahoma, leasing the land from the government. After Oklahoma became a state, they began buying acreage across the border in Texas. And buying. And buying.

W. T. Waggoner was asked: "My God, Tom, are you going to buy all of Texas?"

Tom is said to have replied: "No. Only the land bordering ours."

By 1909, Tom Waggoner had bought up over 500,000 north Texas acres—the largest ranch under one fence in the United States. He had also sired five children: Dan; Willie; Guy; E. Paul; and Electra, the girl with the electric name.

His wife, the former Sicily Halsell, named their darling daughter for her father, Electius Halsell . . . and there has been an Electra in the family every generation since.

Electra was not only the family darling, she was the toast of northwest Texas. By 1902, when she was twenty, townsfolk of Waggoner pe-

Electra Waggoner I at Palm Beach.

titioned that the post office title be changed to Electra, Texas. A birthday surprise for her.

And that wasn't the only very special birthday present she was to receive. On another natal anniversary her daddy gave Electra a big ranch in Wilbarger County. She called it Zacaweista, the Indian name for tall grass, where her grandson Bucky Wharton lives today.

She went on to become an international hostess, intimate of J. P. Morgan scions and Teddy Roosevelt. She had a palace in Dallas, furnished with objects d'art she had collected kicking up her heels around the world.

Her dressing room appeared almost an annex of Neiman-Marcus. In her shoe cabinet, 350 pairs of shoes stood on-the-ready. She had a new pair delivered daily, if not from Neiman's, then from Manhattan. Word circulated that the store had a standing order to deliver a large stock of dresses for her to choose from before any other customer could get her clutches on them. To be sure that no one else had tried on the dress, each had to come to her in its original box from Paris or New York.

Along the way, she collected husbands, too.

First was Philadelphia socialite Albert B. Wharton, Sr. They had met on an around-the-world cruise, becoming engaged in the Far East. They had two sons, Tom and Albert, Jr. (Buster). Son Tom collected a few mates himself. Eight, to be exact. Incidentally, his uncle Guy Waggoner married and divorced eight times, too. It sort of ran in the family. Albert, Jr. (Buster) Wharton married four times. Buster and his cousin, Electra II, are co-owners of the ranch today.

Electra I died in 1924, passing along her name to her brother E. Paul's daughter, who "immortalized" the name even more. The Buick Electra and Lockheed's Electra jet were named for *her*. But Electra II is best known as an internationally acclaimed sculptor—and rancher.

Electra Waggoner Biggs, Electra II, may be Texas' top lady rancher, but if you're expecting an Annie-Get-Your-Gun, forget it. A Southern Mrs. Miniver, she is. More silk-and-satin than suede.

Even though Electra Biggs was bred on her papa's half-million-acre spread in northwest Texas, she was sent off to boarding school when she was barely old enough to roller-skate. She spent most of her youth, and married life, in New York. Consequently, when she inherited her family's whopping big Waggoner Estate, she returned a city girl, owner of more ranch acres than any other woman in America. She was also the most noted society sculptor since Gertrude Vanderbilt Whitney. Both these very feminine, elegant women were to sculpt two of the world's most macho monuments to cowboys: Mrs. Whitney's *Buffalo Bill* in Cody, Wyoming, and Mrs. Biggs' *Will Rogers. Buffalo Bill* bucks his steed in front of Cody's Buffalo Bill Historical Center complex. *Will Rogers* rides his horse, Soapsuds, into the sunset at Claremore, Oklahoma's Cowboy Hall of Fame, the Coliseum in Forth Worth and on the campus of Lubbock's Texas Tech.

Electra the Second became a sculptor to avoid taking a business course at Columbia. She loathed math, you see. At the time, she was living the life of a New York debutante . . . belle of the ball at coming-out parties and college proms . . . trotting to Long Island, Newport, Virginia, and all points Southwest. Beautiful, fun and very rich, she was a star in the social firmament. Since she was the only child of E. Paul Waggoner and would someday inherit a ranching empire that spread over six counties, her parents wanted her to learn a little about business, too.

Boarding at exclusive Miss Wright's School in Bryn Mawr had broadened her scope socially. When it came time for college, Electra chose Columbia University in New York to study business management. Just across town from her family's apartment at The Carlisle, Columbia seemed the most convenient campus. Besides, her most devoted beau of the moment was a student there, and could help with her math while they did their homework together.

Business Administration, as it turned out, was just not Electra's bag. When she asked a prep-school pal in desperation, "What can I do so I can stay in New York and study?" She was told, "Take a class in sculpturing. It's divine. You squeeze a lot of mud through your fingers, and before you know it . . . voilà . . . you've created an image."

Electra not only created an image, before long she was receiving more commissions from friends than she could handle. One of her earliest was a statuette of little Jimmy Robinson, son of Atlanta friends, the James Robinsons. Recently, that Jimmy Robinson, now chairman of American Express, was one of the first to buy her scaled-down, table-size, limited-edition *Will Rogers.* Only 100 castings were struck, and before they were cast, 85 had been ordered by a who's-who of Western art collectors.

Early on, Electra proved to be an exceptional artist. Before she was twenty, studying in Paris, her black marble head of a woman copped third prize in the Salon d'Automne.

"Parisians compared the enigmatic expression on my piece's black marble face to that of the Mona Lisa," Electra said. "Actually, the model was my maid Ida, who was terribly bored and always got sleepy when she was posing. The Huntington Museum and Library in Pasadena bought it for three thousand. I've tried to buy it back, but they won't sell."

Over the years, her commissions have included portrait heads of Eisenhower, Truman, Knute Rockne and her close chum, Mary Martin. When Mary Martin left *South Pacific* she personally inscribed medallions with her portrait head by Electra, and gave them as parting gifts to 400 members of the cast and crew.

Electra first established her studio in a building near the mayor of New York's Gracie Mansion. This turned out to be most convenient at the time she went to Mayor La Guardia for a favor. She asked to borrow from her noted neighbor, not a cup of sugar, but a police horse . . . to pose for her life-size Will Rogers statue. Mayor La Guardia obliged.

Every day, a New York mounted policeman trotted across town to deliver his equine model. Then he had to wait until the horse had finished posing. To pass the time, the cop would visit a nearby tavern and tipple. Each night, he'd ride back to the police stables swaying in the saddle.

Electra didn't have as many problems with the model for Will Rogers himself. His wife and Will, Jr., helped.

She had never met Will Rogers personally. He had, however, visited her father's horse operation. E. Paul, who had the title "Leading Quarter Horse Breeder of America," was a frequent host to Hollywood celebrities as well as sportsmen, ranchers and horsemen. Mr. Waggoner's stallion, Poco Bueno, was idolized like a movie star himself. Hordes would travel to the ranch just to see him in person. Every two years Poco brought in $5,000 in stud fees and a half-million dollars in colts. E. Paul refused a half-million dollars offered for him. Poco Bueno was somewhat of an equine Barrymore. Photographed often, he would instantly strike a pose the moment he caught sight of a camera.

Racing and breeding thoroughbreds was E. Paul's great joy. He established Arlington Downs, which was flourishing near his Santa Rosa Ranch before Texas repealed the bill permitting pari-mutuel betting in June of 1937.

While E. Paul was raising champion horses, his wife, Helen Buck Waggoner, was growing gorgeous gardens on her palatial Santa Rosa estate. From front gate to the front door of her rambling tile-roofed Mediterranean villa, the distance is four miles. Approaching the white mansion, high on a hillock, is a heaven of horticulture . . . seemingly miles of velvety green grass, exotic shrubs, ponds, walkways, gazebos, a swimming pool, rare trees, Helen's gardens and a swan lake. This is the view from her daughter Electra's sculpture studio, today—and as far as the eye can see, she owns with her cousin.

Returning to the solitary splendor of Santa Rosa Ranch after the glamour and bustle of New York and Washington, Electra experienced a slight case of culture shock. Not so for her husband, John Biggs. Having been brought up in Sherman, Texas, he felt right at home being back in the saddle again. He had left Texas to attend VMI, the famed military college in Lexington, Virginia. Stonewall Jackson and General George Marshall had preceded him there. As athletic star and commandant of cadets in his senior year, Biggs lived up to his name and had been Big Man on Campus in the eyes of the corps. He met Electra in New York when he was a top executive for International Paper Company. After they were married, they lived in Manhattan with their two daughters, Electra III and Helen, who was named for her gardening grandmother.

John Biggs found running the Waggoner Estate not too different from the corporate scene headquarters in any suburb. His command center was not a rustic ranch house but an office building seemingly as big as Fort Knox. Private planes made commuting from coast to coast comparatively simple, since he had practically door-to-door service. The ranch was one of the first to employ helicopters for herding cows, saving valu-

Section of Electra Waggoner Bigg's Santa Rosa Ranch, near Vernon, Texas. Waggoner Estate spreads over 500,000 acres all under one fence.

able time. The late Tony Hazlewood, then head of the Waggoner Ranch operations, once estimated that a helicopter could "do the work of fifteen to twenty cowboys on good horses in heavy brush." Mr. Biggs had been an army colonel during World War II, so "whirly-herding" was not too far removed from his reviewing troop movements. When he had first come to the ranch in 1946, after being released from his colonel's duties in Washington, he found a smoothly run empire. R. B. Anderson was then general manager of the entire W. T. Waggoner estate, which encompassed oil, cattle, agriculture, and banking and financing. Biggs served as his assistant general manager until Anderson left in 1953 to become Eisenhower's Secretary of the Navy, and later, Secretary of the Treasury. Then Biggs took over, and held the post until he died of cancer in 1975.

He and Electra II had been married for over 30 years. Visiting her Santa Rosa mansion today, guests feel they are in a house of happy memories. Here and there are reminders of annual jaunts to Hong Kong and the Far East; snapshots taken at their traditional New Year's Eve house parties on the ranch and on hunting trips, or with children and grandchildren. Electra's studio wall is covered with photographs of faces she has sculpted—famed Texans like Amon Carter, Sid Richardson; Sam Rayburn and Robert Kleberg, Jr.; Presidents Truman and Eisenhower; Bob Hope; Victor McLaughlin; Will Rogers and Knute Rockne, among them.

Ladies named Electra seem destined to light up the sky.

When Electra was married in 1933 at New York's St. Bartholomew's church, it was a glamorous social event. Norell, then with Hattie Carnegie, designed the bridal gown and bridesmaids costumes. The reception was held at the Waldorf-Astoria, in the Empire Room. Emil Coleman played. Electra wore her Aunt Electra's $10,000 lace veil bought on the round-the-world cruise where she first met A. B. Wharton. Steichen photographed the bride for *Vogue*'s July issue. The picture appeared as a full page, captioned: "AUREOLE OF TULLE. One of the most dramatic brides of the early summer was Miss Electra Waggoner," it read. ". . . Great drifts of tulle swirled about her—for, besides a veil of tulle and rose-point lace, yards and yards of tulle were attached to the shoulders of her ivory satin dress and flared out like an aureole. Her bouquet of white orchids was by Max Schling."

The *Vogue* portrait of Electra the bride was one of Edward Steichen's most famous photographs. Almost fifty years later, June 25, 1982, the original was auctioned at Sotheby's in London as part of Steichen's estate. It brought an impressive sum.

The bridal veil, a lace masterpiece, was worn by Electra I, Electra II and her daughters Electra III (Mrs. Charles Winston) and Helen (Mrs. Gene Willingham) when they married. It just wouldn't be a Waggoner wedding without Aunt Electra's veil.

In Greek myth there was an Electra, one of Atlas and Pleione's seven daughters. She and her sisters were transformed into bright stars, the Pleiades of constellation Taurus. Occasionally in the heavens, the star Electra shows herself to mortals as a comet.

★ THE WAGGONER FAMILY ★
Some Forebears and Descendants of Electra Waggoner Biggs

GENERATIONS

1st	2nd	3rd	4th	5th	6th	
Solomon Waggoner *married* Elizabeth McGaugh						
	Dan Waggoner					
	married (1) Nancy Moore					
		William Thomas (Tom) Waggoner *married* Ella Halsell				
		Daniel Waggoner				
		Electra Waggoner *married* Albert Wharton, Sr.				
		Willie Waggoner				
		Guy L. Waggoner				
		E. Paul Waggoner *married* Helen Buck				
			Electra Waggoner *married* John Biggs			
				Electra Waggoner Biggs *married* Charles F. Winston		
					Electra Winston	
				Helen Dale Biggs *married* Gene W. Willingham		
					Jennifer Willingham	
					John Waggoner Willingham	
	married (2) Sicily Halsell					

Electra Waggoner II (Mrs. John Biggs), photographed for Vogue *in 1933 by Edward Steichen.*

VIII

King
of the Keyboards

IN THE PEERAGE of concert pianists, Van Cliburn is Texas' Prince
Charming. On April 14, 1958, when it was announced that Van
Cliburn of Kilgore, Texas, had won the First Prize Gold Medal in the
International Tchaikovsky Piano Competition in Moscow, he became an
international hero. Khrushchev, who had been in office only 17 days,
gave him the famous bear hug and New York gave the twenty-three-
year-old Texan a ticker-tape parade. In presenting him the keys to the
city, Mayor Robert Wagner lauded: "The impact of Van Cliburn's triumph goes far beyond music and himself as an individual, and is a dramatic testimonial to American culture ... with his two hands Van Cliburn struck a chord which has resounded around the world, raising our
prestige with artists and music lovers everywhere." President Eisenhower invited Van Cliburn and his parents to visit the White House.
The Russians showered him with so many gifts, he left Moscow with 17

pieces of luggage to carry them all home. His first recording for RCA Victor, Tchaikovsky's B-flat Minor Concerto, broke records in classical record sales. Six feet four with modest, friendly manners and thick, curly hair, he immediately captured the adoration of his audiences.

Van Cliburn is of English, Scottish and Irish ancestry. His mother's parents, William Carey O'Bryan and Sirrildia McClain O'Bryan, were prominent socially, and Col. O'Bryan served three terms in the Texas legislature. Col. O'Bryan's father, Dr. Solomon Greene O'Bryan, was a cofounder and president of Baylor University of Waco. On Van's father's side, his ancestors hailed from Cliburn Village in Northern England.

An only child, Van Cliburn was born in Shreveport, Louisiana, and named for his father, oil executive Harvey Lavan Cliburn, later shortened to Van. The Cliburns moved to Kilgore when Van was six years old. Van's mother, Rildia Bee O'Bryan Cliburn, a talented pianist, had studied under Arthur Friedheim, a pupil of Franz Liszt. When Van was only three, long before he had learned to read words, she began to teach him to read music. She remained his only instructor until he went to study with Juilliard's legendary Russian, Madame Rosina Lhévinne in New York.

Van Cliburn played first in public at the age of four, at Shreveport's Dodd College. By the time he was six, it was obvious that Van was destined for a concert career. He was to win many musical accolades and prizes before his history-making journey to Moscow. At the age of twelve, as winner of a statewide young pianists' competition, he made his orchestral debut with the Houston Symphony, playing the Tchaikovsky B-flat Minor Concerto. The following year, he bowed at Carnegie Hall as winner of the National Music Festival Award.

In 1952, he won the G. B. Dealey Award in Dallas, bringing with it an appearance with the Dallas Symphony and, in the same year, won the Kosciuszko Foundation Chopin Award. He added to his laurels by winning a grant from the Olga Samaroff Foundation and the Juilliard Concerto contest in 1953, and in 1954 upon his Juilliard graduation with highest honors, he received the Carl M. Roeder Memorial Award and the Frank Damrosch Scholarship, which enabled him to go on to graduate work. Further honor was bestowed when he was invited to be the 1978

Juilliard Commencement speaker, making him only the second graduate to be so honored (the first was Leontyne Price).

A most important victory came in 1954 when he won the Edgar M. Leventritt Foundation Award, playing the Liszt Twelfth Rhapsody. This competition gave the winner the privilege of playing in concert with the New York Philharmonic, as well as four other major American orchestras—the Cleveland, Pittsburgh, Denver and Buffalo symphonies.

His debut with the New York Philharmonic in 1954 was a huge success. Playing the Tchaikovsky First Piano Concerto, cheers broke out at the end of the first movement. The performance was recalled by critic Louis Biancolli of the *World Telegram and Sun,* who predicted: "This is one of the most genuine and refreshing keyboard talents to come out of the West—or anywhere else—in a long time. Van Cliburn is obviously going places, except that he plays like he had already been there."

When Van Cliburn triumphed in Moscow five years later, he immediately won the hearts of the Russian people. Tickets to Cliburn auditions were in such demand that people queued up for three or four days in advance. Word seeped back to America, which up to then had been fairly oblivious to the Moscow Competition. By the time Van was proclaimed the winner, he was front-page news all around the world and the idol of millions.

After the competition was over, Premier Khrushchev asked to hear Cliburn, and invited him to play several concerts in the Soviet Union, each one to sold-out houses and tumultuous acclaim. The international cables and telephones buzzed with offers. Overnight his concert schedule was miraculously filled.

Reviewing his first concert in New York after winning the medal in Moscow, *The New York Times* critic wrote: "The pianist had lived up to expectations, something that hardly seemed possible after so great a buildup."

A month later, Van returned to Europe. Performing in England, France, Italy and Brussels, his personal warmth and enthusiasm made him a good-will ambassador for America. Recording with RCA, his first album, the Tchaikovsky First Piano Concerto, became the first classical album in history to sell one million copies. During this period, he studied conducting under maestro Bruno Walter. He appeared in concert with the Moscow State Symphony. At the podium was his old friend, Kiril Kondrashin, with whom he had performed in Moscow.

Cliburn returned to the Soviet Union that same summer sponsored by the U. S. State Department as part of the Cultural Exchange Program. Again, enormous crowds gathered to hear him play in Moscow and also in Leningrad, Kiev, Tbilisi, Yerevan and Baku. His final appearance in Moscow's huge Sports Palace attracted more than 20,000 persons. Thousands were turned away. So great was the ovation at the concert's close that the ushers had to surround the stage to protect the artist from crowds. Ecstatic admirers thrust flowers and gifts into his arms. While in Moscow, he also played an Independence Day concert on July 4 at the American Embassy. Returning to the Soviet Union in 1962, in 1965 and 1972, he met with the same fervent enthusiasm.

In April 1983, the 25th anniversary of the Tchaikovsky Competition triumph, Van Cliburn was presented with the 1983 Albert Schweitzer Music Award "for a life's work dedicated to music and devoted to humanity." The Schweitzer Award, which is the major American award presented to performing musicians, was given to Van Cliburn "for helping humankind transcend its national boundaries and ideologies through a profound respect for musical excellence."

IX

Polo Peerage

WHEN H.R.H. The Prince of Wales visited Texas, he was entertained royally—at a polo picnic.

Texans have a passion for polo.

Right from the beginning of polo in America, San Antonio has been the major center for training polo ponies.

Supposedly, James Gordon Bennett, publisher of the *New York Herald*, first brought polo to the United States in 1876. However, in 1872, Captain Glynn Tourquant and a group of fellow Englishmen were whacking mallets-to-ball from horseback on his Boerne, Texas, ranch. Tourquant, a victim of English primogeniture, had come to Texas seeking his fortune. Having played polo in England, he quickly saw that properly trained Texas wild horses were naturals for the game. Texas mustang and cayuse breeds, descended from Moorish and Arabian

*Spaniards brought the horse to the New World in the eighteenth century;
polo was first introduced in San Antonio in the mid-1880s.*

horses brought over by Cortez, had run wild for generations. Having to
struggle for their lives daily, they had developed extraordinary speed
and endurance. Later, bred with racing stock, they developed into remarkably swift steeds that could stop and turn on a dime.

Polo farms flourished around San Antonio. In 1884, Pat Jones
started a polo training business on his Salado Creek Ranch. A neighbor,
Harry Tappan, followed suit, adding a polo field. Wealthy polo enthusi-
asts from the East, Jay Gould, August Belmont and Harry Oelrichs, obtained "bucking broncos" from the ranches, and borrowed their cowboys to help break them. In 1879, San Antonio-trained polo ponies
participated in the first regular match between Westchester Polo Club
and Queen's County Hunt Club.

Among Texas polo players, Llano-native Cecil Smith was the all-time champ. Discovered by Austin polo whiz George Miller, in 1925, Cecil Smith went on to hold a 10-goal handicap for 25 years in succession (1934–1959). No other man in the history of polo has ever equaled his record.

Texas polo was at its zenith in the thirties. Its biggest year, 1933, when Cecil Smith and Rube Williams, also a Llano future 10-goaler, teamed with two Californians and participated in the East-West All-Star Series at the Chicago World Fair. They played against Tommy Hitchcock, the only U.S. 10-goal player at that time, and his highly favored Eastern team. To everyone's surprise, the West won.

Cecil and his crew took the first match 15–11. In the second go-round, Rube Williams was taken off the field with a broken leg, and the West team lost 12–8. Cecil Smith became the hero of the third match, winning six of the 12 goals scored by his team.

Final score, West 12, East 6.

From then on, all through the thirties, polo boomed in San Antonio. Crowds of 7,000 came to see Cecil and Rube play. Then World War II called it all to a whoa. The army abolished the cavalry. Many players, including the great Tommy Hitchcock, were killed in action.

In the past decade, Texas polo has had a great revival, spearheaded by Will Farish III of Houston's Bayou Club; Norman Brinker of Willow Bend Polo Club in Dallas; Carlton Beal, co-founder of Midland Polo Club; and Steve Gose, with his Retama Polo Center going strong in San Antonio. Gose's multi-million-dollar Retama Polo Center has 16 polo fields, stables for over 400 horses and a double-sided stadium that seats 4,000. Steve Gose is Southwest Circuit majordomo for the U. S. Polo Association, and his Retama Club is home for the U. S. Open, highest-goal polo tournament sponsored by the U.S.P.A., played in the fall.

Ever since James Gordon Bennett brought polo to the United States from England, San Antonio has been America's major center for training polo ponies. In 1983, the city celebrated its centennial year in polo. Now, with Retama, it is becoming an international polo mecca. Players from South Africa, Australia, England, Argentina, Mexico and Spain have been swooping in. Mallet men who have whopped the willow-root ball there include:

San Antonio's Retama Polo Center, with 16 polo fields, stables for over 400 horses, a 4,000-seat stadium, is mecca for the game's top international teams and tournaments.

NAME	TEAM
Hernan Agoti, Buenos Aires, Argentina	Argentina
Dick Albert, Tulsa, OK	Tulsa
Red Armour, Blanco, TX	Boca Raton
Charles Armstrong, San Benito, TX	San Antonio
Stuart Armstrong, Kingsville, TX	San Antonio
Jeff Atkinson, Seguin, TX	San Antonio
Joel Baker, Carpinteria, CA	Rolex A&K
Bob Barry, New Braunfels, TX	Thunder
Joe Barry, San Antonio, TX	Retama
Roy Barry, New Braunfels, TX	Twelve Oaks
Alston Beinhorn, Houston, TX	San Ysidro

Toti Bordeu, Buenos Aires, Argentina	Argentina
Rick Bostwick, Old Westbury, NY	Southern Hills
Mike Carney, Wichita, KS	Boca Raton
Tom Corbett, Dallas, TX	Thunder
Fred Dearborn, Lexington, KY	Saxony Farms
José Ignacio Domecg, Jerez, Spain	Madrid
Nacho Domecg, Jerez, Spain	Sotogrande
Pedro Domecg, Jerez, Spain	Madrid
John Donaldson, Lexington, KY	Saxony Farms
Gaston Dorignac, Buenos Aires, Argentina	Santa Ana
Podger El Effendi, Barrington, IL	Tulsa
Bart Evans, Midland, TX	Fort Lauderdale
Ken Fransen, Spokane, WA	Valdina
Alonzo Galindo, Midland, TX	Y Bar O
Carlos Galindo, Midland, TX	Y Bar O
Hector Galindo, Midland, TX	Y Bar O
Pablo Rincón Gallardo, Mexico	Mexico
Fortunato Gomez, Midland, TX	Tulsa
Roberto Gonzales, Mexico City	Tecamac
Matt Gose, San Antonio, TX	Valdina
Steve Gose, San Antonio, TX	Retama
Tom Gose, San Antonio, TX	Valdina
Carlos Gracida, San Antonio, TX	Retama
Memo Gracida, San Antonio, TX	Retama
Ruben Gracida, Carpinteria, CA	Fort Lauderdale
Alberto Heguy, Colonel Suarez, Argentina	Colonel Suarez
Seth Herndon, Tulsa, OK	Southern Hills
Antonio Herrera, Mexico	Rolex A&K
Julian Hipwood, West Palm Beach, FL	Southern Hills
Bruce Hundley, Versailles, KY	Saxony Farms
Geoffrey Kent, Oak Brook, IL	Rolex A & K
Dr. John Kuhn, Chicago, IL	San Antonio
Corky Linfoot, Sutherland Springs, TX	Twelve Oaks
Reggie Ludwig, Sonoita, AZ	San Ysidro
Stuart Mackenzie, New Zealand	Rolex A & K
Jimmy Newman, Cibolo, TX	San Antonio
John C. (Jack) Oxley, Tulsa, OK	Fort Lauderdale
John T. Oxley, Tulsa, OK	Boca Raton
Nick Rennekamp, Prospect, KY	Saxony Farms
Owen Rinehart, Plano, TX	Boca Raton
Javier Rodriguez, Mexico	Tecamac

Jake Sieber, Cincinnati, OH	Fort Lauderdale
Charles Smith, Fort Worth, TX	Twelve Oaks
Samuel Solorazano, Brownsville, TX	San Ysidro
Michael Sparks, Arlington Heights, IL	Twelve Oaks
Henry J. M. Taub, Houston, TX	Blanco
James Uihlein, Meguon, WI	Blanco
Robbie Uihlein, Brandon, FL	Blanco
Louis Valdes, Madrid, Spain	Sotogrande
Rob Walton, Modesto, CA	Tulsa
Tommy Wayman, Adkins, TX	Southern Hills
David Wigdahl, Bartlett, IL	San Antonio
Jimmy Yarborough, Midland, TX	Y Bar O
William T. Ylvisaker, Barrington, IL	San Antonio

For the first time, too, since Cecil Smith's reign, two Texans have been knighted as ten-goalers: Tommy Wayman and Memo Gracida, of San Antonio.

The Royal Team

In 1977, when the Prince of Wales visited the ranch of Tobin and Anne Armstrong, former U. S. Ambassador to the Court of St. James's, the guests enjoyed a royal polo match.

These were the players:

> H.R.H. The Prince of Wales, Britain
> Tobin Armstrong, Armstrong Ranch
> John Armstrong, King Ranch
> Charles Armstrong (John's son), King Ranch
> Bobby Beveridge, San Antonio, Retama Polo Club
> Norman Brinker, Dallas, Willow Bend Polo Club
> Will Farish, Houston, Houston Polo Club
> Steve Gose, San Antonio, Retama Polo Club

Tobin and Anne Armstrong first met the Prince of Wales when Anne served as U. S. Ambassador to Great Britain during 1976–1977. At

*H.R.H. The Prince of Wales in polo match
at Armstrong Ranch, near Kingsville,
Texas, 1977.*

the time, Tobin was helping to raise funds for restoring bombed-out Canterbury Cathedral. Tobin's brother, John, and three of his boys had played in a match with the Prince on his home turf. But Tobin couldn't work polo into his schedule during their days at the Court of St. James's. So the Armstrongs invited Prince Charles to play at their ranch on his U. S. visit.

The Prince not only loved polo, he was most interested in seeing a roundup. In his student days, he had worked cattle on a large ranch in

Australia, one that bought prize Santa Gertrudis cattle from the Arm-strongs' ranch. So when he arrived on their 50,000-acre spread near Kingsville, his hosts not only had a polo game awaiting him, but also a pair of red chaps, their welcome gift for riding the range. On an English saddle, of course.

Before the Prince doffed his cowboy clothes and slipped into his white polo livery, private planes began descending like a sudden plague of locusts. Over 250 prominent Texans showed up to meet the royal visitor, watch him in action, and enjoy a South Texas barbecue under a yellow-and-white striped tent. The Armstrongs' daughter, Katherine, announced the polo match—and it was a spirited game. The Prince made a big hit with all the Texans . . . as had the Armstrongs with the British during their Embassy days. One news magazine at the time reported: "She's highly attractive, and her husband is a 'Zane Grey' ideal." The *London Daily Mail,* citing her reputation as an international hostess, crack-shot and horsewoman, declared Ambassador Armstrong "America's most romantic diplomat." To the British press, "Uncle Sam" became "Auntie Sam" while she was in London.

If Mayfair expected a lady in fringed skirt and ten-gallon hat, they were in for a surprise. Madame Armstrong was as much at home in a Halston as a Stetson. Daughter of an aristocratic New Orleans coffee importer, Armant Legendre, she had met Armstrong on a visit to King Ranch with Helenita Kleberg, her classmate from both Foxcroft and Vassar. Tobin Armstrong lived on the ranch "next door." His brother, John, was married to Helenita's sister, Henrietta Kleberg, and was second in command at King Ranch. A year after she met Tobin, they married. She became mistress of his eight-by-ten-mile spread. While presiding over its handsome adobe homestead, she raised five children, including a set of twin boys, Tobin, Jr., and James.

Mrs. Armstrong adapted quickly to all aspects of ranch life, occasionally working cattle as well as keeping books. Noted for the ranch's hunting and fishing parties, which she organized, she also took a lively interest in Republican politics, becoming known as a champion of women's rights. "Anne Armstrong was for women's rights when it meant not very much to anybody," said Jill Ruckelshaus, who worked with her on Republican committees in Washington. "She's primarily responsible for getting women into the military academies. She convinced the White House that women are the future."

Despite all her contributions to her government, she will no doubt go down in history as America's first woman Ambassador to Great Britain, and the "lady who played hostess to Prince Charles on the ranch."

Surrounded by macho cowboys, polo players and politicians, Anne Armstrong took all her challenges in stride.

As she often quoted, with a wink: "The cock croweth, but the hen delivers the goods."

X

Merchant Princes

The Marcus Family

NEIMAN-MARCUS has become a symbol of Texas affluence and glamour. No store in America has so influenced the style and taste of its city and state. Stanley Marcus, former chairman of the board, is "the legend" of fashion retailing. "I have the simplest tastes," says Marcus, paraphrasing Wilde. "I'm easily satisfied with the best."

Neiman-Marcus was born in 1907 when Herbert Marcus, Sr., joined his sister, Carrie, and her husband, Al Neiman, and opened a quality store. At the time, Dallas was everything but "quality." Rip-roaring, it was. A cotton and railroad town, boasting 222 saloons and the best little whorehouses in Texas. In 1913, a fire destroyed the building and the store was rebuilt at its present location on Main and Ervay streets. Herbert had four sons: Stanley, Edward, Herbert, Jr., and

Stanley Marcus presents cowboy hat to Earl Mountbatten as his Countess looks on.

Lawrence, in that order. When Stanley graduated from Harvard Business School, he joined the firm. His fashion expertise, dedication to quality and savvy showmanship gave the store international celebrity. Its spectacular International Fortnight store promotion became The Big Event in Dallas. Originated in 1957, each year the Fortnight honors a different country. To kick it off, a gala benefit is held, raising big bucks for Dallas charities and cultural projects. The whole city gets into the act, with concerts, art exhibits and film festivals tying in. For the Italian Fortnight, the guest of honor was Sophia Loren, and leading Italian designers flew in to present their fashions. The 1977 Fortnight saluted France. An abandoned air terminal at Love Field was transformed into the streets of Paris, including a replica of Regine's discothèque—with Regine, herself, greeting guests. Ambassador Jacques Kosciusko-Morizet and his wife were there, too. And, of course, lots of cancan girls and champagne.

For over 50 years, the Neiman-Marcus Christmas catalog has made news with its extravagantly fun "His and Her" gifts. One year, it was matching airplanes.

Now Neiman-Marcus has stores spread out around the country. Stanley and Lawrie are retired. Eddie and Herbert, Jr., are gone. However, the Marcus genius is still on tap. Richard, Stanley's son, is chair-

Neiman-Marcus' first Dallas building.

man and CEO, and Lawrie, a consultant, is still making sure that Dallas continues to have "the best-dressed women in America."

NEIMAN-MARCUS FORTNIGHTS

1957	French	1970	Ruritania
1958	British	1971	*Fête des Fleurs*
1959	South American	1972	French
1960	Italian	1973	British
1961	American	1974	Japan
1962	Far Eastern	1975	Italian
1963	Swiss	1976	Irish
1964	Danish	1977	French
1965	Austrian	1978	Brazil
1966	French	1979	British
1967	British	1980	Spanish
1968	Italian	1981	Oriental
1969	East Meets West	1982	The Odyssey

TWO DECADES OF NEIMAN-MARCUS HIS-AND-HER CHRISTMAS GIFTS

1960: *His and Her Airplanes*

His—a 7-seat Beechcraft Super G18. Hers—the 4-seat Beechcraft Bonanza; both 3 miles a minute; choice of color, style, cabin arrangement, and any number of combinations of individual navigational equipment.

1961: *Ermine Bathrobes*

Made of Canadian white ermine, bleached to an even greater whiteness. Full-length, lined with pink taffeta.

1962: *Chinese Junks*

A real Chinese junk, made in Hong Kong according to the finest U. S. yacht standards. Thirty feet long, teakwood decks, mahogany planking, three sails, 30 horsepower. Choice of brightly painted or natural wood.

1963: *His and Her Submarine*

The MiniSub Mark VII, a freely flooded underwater craft, designed to carry two people and cruise at a speed of 3 to 7.3 m.p.h. A hull of plastic-impregnated, laminated glasscloth. Fourteen feet long, 46 inches high and 90 inches wide.

*The late Billie Marcus and husband, Stanley, host Coco
Chanel at Marcus ranch on her one and only visit to the
United States.*

1964: *His and Her Balloons*
Free-flying balloons, utilizing the principle of the original Mont-
golfier hot-air balloon, but generating heat for buoyancy by a pro-
pane burner. Acrylic coated in rip-stop nylon.

1965: *His and Her Para-Sails*
They sailed from land or water skyward and back again with an as-
cending nylon parachute, flying from 100 to 300 feet in the air, lift-
ing between 80 and 225 pounds at airspeeds from 10 to 20 m.p.h.

1966: *His and Her Bathtubs*
Luxurious side-by-side bathtubs adapted from the French bathroom of Louis XIV and set in a lacquered-wood base with marble
top and backboard; in porcelain with 24-karat gold-plated French
rose scrollwork and control valves.

1967: *His and Her Camels*
"For people who have been promising themselves to slow down: a
matched pair of the slowest, surest beasts on land will be flown
from California to your private oasis (anywhere in the Continental
United States)."

1968: *His and Her Jaguars*

A pair of Neiman-Marcus pussycats: for him, Britain's magnificent Jaguar XKE Grand Touring Coupe; for her, a natural Brazilian jaguar coat trimmed in natural ranch mink.

1969: *His and Her Vasarely Collection*

Artist Victor Vasarely, genius of optical design, was commissioned by Neiman-Marcus to compose "Vega MC Negative and Positive": for him, the negative color values mounted in plexiglass and brushed aluminum; for her, a scarf of the positive color values.

1970: *His and Her Thunderbirds*

With luxury options designed by Neiman-Marcus to make each an individual, private world on wheels, cars included: custom grille and paint treatment to distinguish it as a Neiman-Marcus Thunderbird, a complete tape center (including four languages), sun roof, Neiman-Marcus graphic design fabric top and trunk interior. Also, for him: a dictating machine, electric razor, and locking safety box; for her: console cosmetic case, telescoping fluorescent makeup mirror, and sewing kit (with 14-karat gold thimble).

1971: *His and Her Mummy Cases*

From the ancient land of Mother Nile: richly adorned, but gratefully vacant, authenticated mummy cases, both approximately 2,000 years old.

1972: *His and Her Mannequins*

Full-dimensional, life-size mannequins are facsimiles of the person of your choice and programmed to laugh as long as you like at your jokes or say yes in any language you specify, via remote control.

1973: *His and Her Greek Kraters*

Pair of genuine Greek bell-kraters (double-handled urns), unearthed in Southern Italy, date from the mid-fourth century, B.C.: one krater adorned with a male figure and one with a female figure.

1974: *His and Her Hoverbugs*

A revolutionary two-passenger craft, licensed as a marine vehicle, which moves on a bed of air, 6 to 8 inches off the ground or water, cruising at an average speed of 35 to 45 m.p.h., depending on the surface you travel.

1975: *His and Her Dinosaur Safari*

A ten-day safari into the wilds of east central Utah to search for the remains of allosaurus—the giant carnivorous dinosaur. Guaranteed finding a skeleton in a realistic pose with a suitably inscribed donor plaque; the skeleton to be placed in the museum or institution of your choice and price included a bronze skull for the hunter to keep.

1976: *His and Her Buffalo Calves*

A pair of American bison: male and female buffalo starter calves, six months old, from the herd of Bison Enterprises, Ltd. in Hartsel, CO, the first certified 100% purebred buffalo herd in the United States, and certified by the American Buffalo Association.

1977: *His and Her Windmills*

For the energy conserver, urban windmills to provide a non-polluting, noiseless, environmentally safe way to enjoy electrical appliances and gadgets without overtaxing public power supplies or family utility bills. Each windmill operates independently, with its own storage batteries and an alternator to convert to alternating current when needed.

1978: *His and Her Natural Safety Deposit Boxes*

Deep within a 9,000-foot mountain of granite in Utah's Wasatch Range, a cavern, over 150 feet long, for those seeking maximum security and preservation for their really valuable possessions. Temperature and humidity never vary. Security is assured by an elaborate system of surveillance, closed circuitry, and hair-triggered alarms—all powered by waterfall-generated electricity. Available for a 50-year lease.

1979: *His and Her Dirigibles*

Hot-air dirigibles with a compartment to comfortably accommodate two passengers and a well-stocked picnic basket. A 72-hp engine enabled each dirigible to cruise at 25 m.p.h., and all 120 feet of each craft were collapsible and portable. Full flight instructions were included, and the dirigibles could be had in any color and design.

1980: *His and Her Ostriches*

A pair of young ostriches, "a link in the chain to save these great flightless birds, which for all their strength and hardiness, are rapidly disappearing from their last natural habitats in Africa." The Neiman-Marcus blurb pointed out: "These gracefully gangly birds are perfectly suited to a ranch life; they lay about 30 or 40 eggs a year (each equal to about 23 grade A large chicken eggs), it wouldn't take long to establish a herd."

The Sakowitz Family

Robert Tobias Sakowitz and his sister Lynn, Mrs. Oscar Wyatt, Jr., are "beautiful people" superstars. They are the only sister and brother on the Best-Dressed List. Both are constantly on-the-scene and on-the-boards of all the best galas and jet-set gatherings. Lynn, whose husband is the Coastal States Oil magnate, bought Somerset Maugham's Villa Mauresque in Cap Ferrat. Her Riviera neighbor and friend, the late Princess Grace, was often there. Bob, formerly married to Peter Duchin's sister-in-law, Pam Zauderer, seems right out of central casting in the part of "handsome, dynamic, top-fashion executive." Only he's the real thing. Chairman of the board, president and chief executive officer of the swank Sakowitz fashion empire. Sakowitz, Inc., is one of America's last privately held specialty stores still operated by the founding family. There's been a Sakowitz emporium in Texas since Louis Sakowitz operated a store in Galveston before 1900. Two of his sons, Tobias and Simon, started Sakowitz Brothers in 1902, and moved to Houston. It came to prominence by featuring "carefully selected merchandise specifically selected for their area's carriage trade." Tobias' son, Bernard, entered the business in 1929, and was active as chairman until his death in 1981. Robert, born in 1938, joined the firm in 1960. But first he went in a different direction from being Number One Son of the Store. After graduating cum laude from Harvard, he went to work for a bank in Europe. In Paris, he joined the largest department store chain in France, Galleries Lafayette. There, he met such giants of French design as Yves St. Laurent and André Courrèges, later convincing them to design ready-made clothes for the American woman. In 1963, Bob returned to Houston and his family stores, after a brief sojourn in New York City with Macy's, and pushed Sakowitz into high fashion. Visability. Image. Publicity. All play a big part in Bob Sakowitz's marketing philosophy. His greatest publicity gimmick, usually making the columns and the newsmagazines each Christmas, is Sakowitz's Ultimate Gift. One, "To Be Bathed in a Bathtub Full of Your Own Real Diamonds," had a price tag of $118,335,000. On the Texas fashion scene, Bob Sakowitz is unquestionably "the crown prince of panache."

The Hunt
Behind the Hotel

MENTION "heirs of H. L. Hunt" and visions of cornering world markets—silver, soybeans, World Tennis, thoroughbreds—come immediately to mind.

Although H. L.'s billion-dollar babies hate being in the headlines, they are seldom out of them. It's the cross they have to bear being members of a family bequeathed a fortune from their father.

Now another Hunt is very much in the news. Caroline. She's the Hunt behind THE hotel: Dallas' The Mansion on Turtle Creek, an intimate, world-class hotel with an award-winning restaurant.

Discreet, modest, unassuming, unpretentious, Caroline Hunt Schoellkopf has given her hometown a hotel as chic as The Ritz. Seductively, subtly patrician, The Mansion adds the most dash to Dallas since Neiman-Marcus opened its doors in 1907.

Going into the hotel business was her eldest son Stephen Sands' idea. "Stephen felt Dallas needed a Connaught-type small hotel," she says in her soft Southern drawl. "We all liked the idea of preserving a palatial mansion which could be enjoyed, not as a museum, but in its original spirit."

Few had heard of the Caroline Hunt Trust Estate before The Mansion on Turtle Creek came to life. While her father, H. L. Hunt, was out making, reportedly, a million dollars a day in the oil fields, Caroline Hunt had grown up doing much the same things other well-bred Dallas girls did. She attended exclusive Hockaday School for Girls, then Mary Baldwin College in Staunton, Virginia, alma mater of her great-grandmother, and her older sister, Margaret. Some Hunt cousins and nephews, as well as her brother Herbert, matriculated at Washington and Lee nearby.

After graduating from college, Caroline married oilman Lloyd "Boomer" Sands, and devoted most of her time to raising their five children. Teaching Sunday school, she headed the Early Childhood Education Department of her Highland Park Presbyterian Church, and was appointed the church's first woman deacon. While her children were young, she also served on boards of the Junior League of Dallas, the Child Guidance Clinic and West Dallas Community Centers . . . even wrote a 275-page cookbook, *The Compleat Pumpkin Eater.* Her special interest is cooking, and her specialty, pumpkin. In the world of cuisine, she was one of three American women elected to the Commanderie des Cordons Bleus de France.

Later she was active on the boards of the North Texas Arthritis Foundation, the Dallas Symphony League and the Dallas County Heritage Society, donating and having moved a root cellar, curing shed and barn to the Heritage Society's Old City Park, a museum of authentic structures dating from the early days of Dallas. As a member of Mary Baldwin's executive committee, she was instrumental in having several buildings at the college added to the registry of Historical Landmarks of Virginia.

But it was only after divorcing "Boomer" Sands in 1973, that she went into business, and while at it, preserved, in a very special way, Dallas' historically significant Sheppard King mansion.

After the divorce, she began casting about for an enterprise that

*Miss Ela Hockaday with members of her Hockaday School's 1947
graduating class.*

*Caroline Hunt Schoellkopf at her chic hotel in Dallas, The Mansion on
Turtle Creek.*

would be interesting, productive and pleasurable for her sons and daughter to share as a family. Except for her youngest son, Patrick, all the Sands offsprings worked for her Caroline Hunt Trust Estate. Stephen, the oldest, was in charge of real estate; Bunker, ranching and farming; David, timber, oil and gas. Her only daughter, Laurie, bought old homes and remodeled them for resale.

To real-estate son Steve, hotel returns looked better than the standard real-estate transaction. Also, her only sister, Margaret Hunt Hill, matriarch of H. L.'s heirs, had found owning Colorado's Garden of the Gods Club most rewarding. So Caroline and family decided to embark in the hotel business full sway.

They chose the name Rosewood Hotels, Inc., Rose being Caroline's middle name. For their first venture, they found a baroque Mediterranean mansion, one that looked right out of *Sunset Boulevard*. It had great mystique, plus a fashionable address: Turtle Creek. Cotton titan Sheppard King had built it in 1925, when money was no object and owning a Mediterranean palazzo was the thing. King, no relation to the King Ranch clan, traveled to Europe for ideas. He then modeled his mansion on a sixteenth-century Italian villa. When William Randolph Hearst was sending home innards of castles for furbishing his San Simeon, Sheppard King began collecting for his own palace in Dallas.

He shipped back a sixteenth-century German mantel for his oak-paneled library, which is now part of the hotel's main dining room. Noted Swiss wood-carver Peter Mansbendel was brought to Texas to execute the library's carved wood ceilings and mantel. Since Mrs. King was a descendant of King Edward III, the Kings had installed a set of stained-glass library windows depicting the British barons signing the Magna Carta at Runnymede. This had special appeal to Mrs. Schoellkopf, who through her mother's Nantucket Starbuck side traces her ancestry back to King Edward, too.

Rosewood Hotels purchased the King mansion and its four and a half acres for $1.6 million. Then they invested $19.4 million in renovating and building a 143-room hotel addition. Dallas architects Shepherd & Boyd designed it. To create "timeless classic interiors with understated elegance," they turned to Robert Zimmer, of Howard Hirsch and

Associates in Santa Monica, California. He didn't skimp anywhere. The Mansion on Turtle Creek's bathrooms are lavished with Roman marble and real brass fixtures, requiring two full-time brass polishers. Each dressing room features a movie-star glamorous makeup table outlined in 16 bulbs. Guests luxuriate in beds with 100-percent cotton sheets. Bedspreads and drapery fabrics are by Clarence House. Rugs were specially handwoven in Portugal and the Orient. Elevators have been paneled in solid oak. Suites, furnished with antique armoires and original art, have French doors opening onto a balcony.

Zimmer sought to give his interiors a residential feeling, a sense of arrival, of coming home to a very elegant mansion. Rooms have fresh flowers and the latest *Fortune* and *Architectural Digest* on the coffee table. Awaiting in the bathroom is a handsome wicker bath tray neatly packed with fluffy terry towels, mat, terry-cloth bathrobe, milled soap, Polo shampoo and bath gel. Even the smallest suites contain six telephones, two TVs, two marble bathrooms and a stereo system.

Robert Zimmer, now Rosewood's president, was so successful in achieving his goal that Mrs. Schoellkopf almost thinks of The Mansion on Turtle Creek as home . . . and all those handsome, chic guests as part of a continuing house party.

In fact, the hotel had a house party for its opening. A gala "Weekend at the Mansion." People paid a handsome sum to be the first to weekend at The Mansion on Turtle Creek. Southern Methodist University and TACA—an organization benefiting the performing arts of Dallas—were $110,000 richer for it. During the week after, the likes of Alan Alda, Larry (J. R.) Hagman and Lee Grant were checking in at the reception desk.

For someone as fascinated with cooking as Mrs. Schoellkopf, The Mansion on Turtle Creek's 40-man kitchen is pure heaven. Sometimes she sits contentedly knitting in the corner watching the ballet of the cooks among the clatter, clash and bubbling cauldrons.

Her second husband, Hugo "Buddy" Schoellkopf, scion of a prominent old Dallas German family, feels very much a part of the hotel, too. No doubt because some of his hunting trophies—heads of deer, pronghorn antelope and mountain sheep—are in the wood-paneled bar.

WILLIAM I

MATILDA OF FLANDERS

Chart of Descent from William the Conqueror

30 **W**illiam the Conqueror, son of Robert, D of Norman-
cy, & Arletta, b 1027-28 at Falaise, Normandy, d.Sept.
9,1087 at Rouen, France; defeated King Harold at
Hastings, & crowned KING OF ENGLAND Dec.25,1066 at West-
minster Abbey; m. Matilda or Maud of Flanders

29 Henry I (Beauclerc), K. of England, b 1068; d. Dec.1,1135; m
1st Matilda of Scotland, d. 1118

28 Matilda or Maud, Q. of England & Empress, b.1102, d.
Jan 30,1164; m 2nd,1127, Geoffrey V. Plantagenet, C of Anjou & Maine

27 Henry II, K. of England, b Mar 25,1133, d July 6,1189, m.
1152, Eleanor of Aquitaine

26 John (Lackland), K of England, b Dec 24,1167, d. Oct 19,1216, m 2nd Isabel
of Angoulême

25 Henry III, K. of England, b Oct 1.1207; d. Nov. 16,1272, m., 1236,
Eleanor of Provence

24 Edward I (Longshanks), K. of England, b June 17,1239, d. July 7,
1307; m. 1st,1254, Eleanor of Castile, d. Nov. 28, 1290

23 Princess Elizabeth Plantagenet, b Aug, 1282; d. May 5,1316; m.
2nd, Humphrey de Bohun, E. of Hereford & Essex

22 Margaret de Bohun m Sir Hugh de Courtenay, E. of Devon, K.G.

21 Sir Philip Courtenay of Powderham Castle, K.G., m. Anne Wake

20 Sir John Courtenay m. Agnes, Joan or Isabel Champernoun

19 Sir Philip Courtenay m. Elizabeth Hungerford

18 Sir William Courtenay m. Margaret Bonvile

17 Edward Courtenay m. Alice Wotten

16 Alice Courtenay m. Reginald Gayer

15 John Gayer, d. 1593

14 Stephen Gayer m. Jane Tembrace

13 John Gayer m. Sibell Treffrey

12 Thomas Gayer

11 John Gayer m. Margaret Trelawney

10 Humphrey Gayer m. Jane Spark

9 William Gayer came to America from Devonshire, England, d. 23rd
7mo,1710 at Nantucket; m. 1st Doris Starbuck

8 Dorcas Gayer m. Jethro Starbuck

7 Thomas Starbuck m. Rachel Allen

6 Thomas Starbuck m. Dinah Troll

5 Reuben Starbuck m. Deborah Folger

4 John Starbuck m. 2nd Sophia (Whipple) Horton

3 Lydia Starbuck m. Charles Waldo Bunker

2 Nelson Waldo Bunker m Sarah Rebecca (Hunnicutt) Kruse

1 LYDA BUNKER m. Nov. 26,1914, Haroldson Lafayette Hunt II

I Margaret Hunt, b. Nov. 19,1915; m Oct.15,1938, Albert Gallatin Hill
II Haroldson Lafayette Hunt, III, b Nov. 23, 1917
III Caroline Hunt, b. Jan. 8, 1923
IV Lyda Bunker Hunt, b. Feb. 20,1925; d. Mar 20,1925
V Nelson Bunker Hunt, b. Feb. 22,1926 VI William Herbert Hunt, b. Mar 6,
1929 VII Lamar Hunt, b Aug. 2, 1932

**WILLIAM I
THE CONQUEROR**

HENRY II

**GEOFFREY V
PLANTAGENET**

AQUITAINE

⭐ *THE HUNT FAMILY* ⭐
The Family of Caroline Hunt Schoellkopf

GENERATIONS

1st	2nd	3rd	4th
H. L. Hunt,	Jr. *married* Lyda Bunker		
	Margaret Hunt *married* A. G. Hill		
	Haroldson Lafayette Hunt III		
	Caroline Hunt		
	married (1) Lloyd Sands		
		Stephen Hunt Sands *married* Marcelene Snorf Wilson	
			Wilson Lloyd Sands
			Lowell Hunt Sands
			Stephen Storm Sands
			John Bowmer Sands
		John Bunker Sands *married* Ramona Stark	
			Haven Starbuck Sands
			Jacob Cayce Sands
			Stark Bunker Sands
		David Keith Sands *married* Nancy Goldman	
			Lydia Ligon Sands
		Laurie Sands	
		Patrick Brian Sands	
	married (2) Hugo W. Schoellkopf		
	Lyda Bunker Hunt		
	Nelson Bunker Hunt		
	William Herbert Hunt		
	Lamar Hunt		

Mr. Schoellkopf, after retiring from his sporting goods company, started a second career himself: Pumpkin Air. He named it for Caroline's passion for pumpkin. Even his fleet of helicopters and Cessnas are painted pumpkin-orange.

The success of The Mansion started a whole chain of events, and a Rosewood chain of hotels.

In 1982, Rosewood Hotels opened another hotel in Houston, The Remington on Post Oak Park. Although there was no old mansion, it is another classic world-class hotel with the great attention to detail. A third Rosewood hotel, exclusive Hotel Bel-Air with its famous garden setting in Los Angeles, is also being renovated with Mansion touches.

The Mansion on Turtle Creek is only one flower in Caroline Hunt Schoellkopf's Dallas garden patch. Ride through downtown Dallas with her and she points out family projects in the works in much the way your Aunt Minnie would show you her petunias and perennials. "See that skyscraper, Thanksgiving Tower? It's the family's new Placid Oil headquarters building. Pretty, isn't it? And that vacant lot? That's the one we leveled for our 13-acre shopping mall. It'll have a hotel and office complex, too. Philip Johnson is designing it for us," she states matter-of-factly.

"We hope to eventually have hotels in other cities, perhaps New York, New Orleans, San Francisco or Denver. But The Mansion on Turtle Creek, I'm sure, will always have a special place in my heart."

It is, after all, her firstborn. Besides that, it's painted a beautiful shade of pumpkin.

XII

The King and Queen of Clubs

AMONG THE PRIVATE CLUBS of Texas, two stand right at the top: Houston's Bayou Club and The Argyle of San Antonio.

The Bayou came first, in 1940. Hugo "Baron" Neuhaus, Harry Wiess and Stephen Farish were the chief organizers. Most of Houston's old guard were charter members, including Stephen's brother, Will Farish, Roy Cravens, Jay Ray, Craig Cullinan, Malcolm Lovett, Leslie Dufton, Charles Wrightsman and others in the inner circle of The Stables Set.

Though most of these friends owned handsome country places for entertaining, "Baron" Neuhaus thought that "a club for those who haven't a country place" was needed. He envisioned a central spot, near the key estates, where the group could gather for polo, tennis, swimming and informal dining.

Neuhaus, Farish and Texas society's "court architect" John Staub

Hugo "Baron" Neuhaus, shown here with his wife, the former Kate Rice, started The Bayou as "a country place for those without a country place."

spent many mornings on horseback searching for a suitable site off Houston's Post Oak Road. When they came upon a clearing of magnolia, loblolly and live oak trees, they knew they had found their spot. Fortunately, friend Will Hogg's father, Texas famed governor, had great pull with the University of Texas, which held title to the property. With Will pushing it through, their choice acreage was acquired.

John Staub, a charter Bayou member himself, had built the mansions of most of those who would frequent the club. He knew they had the highest standards of taste, and that every detail would be noticed almost daily. So he and Mr. Neuhaus created an environment almost certain to be pleasing to this privileged few.

Staub's design for the clubhouse was derived from a classic eighteenth-century Louisiana parish plantation house, Saint John's Legacy. Since Houston is climatically associated with Louisiana, rather than the Southwest or New Mexico, his choice seemed ideal. It had handsome touches. Old brick. Double-hung shuttered windows. Tall, slender Ionic columns. A formal Grecian pediment. An upstairs gallery sweeping over the entranceway porte-cochere.

Results of their labor of love received high accolades at the club's grand opening in 1940. A luncheon was held alfresco around the new swimming pool. Impeccably white linen suits were the order of the day for all gentlemen present. Their crisp whiteness was accentuated by the newly painted spoked-back captain's chairs at all the tables. Unfortunately, those freshly painted chairs hadn't dried. When the charter members rose to applaud the dedication speech, their backsides resembled those of convicts from a Georgia chain gang.

The Bayou Club of Houston

CHARTER MEMBERS, JULY 2, 1940

Anderson, James A., Jr.	Farish, S. P.
Armstrong, Mrs. E. M.	Farish, W. S.
Arnold, Isaac	Fay, Albert Bell
Asche, Fred B.	Fay, Ernest Bell
Benedum, Paul	Fleming, Lamar, Jr.
Blaffer, R. L.	Francis, Charles I.
Bonner, B. F.	Franzheim, Kenneth
Broun, George T.	Gardiner, J. W.
Burns, Edward	Garwood, St. John
Burroughs, Julian S.	Godwin, Herbert
Butler, George A.	Goldston, W. J.
Campbell, W. T.	Hammon, George F.
Carter, W. T., Jr.	Hammon, John
Childs, W. L.	Hanszen, H. C.
Clayton, W. L.	Heyer, George S.
Coates, Frank G.	Hill, George A., Jr.
Cravens, J. R.	Hogg, Miss Ima
Crotty, John T.	Hogg, Mike
Cullen, H. R.	Johnson, J. M.
Cullinan, Craig F.	Jones, Jesse H.
Davis, John B.	Kuldell, R. C.
Dorrance, John K.	Link, J. W.
Elkins, J. A.	Link, J. W., Jr.
Ellwood, D. C.	Lykes, J. M.
Farish, R. D.	McAshan, S. M., Jr.

Meredith, Otis
Neal, Mrs. Marion
Neff, Mrs. Laura
Nelms, H. G. (Chad)
Neuhaus, H. V. (Hugo)
Nolan, E. J.
Potter, Hugh M.
Pyron, W. B.
Randolph, R. D.
Rice, W. M.
Scott, J. Virgil
Sharp, D. C.
Sharp, Mrs. Estelle
Sharp, W. B.
Showers, E. A.

Smith, Howard
Staub, John F.
Taylor, Dr. Judson L.
Underwood, Milton
Vinson, W. A.
Weems, Wharton
Wier, R. W.
Wiess, H. C.
Wilson, W. D.
Winston, J. O., Jr.
Womack, K. E.
Womack, K. E., Jr.
Wray, A. J.
Wrightsman, C. B.

Recipe for The Bayou Club's famed cocktail:

BAYOU BREEZE
5 jiggers light rum
4 limes
3 teaspoons sugar

Fill blender with crushed ice and a handful of loose mint leaves. Blend until a deep frost, then pour into cocktail glass. (Baron Neuhaus liked to make his in a *clear* glass shaker so one and all could see what was going on inside. It added to the suspense.)

The Argyle of San Antonio

San Antonio's most exclusive, and unique, club is The Argyle. Unique in that it is a private club devoted to supporting basic biomedical research and man's battle against disease. Article I of the club bylaws emphasizes that the purpose of the club is "to support, encourage and foster the Southwest Foundation for Research and Education."

Housed in a stately Southern mansion fronted with two stories of verandas, it bespeaks gracious splendor. The house was built before the

The Argyle, club of San Antonio aristocracy, proved the perfect setting to introduce Sarah Johnson, great-great-granddaughter of King Ranch founder.

War Between the States by Scottish ranchers, who named it "The Argyle" for their clan homeland back in Scotland. Later it was the scene of lavish entertaining. Generals Robert E. Lee and John J. Pershing were distinguished guests here.

Before becoming a club, in 1956, The Argyle mansion had fallen on bad times and was in great need of repair.

Then along came Mrs. Lewis J. (Betty) Moorman, Jr. As a trustee of the Southwest Foundation, she and the Foundation president, Dr. Harold Vagtborg, were seeking ways to interest more local ladies in supporting its medical research programs. First, Betty Moorman recruited a group of other prominent San Antonians. Mesdames Edgar (Mag) Tobin, William (Carolyn) Negley and Frank (Rena) Huntress became Foundation trustees with her. Betty Moorman suggested they establish a high-caliber club with carefully chosen members who would make a substantial annual contribution to the Foundation. All greeted the idea with great enthusiasm. Only Mrs. Moorman's brother, Tom Slick, and her mother, Mrs. Charles F. (Bernice) Urschel, remained skeptical. Later they became enthusiastic about it.

With such powerhouses behind the idea, the Southwest Foundation arranged to acquire the dilapidated Argyle property. To get it appropriately zoned by the city of Alamo Heights, they had the services of powerful attorney Jesse H. Oppenheimer, of the distinguished Oppenheimer Bank family. He was assisted by H. B. "Pat" Zachry, a next-door neighbor, who helped in getting the property rezoned as a private club, despite active opposition. Through Oppenheimer's and the founders' perseverance The Argyle was deemed a tax-exempt, private organization. Owned by, and dedicated to, the support of the Southwest Foundation, The Argyle avoids a ten percent tax on dues and initial contributions paid by members.

More ladies with clout joined the board: including Mesdames John M. (Eleanor) Bennett, Dale H. (Jean) Dorn, Albert F. (Janet Shook) LaCoste and Charles F. (Betty) Urschel, Jr. For the next two years, they all set about restoring and redecorating the 1854 building.

Furnishings were contributed to the Foundation by Argyle members for use in the club. All tax-deductible gifts. Several San Antonio interior designers aided in the redecorating.

Lew and Betty Moorman gave The Tree Room in memory of his father, Dr. Lewis J. Moorman.

Mr. and Mrs. Charles F. Urschel donated another addition, which was named The Urschel Room.

In 1969 an elegant dining room was authorized by action of the Board of Governors, to be called the Tom Slick Room, in memory of the man whose foresight and gifts made the Southwest Foundation for Research and Education possible.

During the winter of 1981, The Argyle's distinctive veranda was completely rebuilt. All the planning, building and restoration through the years was under the supervision of Vaughan Meyer.

The Argyle has never been more thoroughly covered, by both society editors and decorators, than at the 1982 debutante gala for Sarah Johnson, great-great-granddaughter of King Ranch founder Richard King. The theme of the party was "The Great Balloon." Guests were

Sarah Johnson is shown with her brother, Kley (for Kleberg), at her glamorous bayou-bash debut given by her parents, the B.K. Johnsons. Lester Lanin and orchestra popped down from New York to play.

welcomed in the parking lot with champagne served from the straw gondola of a real Around-the-World-in-80-Days hot-air balloon. Helium-filled balloons, anchored with baskets of red and yellow tulips, outlined walks and centerpieced tables. Balloons and bouquets swirled over The Argyle grounds, porches and interiors. Tiny white lights outlined trees and shrubs, creating a Midsummer Night's Dream woodland. Couples strolled down newly created paths bordered with red geraniums on one side and red and pink azaleas on the other. Dancers swirled to the music of Lester Lanin under a huge party tent. Hosts B.K. and Patsy Johnsons' 900 guests dined on lobster, veal and other goodies in a separate dining tent. Both tents were decorated with more balloon fantasies. Inside the club, where a rock band blasted away, walls were covered with witty murals and soft sculpture of more up-up-and-away delights. Even Sarah's yellow taffeta ball gown, created for the occasion by designer Oscar de la Renta, was hand-painted with, what else . . . bubbly balloons.

With 775 resident, 412 nonresident, 15 honorary and 28 special members, The Argyle contributes over $350,000 to Southwest Foundation annually—the equivalent of the income from a three-million-dollar endowment.

The Argyle Club had its formal opening on Friday, April 13, 1956. The Charter Members list reads like a cross section of South Texas society:

REGULAR MEMBERS

Abbey, Mr. William C.
Achning, Mr. and Mrs. Walter J.
Alexander, Mr. and Mrs. Donald
Allen, Mr. and Mrs. Hugo
Altgelt, Dr. and Mrs. James E.
Ames, Mr. and Mrs. Eugene L.
Ansley, Mr. and Mrs. Joe C.
Arneson, Mrs. E. P.
Atherton, Mr. and Mrs. Holt
Ayres, Mr. and Mrs. Robert M., Jr.
Bahan, Mr. and Mrs. Merle W.
Bain, Mr. and Mrs. Willard S.
Bakke, Mr. and Mrs. W. E.
Balthrope, Mr. and Mrs. Charles W.
Barclay, Mr. and Mrs. Robert D.
Barclay, Mr. Robert D., Jr.
Barnard, Mr. and Mrs. James R.
Barnes, Mr. and Mrs. T. E., Jr.
Barrett, Mrs. Charlotte Osborn
Barrett, Mr. and Mrs. Thurman, Jr.
Baskett, Mr. and Mrs. John L.
Bass, Mr. and Mrs. Harper H.
Basse, Mr. and Mrs. E. A., Jr.
Becker, Mr. A. L.
Becker, Mr. and Mrs. Charles Lee
Becker, Mr. and Mrs. E. C., Sr.
Beinhorn, Mr. and Mrs. William A., Jr.
Bennett, General and Mrs. J. M., Jr.
Berman, Mr. and Mrs. Willard

Biedenharn, Mr. and Mrs. Albert M., Jr.
Bird, Mr. and Mrs. Arthur S.
Bonnet, Dr. Edith M.
Bowermaster, Mr. and Mrs. Walter
Bowman, Mr. and Mrs. Jack T.
Bray, Mr. and Mrs. Charles W.
Bredenberg, Mr. and Mrs. Fred D.
Briggs, Mr. and Mrs. Robert W.
Britt, Mr. William D., Jr.
Brooks, Mr. and Mrs. David
Brown, Mr. and Mrs. Fred H.
Brown, Mr. and Mrs. H. Lutcher
Browning, Mr. and Mrs. C. L., Jr.
Bryant, Mr. and Mrs. Henry H.
Buchek, Mr. V. F.
Bunting, Mr. and Mrs. Bruce B.
Burney, Mr. Todd D.
Burns, Mr. and Mrs. Charles H.
Byrd, Mr. and Mrs. Edward
Cade, Mr. and Mrs. Lawrence
Cadwallader, Mr. and Mrs. A. H., Jr.
Cahill, Mr. and Mrs. Robert E.
Calvert, Mr. and Mrs. James H.
Campbell, Mr. and Mrs. Colin D.
Campbell, Mr. and Mrs. Trent
Casey, Mr. and Mrs. Martin F.
Chamberlain, Mr. and Mrs. F. G., Sr.
Chamberlain, Mr. Fidel G., Jr.
Chapman, Mr. and Mrs. Guy E.

Cheever, Colonel and Mrs. Charles
Clark, Colonel and Mrs. Charles A., Jr.
Clark, Mr. William K.
Clemens, Mr. and Mrs. Ernest W.
Clifton, Mr. and Mrs. George
Coates, Mr. and Mrs. George H.
Cocke, Mr. and Mrs. Bartlett
Cohagan, Mr. and Mrs. Stanley R.
Condos, Mr. and Mrs. George J.
Cox, Mr. and Mrs. John J.
Coyle, Dr. and Mrs. E. W.
Creighton, Mr. and Mrs. Victor E.
Cross, Mr. and Mrs. Dalton
Cushing, Dr. and Mrs. Daniel N.
Danvers, Mr. and Mrs. Don
Dauchy, Mr. and Mrs. C. C.
Davis, Mr. and Mrs. Richard T.
Denman, Mrs. Gilbert M.
Denman, Mr. Gilbert M., Jr.
Dewar, Mr. and Mrs. H. H.
Diseker, Dr. and Mrs. Thomas H.
Dittmar, Mr. and Mrs. Elmer A.
Dorn, Mr. and Mrs. Dale H.
Dugger, Mr. and Mrs. William L., Jr.
Duncan, Mr. and Mrs. G. Cameron
Eiband, Mr. and Mrs. Ernest G.
Fair, Mr. and Mrs. Ralph E.
Feagin, Colonel and Mrs. John A.
Fehr, Mrs. Charles J.
Ferrando, Mr. and Mrs. Al
Finesilver, Mr. and Mrs. Mervin
Fitz-Gerald, Colonel and Mrs. Hugh J.
Fitzsimmons, Mr. and Mrs. Hugh, Jr.
Fitzsimons, Mrs. H. A.
Folks, Mr. and Mrs. Harold R.
Ford, Mr. and Mrs. O'Neil
Ford, Mr. and Mrs. R. Russell
Frasher, Mrs. Francis M.
Frates, Mr. and Mrs. Earl C.
Freeman, Mr. Joe
Friedrich, Mr. and Mrs. George

Friedrich, Mr. and Mrs. R. H.
Frost, Mr. and Mrs. Jack
Frost, Mr. and Mrs. T. C., Sr.
Gaines, Mr. and Mrs. James M.
Galt, Mr. and Mrs. Edward
George, Mr. and Mrs. Charles
George, Mr. and Mrs. Gordon N.
Gill, Mr. and Mrs. Richard
Gillespie, Mr. and Mrs. Frank M., Jr.
Gillespie, Mr. and Mrs. James V.
Givens, Mr. and Mrs. Ben F.
Goad, Mr. and Mrs. Thomas J.
Goldsbury, Mr. and Mrs. Christopher
Goldsmith, Mr. and Mrs. Nat
Gossett, Dr. and Mrs. Robert M.
Grant, Mr. and Mrs. George W.
Green, Miss Mary V.
Green, Colonel and Mrs. Winfred C.
Gregory, Mr. and Mrs. Claiborne B.
Gresham, Mr. and Mrs. R. N.
Grindal, Mr. and Mrs. H. W.
Groos, Mrs. Franz C.
Gunn, Mr. and Mrs. C. C.
Guthrie, Mr. and Mrs. J. E.
Guthrie, Mr. and Mrs. R. K.
Halff, Mrs. Hugh A. L.
Halsell, Mr. and Mrs. Ewing
Hardie, Mrs. Gunter
Harris, Mr. and Mrs. George M.
Harris, Mr. and Mrs. Jerome K., Sr.
Harrison, Mr. and Mrs. K. D.
Harrison, Mr. and Mrs. William J.
Hartman, Dr. and Mrs. Albert W.
Heard, Mr. and Mrs. Cyrus L.
Helland, Mr. and Mrs. Archie
Henderson, Mr. and Mrs. John P.
Henshaw, Mr. and Mrs. Walter A.
Hensley, Mr. and Mrs. Jilson H.
Heppes, Mr. and Mrs. Julien O.
Herff, Dr. and Mrs. Ferdinand P.
Herff, Mrs. Lucie Frost

Hill, Mr. and Mrs. Luther H.
Hill, Mr. and Mrs. Roger C.
Hixon, Mr. and Mrs. F. C.
Hobbs, Mr. and Mrs. W. G., Jr.
Holland, Mr. and Mrs. Edward W.
Holmes, Mr. and Mrs. Christian R.
Holt, Mr. and Mrs. Peter
Holt, Mr. William K.
Houston, Mr. and Mrs. Frank K.
Howeth, Mr. and Mrs. Ike K.
Hudson, Mr. and Mrs. Harold W.
Huey, Mr. and Mrs. Charles M.
Huff, Colonel and Mrs. Roy
Huntington, Colonel and Mrs. Frederick W.
Huntress, Mr. and Mrs. Frank, Jr.
Hyman, Mr. and Mrs. Vance
Jackson, Dr. and Mrs. Dudley
Jergins, Mr. and Mrs. Allen A.
Jersig, Mr. and Mrs. Harry
Johnson, Mr. and Mrs. Albert D.
Johnson, Mr. and Mrs. Carl Wright
Johnson, Mr. and Mrs. Gordon W.
Johnson, Mr. and Mrs. Stewart C.
Jones, Mrs. Edwin M.
Jones, Mr. and Mrs. Gus T.
Kampmann, Mr. and Mrs. Ike S., Jr.
Kayton, Mr. and Mrs. Lewis
Killen, Mr. and Mrs. Smokey
Kocurek, Mr. and Mrs. Louis J.
Koehler, Mr. and Mrs. Otto A.
Kraus, Dr. and Mrs. B. W.
Kuntz, Mr. and Mrs. John J.
Kuper, Mr. and Mrs. Charles A.
Lackey, Mr. and Mrs. Vachel
Lang, Mr. and Mrs. Gilbert
Lang, Mr. and Mrs. Sylvan
Lanham, Mr. and Mrs. R. E.
Lawrence, Mr. and Mrs. Jack G.
Lee, Mr. and Mrs. Kenneth E.
Lentz, Mr. and Mrs. Leslie L.
Leopold, Dr. and Mrs. Henry N.

Lewis, Mrs. Frank M.
Lindsay, Mr. and Mrs. Sidney A.
Lipscomb, Mr. and Mrs. Robert C.
Locke, Mr. and Mrs. John R.
Loftin, Mr. and Mrs. Roy B.
Loring, Mr. and Mrs. Porter, Jr.
Luke, Mr. and Mrs. Edward S.
Lupe, Mr. and Mrs. William B., Jr.
Mallory, Dr. and Mrs. Meredith, Jr.
Mangum, Mrs. E. Pryor
Mathews, Mr. and Mrs. Irving
Mathis, Mr. Walter Nold
Matteson, Mr. and Mrs. Barney T.
Matthews, Mr. and Mrs. Dudley M.
Matthews, Mr. and Mrs. Wilbur L.
McAllister, Mr. and Mrs. Walter W.
McCampbell, Mrs. Marilou
McFarlin, Mr. and Mrs. E. B.
McFarlin, Mr. and Mrs. John R.
McFarlin, Mr. and Mrs. R. B.
McGoodwin, Mr. and Mrs. James V.
McLean, Mrs. Marrs
McNab, Mr. and Mrs. I. A.
Meadows, Dr. and Mrs. John C., Jr.
Meyer, Mr. and Mrs. Vaughan B.
Miller, Mr. and Mrs. Wynn D.
Minter, Dr. and Mrs. Merton M.
Montgomery, Dr. and Mrs. William D.
Moorman, Mr. and Mrs. Lewis J., Jr.
Morrison, Mr. and Mrs. Alfred
Muir, Mr. and Mrs. Edward D.
Murchison, Mr. and Mrs. John W.
Musgrave, Colonel and Mrs. Thomas
Neal, Mrs. Jack
Neal, Mr. and Mrs. Leslie R.
Negley, Mr. and Mrs. Alfred W.
Negley, Mr. and Mrs. Richard V. W.
Negley, Mr. and Mrs. William
Nelson, Mr. and Mrs. James Cecil
Netter, Mr. and Mrs. Norman
Newman, Mr. and Mrs. John E.

Newman, Mr. and Mrs. William C., Jr.
Newton, Mr. and Mrs. Carl
Newton, Mr. and Mrs. Frank R., Jr.
Nix, Mr. and Mrs. Joe J.
Nixon, Mr. and Mrs. R. S.
Noble, Colonel and Mrs. Charles H.
Nordan, Mr. and Mrs. L. A.
Norman, Dr. and Mrs. Ruskin C.
Northrup, Mr. and Mrs. Preston G.
O'Brien, Mr. and Mrs. Jerome J.
Oliver, Dr. and Mrs. David R.
O'Neill, Mrs. J. E.
Oppenheimer, Mr. and Mrs. Alexander
Oppenheimer, Mr. and Mrs. Dan
Oppenheimer, Mr. and Mrs. Frederick J.
Oppenheimer, Mr. and Mrs. Harris K.
Oppenheimer, Mr. and Mrs. Jesse H.
Orsinger, Mr. and Mrs. Charles G.
Osborn, Mr. and Mrs. W. B.
Osborn, Mr. and Mrs. W. B., Jr.
Padgitt, Mr. and Mrs. James T.
Parker, Mr. and Mrs. George
Parker, Mr. and Mrs. Harry J.
Parker, Mr. and Mrs. Joseph B.
Passmore, Dr. and Mrs. G. G.
Pawkett, Mr. and Mrs. Lawrence
Peet, Mr. and Mrs. James A.
Perot, Mrs. O. B.
Peterson, Mr. and Mrs. Hal
Petty, Mr. and Mrs. O. S.
Petty, Mrs. Van A., Sr.
Phillips, Mr. and Mrs. H. Houghton
Porter, Mr. and Mrs. John B.
Power, Mrs. Helen A.
Prassel, Mr. and Mrs. Dick
Prassel, Mr. and Mrs. Frank G.
Price, Mr. and Mrs. C. Stanley
Pridgen, Dr. and Mrs. James E.
Proper, Mr. and Mrs. Datus E.
Pryor, Mr. and Mrs. Ike T., Jr.
Raider, Mr. and Mrs. Harry A., Jr.

Rhame, Mr. and Mrs. William T.
Rife, Mr. and Mrs. Byron
Rigsby, Mrs. William C.
Rives, Mr. and Mrs. John S.
Robertson, Mr. and Mrs. Alton E.
Roe, Mr. and Mrs. E. J.
Rote, Mrs. Tobin
Rowe, Mr. and Mrs. W. Earl
Rowsey, Mr. and Mrs. Gentry L.
Rubin, Mr. and Mrs. Jay Lewis
Russ, Mr. and Mrs. A. McClure
Russ, Mrs. Leon F., Jr.
Russ, Mr. Semp
Savage, Mr. and Mrs. J. Hamilton, Jr.
Scheig, Mrs. Martha A.
Scherr, Mrs. M.
Schoolfield, Mrs. Neil W.
Schreiner, Mr. and Mrs. Charles
Schuhmacher, Mr. and Mrs. Harry C.
Scrimshaw, Mrs. J. B.
Searcy, Mr. and Mrs. Tyson M.
Seeligson, Mr. and Mrs. Arthur A.
Seeligson, Mr. and Mrs. A. A., Jr.
Seeligson, Mr. Frates
Shand, Mr. and Mrs. James, III
Sheerin, Mr. Lawrence
Skinner, Dr. and Mrs. I. C., Jr.
Slater, Mr. and Mrs. Orval A.
Slick, Mr. Tom
Smith, Mr. Robert C.
Smith, Mr. and Mrs. Robert Knox
Smith, Mr. and Mrs. T. Noah, Jr.
Spencer, Mrs. Richard F.
Spencer, Mr. and Mrs. Walter D.
Spires, Mr. and Mrs. Eugene C.
Stanton, Mr. and Mrs. Joe L.
Steen, Mr. and Mrs. John T.
Stephenson, Mr. David P.
Straus, Mr. and Mrs. Joe R.
Stubenbord, Mr. and Mrs. John J.
Sullivan, Mr. and Mrs. Daniel J. IV

Sweeney, Mr. and Mrs. Edward M.
Sweeney, Mr. and Mrs. James D.
Tappan, Mr. and Mrs. Harry
Test, Mr. and Mrs. Donald N., Jr.
Thaddeus, Dr. and Mrs. A. P.
Thiele, Mr. and Mrs. Joe W.
Thomas, Mr. and Mrs. Alex R., Jr.
Tobin, Mrs. Edgar
Tobin, Mr. R. L. B.
Todd, Mr. and Mrs. John W.
Travis, Mr. and Mrs. Robert H.
Urschel, Mr. and Mrs. Charles F.
Urschel, Mr. and Mrs. Charles F., Jr.
Voigt, Mr. and Mrs. Gaines
Walker, Mr. and Mrs. John R., Jr.
Ward, Mr. and Mrs. Lafayette

Whitaker, Mr. and Mrs. Harvey B.
White, Mr. and Mrs. John H.
Wilhelmy, Mr. and Mrs. Christopher B.
Wilson, Mr. and Mrs. Ellis M.
Wine, Mr. and Mrs. Russell B.
Wingerter, Mr. and Mrs. Lawrence
Witt, Mr. and Mrs. Robert R.
Wofford, Mr. and Mrs. H. Rollins, Jr.
Wood, Mr. and Mrs. John H., Jr.
Woodhull, Mrs. Eloise T.
Wurzbach, Mr. and Mrs. William A.
Zachry, Mr. and Mrs. H. B.
Zander, Mr. and Mrs. Liston
Ziegler, Mr. and Mrs. Thad C.
Zilker, Mrs. Charles A.

OUT-OF-TOWN MEMBERS

Adler, Mr. A. M.
New York, New York
Bates, Mr. and Mrs. John L.
Corpus Christi, Texas
Beck, Mr. and Mrs. Henry C., Jr.
Dallas, Texas
Bellows, Mr. and Mrs. W. S.
Houston, Texas
Bevier, Mr. and Mrs. George M.
Alpine, Texas
Briscoe, Mr. and Mrs. Dolph, Jr.
Uvalde, Texas
Byles, Mr. and Mrs. Axtell
New Braunfels, Texas
Cage, Mr. and Mrs. Richard Grady
Falfurrias, Texas
Carr, Mrs. May Dougherty
Corpus Christi, Texas
Chittim, Mr. and Mrs. J. M.
Leakey, Texas
Christian, Mr. and Mrs. Woods
Mission, Texas

Coiner, Gen. and Mrs. Richard Tide, Jr.
Washington, D.C.
Dall, Mr. Curtis B.
Philadelphia, Pennsylvania
Doane, Mr. and Mrs. Foster B.
Chicago, Illinois
Donnell, Mr. and Mrs. William C.
Marathon, Texas
Dorn, Mr. and Mrs. Forest D.
Bradford, Pennsylvania
Dougherty, Mr. and Mrs. Dudley
Beeville, Texas
Dowd, Mr. and Mrs. W. W.
Chapman Ranch, Texas
Dulaney, Major Gen. and Mrs. Robert
Purcellville, Virginia
Edwards, Mr. and Mrs. O. D.
Corpus Christi, Texas
Eshleman, Mr. and Mrs. Benjamin, Jr.
Corpus Christi, Texas
Finley, Mr. and Mrs. Joe B.
Encinal, Texas

Fletcher, Mr. and Mrs. Clark R., Jr.
Mexico, D. F., Mexico

Francis, Mr. and Mrs. David Gregg
Luling, Texas

Francis, Mr. and Mrs. William H., Jr.
Washington, D.C.

Frates, Mr. and Mrs. C. L.
Oklahoma City, Oklahoma

Hause, Mr. and Mrs. H. Burt
Beeville, Texas

Hawn, Mr. and Mrs. George S.
Corpus Christi, Texas

Hawn, Mr. and Mrs. John D.
Corpus Christi, Texas

Hedrick, Mr. and Mrs. Wyatt C.
Fort Worth, Texas

Hewgley, Mr. and Mrs. J. M., Jr.
Tulsa, Oklahoma

Hill, Mr. and Mrs. Lon C.
Corpus Christi, Texas

Hinkle, Mr. and Mrs. Clarence E.
Roswell, New Mexico

Ivey, Mr. and Mrs. Ben E.
Taft, Texas

Jones, Mr. and Mrs. William W.
Corpus Christi, Texas

Killam, Mr. and Mrs. Radcliffe
Laredo, Texas

Landauer, Mr. and Mrs. James D.
New York, New York

Lasater, Mr. and Mrs. Garland M.
Falfurrias, Texas

Light, Mr. and Mrs. George E., Jr.
Cotulla, Texas

Mars, Mr. Forrest E.
The Plains, Virginia

McCombs, Mr. and Mrs. Holland
Wheelock, Texas

Meyer, Mr. and Mrs. John E.
Birmingham, Alabama

Miller, Mr. and Mrs. W. Frank
Bradford, Pennsylvania

Modesett, Mr. and Mrs. Jack
Corpus Christi, Texas

Morgan, Mr. and Mrs. Arnold O.
Corpus Christi, Texas

Morriss, Mr. and Mrs. Gilmer
Rocksprings, Texas

Musgrave, Brig. Gen. and Mrs. T. C., Jr.
Washington, D.C.

Nixon, Mr. and Mrs. Maston
Corpus Christi, Texas

O'Connor, Mr. and Mrs. Thomas M.
Victoria, Texas

Peterson, Mr. and Mrs. Ernest E.
New York, New York

Plecher, Mr. Wolf H. H.
San Antonio, Texas

Podgoursky, Count Ivan
San Antonio, Texas

Poole, Mr. Hogue
Cotulla, Texas

Raigorodsky, Mr. Paul M.
Dallas, Texas

Russell, Mr. and Mrs. James H.
Sante Fe, New Mexico

Schreiner, Mr. and Mrs. Charles III
Mountain Home, Texas

Seeley, Mr. and Mrs. Herbert Barnum
Bridgeport, Connecticut

Slick, Mr. and Mrs. Earl F.
Winston-Salem, North Carolina

Smith, Mr. Richard Stowers
Hunt, Texas

Sohl, Mr. and Mrs. William J.
Alpine, Texas

Vaughan, Mr. and Mrs. Ben F., Jr.
Corpus Christi, Texas

Waldrop, Mrs. Edna Doak
San Antonio, Texas

Walker, Mr. and Mrs. Bayard
New York, New York

Waltman, Mr. W. D., Jr.
Fort Worth, Texas

Weinert, Mrs. H. H.
Seguin, Texas

Wells, Mr. and Mrs. Robert C.
Kingsville, Texas

Welsh, Mr. and Mrs. J. Leroy
Omaha, Nebraska

West, Mr. Wesley
Houston, Texas

Wood, Mr. and Mrs. Lawrence
Refugio, Texas

Wright, Maj. Gen. and Mrs. Stuart P.
Grapevine, Texas

Wynne, Mr. Angus, Jr.
Dallas, Texas

Wynne, Mr. and Mrs. T. L., Jr.
Dallas, Texas

HONORARY MEMBERS

Lambert, Mr. and Mrs. Joe O., Jr.
Dallas, Texas

Pincus, Dr. and Mrs. Gregory
Shrewsbury, Massachusetts

SPECIAL MEMBERS

Alessandro, Mr. and Mrs. Victor
San Antonio

Bondurant, Colonel and Mrs. W. T.
San Antonio

Capers, Reverend and Mrs. Samuel O.
San Antonio

Craig, Mr. and Mrs. Addison B.
San Antonio

DeCoursey, Brig. General and Mrs. Elbert
Fort Sam Houston, Texas

Erlandson, Mr. and Mrs. Ray S.
San Antonio

Gesick, Mr. and Mrs. Edward J.
San Antonio

Goland, Mr. and Mrs. Martin
San Antonio

Harmon, Mr. Jack
San Antonio

Jacobson, Dr. and Mrs. David
San Antonio

Jones, Bishop and Mrs. Everett H.
San Antonio

Laurie, Dr. and Mrs. James W.
San Antonio

Leeper, Mr. and Mrs. John Palmer
San Antonio

Shook, Mr. and Mrs. Phil
San Antonio

Simpson, Mr. and Mrs. S. H., Jr.
San Antonio

Smith, Mr. and Mrs. C. W.
San Antonio

Swearingen, Dr. and Mrs. Judson
San Antonio

Vagtborg, Dr. and Mrs. Harold
San Antonio

Werthessen, Dr. and Mrs. N. T.
San Antonio

White, Dr. and Mrs. W. R.
Waco, Texas

XIII

Leading Lights in the Lone Star Galaxy

OVETA CULP HOBBY

First in War, First in Peace and First in Houston Media. That's Oveta Culp Hobby, Houston's handsomely groomed business whiz. In World War II, she was the nation's first and only woman to command an army corps—the WACS. After the war, President Eisenhower appointed her America's first Secretary of Health, Education and Welfare. Married to former Texas Governor Will Hobby (1877–1964), 37 years older than she, Mrs. Hobby took over all Hobby interests after his death. During the sixties and seventies she was Houston's First Lady of Media, controlling a Houston-based newspaper-TV empire that included the *Houston Post*, NBC's Houston television outlet KPRC-TV, Nashville's WFTF-TV and Galveston newspapers. She also cofounded the Bank of Texas, a subsidiary of Allied Bancshares. Her son, Lieutenant Governor of Texas, Will, Jr., daughter Jessica Catto of Washington, D.C., and eight grandchildren are heirs to the Hobby throne.

CAMILLA DAVIS BLAFFER TRAMMELL

Daughter of Dallas banker and real estate tycoon Wirt Davis, her debut party in the late forties was such an event *Life* magazine covered it, and Elsa Maxwell directed the revels. Camilla married one of the attendees, John Blaffer, heir to a Texaco-Humble oil fortune. Together they donated a wing to the Houston Museum of Fine Arts and built the auditorium for Kincaid School, Houston's exclusive private school co-founded by John's father, Lee Blaffer. After her husband's death, she married Tex Trammell, of Houston. She and Blaffer had five children: Mrs. John Royall, Mrs. Nicholas Taylor, Joan Blaffer, Mrs. Dan Hrdy, Robert Lee Blaffer, and seven grandchildren.

FORT WORTH'S BASS FAMILY

Fort Worth's Perry Bass was left a fortune by his mother's brother, Texas billion-dollar bachelor Sid Richardson (1891–1959). Uncle Sid had made a mint wildcatting in Texas oil fields during the twenties and thirties. With plenty of money to spend, he bought up every fine Western painting by Remington or Russell that he could get before his pal, oil-rich Amon Carter, beat him to it. Mr. Bass and his firstborn son, Sid Richardson Bass, have taken their Uncle Sid's legacy and built it into a private oil empire that is rivaled only by the Hunt family's. Urbane Yale grad Sid Bass runs the business today. He and his wife, Anne, reside in a contemporary house that is considered one of famed architect Paul Rudolph's triumphs. Best-dressed Anne Bass is a force behind New York's School of American Ballet and the New York City Ballet, serving on the boards of each. Sid heads Bass Brothers Enterprises, a business and investment empire that includes the Americana hotel chain and Fort Worth's $200-million-plus City Center development. Also, Sid Richardson's namesake has made sure his great-uncle will never be forgotten. In March 1982, the Bass family permanently installed the Sid W. Richardson Collection in a downtown, turn-of-the-century building, charmingly restored. Intimate and inviting, it has become a drawing card for

177

*Leading
Lights
in the
Lone Star
Galaxy*

businessmen and shoppers, a pleasant place to pause and contemplate the romantic West in oils by Remington and Russell. Here they can remember, too, the great "natural gentleman," Sid Richardson, and all his oil money that brought them all together. The other Bass sons, Robert, Edward and Lee, keep a low profile, a job in itself when your family's wealth reportedly tops $2 billion.

AMON CARTER'S DAUGHTER, RUTH

Amon Carter's daughter, Ruth, has taken over where her daddy, Fort Worth's biggest benefactor, left off. The son of a blacksmith, Carter rose to own the *Fort Worth Star-Telegram,* radio-TV stations, American Liberty Oil, Remingtons and Russells. Ruth has broadened the paintings collection to include "the best of the West," from Audubon to O'Keeffe, now housed in the Amon Carter Museum, a building designed by Philip Johnson, who, along with John Burgee, also did the mid-city water gardens, a gift of Ruth and her late brother, Amon Carter, Jr. An alumna of Sarah Lawrence, she's a trustee of the National Gallery of Art. In 1983 she married Jack Stevenson, president of the National Gallery's board of trustees and senior partner of New York's prestigious law firm, Sullivan and Cromwell.

GILBERT M. DENMAN, JR.
LEROY G. DENMAN, JR.

From their law firm in San Antonio, first cousins Roy and Gib Denman administer the enormous estates of Texas's most prominent oil land and ranch families. It's been a Denman family tradition ever since grandfather Denman convinced his friend Jim Hogg to serve as the new Lone Star State's first governor. In turn, Denman became Texas' first Judge of the Supreme Court, serving four terms. Bachelor Gilbert Denman, besides being on boards of prestigious institutions and museums, has his own private museum of classical antiquities. His pied-à-terre overlooking San Antonio's picturesque Riverway houses an extraordinary collection of Roman and Grecian marbles, Egyptian burial art and Etruscan ceramics. Dramatically lighted and displayed, it looks as if "The Search for Alexander" wound up on Texas' "Grand Canal."

TRAMMELL CROW

Dallas developer Trammell Crow is said to be the biggest builder and landlord in the United States. His projects are nationwide. They include San Francisco's Embarcadero Center, Atlanta's Peachtree Center, warehouses, hotels, shopping malls, office-residence complexes, housing units and land in Florida, Illinois and Louisiana. Biggest of them all is his Dallas Market Center, which changed the look, ambience and personality of the city. With 7.2 million square feet of commercial space, it outranks Chicago's Merchandise Mart. It includes an Apparel Mart, Trade Mart, Market Hall, Decorative Center and World Trade Center, attracting to Dallas from New York and Chicago a big share of the U. S. wholesale market. This in turn is responsible for Dallas' increasing number of elegant hotels and restaurants. Crow started as a Dallas bank teller, joined an accounting firm, and after World War II managed his in-laws' grain elevator business. From there he went into real estate, and has been buying and building ever since. Besides his Loew's Anatole and Wyndham hotels, he is now developing the Dallas Communications Complex, a series of movie sound studios, making suburban Las Colinas an emerging Texas Hollywood.

ROY CULLEN

Roy Cullen III is named for his grandfather, Houston's king of wildcatters, Hugh Roy Cullen (1881–1957). Starting with only a fifth-grade education, Cullen became one of the world's wealthiest men, right up there with Getty. He first struck oil in 1928, with his wife and five children all dressed in their best clothes looking on. That was only the beginning. He made many major strikes after that, including discovering a mile-deep, billion-dollar oil field on the Tom O'Connor ranch near Victoria. In 1932, Roy Cullen founded Quintana Petroleum. The same year, he also commissioned Houston's high-society architect, John Staub, to build him a "big white house." Big, it was. So big it took 14 servants to maintain it.

Shortly afterward, the Cullens' only son, Roy Gustav, was killed in an oil-field accident, leaving a young wife and three children, Roy III,

179

*Leading
Lights
in the
Lone Star
Galaxy*

Cornelia and Harry. Surviving were four Cullen daughters, Mrs. Corbin Robertson, Mrs. Douglas Marshall, Mrs. Isaac Arnold, all of Houston, and Mrs. Paul Portanova of New York. Before his death in 1957, wildcatter Cullen had given over $200 million to hospitals, cultural institutions and the University of Houston.

Corbin Robinson, Jr., now president of Quintana Minerals, is emerging as a powerhouse in political fund-raising. Another grandson, Baron Enrico de Portanova, and his wife, Alesandra, made news when he attempted to buy New York's famed 21 Club for her as a gift. Their lavish villa Arabesque in Acapulco has 32 bedrooms, 25 bathrooms and four kitchens. The international set buzzes to it in season like bees to the hive. Baron Ricky also acquired another title: Consul General to the United States for the Republic of San Marino.

NINA CULLINAN

Miss Nina (as in Dinah) Cullinan is credited for changing the entire cityscape of present-day Houston.

Seems that Houston's Museum of Art needed to renovate its facade. Miss Nina, whose father started Texaco, had been a generous patron of the arts for decades. She agreed to finance the Museum project stipulating only that an internationally acknowledged great architect be commissioned to do it. With her approval, Mies van der Rohe was selected for the job. This set a new standard of taste in Houston's public buildings. Today, Houston's skyline is a living montage of the best contemporary architects' best works.

CHARLES DUNCAN, JR.
JOHN DUNCAN

Houston's Duncan dynasty, if industry granted noble titles, might have in their lineage a Count of Coca-Cola (Charles); the Grand Duke of Gulf + Western (John) and maybe Marquis of Maxwell House (an uncle). When Coca-Cola bought Duncan Foods from the Duncan family, Charles became president of "The Pause That Refreshes." Later he served in Washington as the first Secretary of Energy and U. S. Deputy

Secretary of Defense. After leaving Carter's cabinet he became chief operating officer for the huge, privately held oil empire of Houston's Jack Warren and Allan King (annual revenues $1.5 billion). John went on to cofound Gulf + Western, which acquired, among other properties, Paramount Studios in Hollywood. An avid collector of contemporary Western art, he is one of the prime movers back of Kerrville's new Cowboy Artists of America Museum.

JAMES ANDERSON ELKINS, JR.

Chairman of Houston's mighty First City Bancorporation, James Elkins, Princeton '41, and his wife, the former Margaret Keith Wiess, are top tout-Houston. Margaret is the youngest daughter of Humble Oil founder Harry Wiess. Jim's father, Judge James Elkins, Sr., helped found Houston's biggest law firm, Vinson & Elkins and Bancorporation's parent company, First City National Bank. The Judge was known as "the secret government of Texas." Besides his banking responsibilities, Jim Elkins serves on many boards, including Eastern Airlines, Cameron Iron Works and Children's Hospital.

WILLIAM STAMPS FARISH III

William Stamps Farish I, a cofounder of Humble Oil, became president of Standard Oil of New Jersey (Exxon) when it acquired Humble. His son, Bill, Jr., married Libbie Rice, whose sister Ella (now Mrs. James Winston) was the first Mrs. Howard Hughes. Bill was killed in a plane crash early in World War II. Today, his son, Will III, is principal heir to the great Farish Exxon fortune. After graduating from the University of Virginia, Will III ventured into investments, oil, and mining and offshore drilling in Africa. Polo is his passion, along with racing and breeding thoroughbreds. A member of The Jockey Club, Will Farish's thriving horse operations are headquartered at his farm, Lanes End, in Versailles, Kentucky. Will's aunt, Martha Farish Gerry, owns Forgate, three times Horse of the Year. Will is married to the former Sarah Sharp, of the Wilmington, Delaware, Sharps.

181

*Leading
Lights
in the
Lone Star
Galaxy*

WILLIAM WALTER CARUTH

Caruth has been a name dear to Dallas since granddad Caruth opened a general store there in 1849. With his profits, he bought land, including a huge cotton plantation. A son, William Caruth, Sr., bought even more, and in 1939 turned it over to his son W. W., Jr. It's what we now call North Dallas. Among W. W. Jr.'s operations: Dallas' North Park Inn, the Caruth Building Service and the Happy Dolphin, along with other properties in Florida. His four children and two nephews might possibly inherit $600 million.

ANNE WINDFOHR SOWELL

Dynamic Dallas–Fort Worth heiress Anne Sowell is the great-granddaughter of legendary Samuel Burk Burnett, who reputedly won the huge Four 6s ranch in a poker game, hence the name. Her mother, the late Anne Burnett Waggoner Hall Windfohr Tandy, was a legend in her own time, too. Married four times, she owned four ranches that spread over a half million acres. Anne was the widow of Charles Tandy, head of Tandy Corporation (Radio Shack stores are part of it). The Burnett family fortune was founded on Fort Worth's First National Bank. No one in Texas had a more exuberant life-style than Anne Tandy. Her everyday diamond was a 48-karat Vargas. I. M. Pei designed her mansion in Fort Worth. Her walls were decorated with priceless Picassos. She had her private plane painted entirely red, to match the shade of her lipstick. Daughter Anne and her husband, James Sowell, a Dallas attorney, have his-and-her planes, too. As sole heirs of Mrs. Tandy, Anne Sowell and her only child, Wendy Meeker, have inherited one of the vastest estates in America.

JOSEPHINE ABERCROMBIE

In 1975, Josephine Abercrombie's mother and father, the James S. Abercrombies, died. She became sole heiress and in control of Cameron Iron Works, manufacturer of heavy equipment, started by her father. Owning 60 percent of Cameron stock, worth an estimated $275 million,

Jo Abercrombie has been involved in its management ever since. In addition, she operates a thriving business marketing beef raised on the Abercrombie ranch. Married four times, she took back her maiden name after divorcing former Cameron president Anthony J. A. Bryan. Prior to Tony Bryan, to whom she was married for 14 years, she was Mrs. James Robinson. They had two sons, Jamie A. Robinson and George Anderson Robinson.

J. ERIK JONSSON

Erik Jonsson has been honored as "Mister Dallas." Driving force behind the Dallas–Forth Worth Airport, he served as mayor of Dallas from February 1964 to May 1971. He is credited as the man who brought Dallas back from the depths of its post-JFK assassination disgrace. His "Goals for Dallas" program, started in 1965, charted the city's development program into the next century. Jonsson and his wife, Margaret, migrated from Brooklyn to Dallas where he served as president, chairman of the board and honorary chairman of Dallas-based mighty Texas Instruments Company. Son Philip Jonsson is a forceful figure in furthering Dallas as a fine arts center.

MARGARET TOBIN

Margaret Tobin *is* Old San Antonio. Her husband, Edgar Tobin, was a direct descendant of the Irish empresarios who started colonies in South Texas. Tobin made a fortune in the 1920s surveying for oil leases with his Tobin Aerial Mapping Company. He would survey oil leases in exchange for a portion of each lease. Mag Tobin is surrounded by Monets and other shrewd art investments of her bachelor son, Robert, a major supporter of the Santa Fe Opera in New Mexico and a board member of New York's Metropolitan Opera.

MARGARET MCDERMOTT

Margaret McDermott, widow of Texas Instruments founder Eugene McDermott, "singlehandedly stocked the Dallas Museum of Fine

183

*Leading
Lights
in the
Lone Star
Galaxy*

Arts," say some members. Before she married Gene McDermott (1899–1973) she was a reporter in India. Today, as the *grande dame* of Dallas, she and her daughter, Mary, supervise two family charities: the McDermott Foundation and the Biological Humanics Foundation. The McDermott contributions to advancing education, health and the cultural environment of Dallas are incalculable.

LON HILL

Lon C. Hill II is credited with opening up South Texas to commerce. He founded Harlingen, Texas, and named it after a friend's birthplace in Holland. When they first heard the name, many pronounced it Holland's Gin, Texas. Lon II headed Central Power and Light Company and worked feverishly getting loans from Northern banks to help finance the highways, railroads, bridges and plants needed for his beloved South Texas. Legend has it that at the peak of the 1930s depression, Mr. Hill pleaded to his Northern bankers: "I tell you, gentlemen, all that South Texas needs is water . . . and a better class of people." The banker is said to have replied: "Mr. Hill, that's all that HELL needs."

Today, with his Corpus Christi advertising agency, Adcraft, his son, Lon III, is carrying on where Lon II left off, promoting big business to "come on down."

ED HARTE

As publisher of Corpus Christi's morning and evening newspapers, *The Caller* and *The Times*, Ed Harte keeps deeply involved in community activities as well as national ones. He's a former chairman of the National Audubon Society, chairman of the board of governors of Corpus Christi's Art Museum of South Texas, and a board member of the Harte-Hanks Communications chain. Mr. Harte also helped organize the Corpus Christi Area Oil Spill Control Association, a group combining his resources of industry and federal and local government to keep his city-on-the-Gulf's oil-refining port the cleanest in America.

PAUL HAAS

President and chairman of Corpus Christi Oil and Gas, Paul Haas is known as "Mr. Foundation." While serving as a trustee for many national, local and state foundations himself, he saw a real need for a single source to get information about specific foundations. Now those seeking seed money for civic, educational or health projects have the Foundation Center to turn to. The Paul and Mary Hass Foundation helps fund it.

MARTHA AND ELTON M. HYDER, JR.

Fort Worth's dynamo duo, Martha and Elton M. Hyder, Jr., seem to accomplish more in 15 minutes than most do in a week. Specializing in oil litigation for over two decades, Elton retired from his lucrative law practice at forty-five for investments—but he started young for both. Passing his bar exam in his third year at the University of Texas Law School, he entered private practice while still in school. He was appointed Assistant Attorney General of Texas at the age of twenty-four. That same year he wrote *Texas Natural Gas Conservation Laws,* a book still cited as the authority on the subject, and other publications on oil and gas. At age twenty-six, after a stint as a Naval officer, he was appointed Associate Counsel for the United States at the International Tribunal in Tokyo, the Japanese equivalent of the Nuremberg trials. He was the youngest special prosecutor among the seasoned lawyers representing all Allied countries. Hyder personally interrogated Tojo. After a year in Japan, with the Japanese war criminals punished and Tojo subsequently hanged, Elton returned to the Attorney General's office and became head of its oil and gas division. He successfully argued his first case in the Supreme Court of the United States at the age of twenty-six. In 1950, he returned to Fort Worth and private practice—and the collecting bug bit him. While a graduate student at Harvard Law School, he had become fascinated with Harvard's famed legal memorabilia and began acquiring paintings, documents, art, pictures, purses of the Lord Chancellors of England, and furnishings associated with famed law history. Now his is one of the largest private collections of important legal

185

*Leading
Lights
in the
Lone Star
Galaxy*

treasures, with some legal instruments dating back to the twelfth century. Over 700 pieces of Hyder's legal rareties and Italian Renaissance furniture enhance five floors of the impressive University of Texas School of Law Building and the Library of the Supreme Court of Texas. Also, many a deserving student has made it through college financially backed by Hyder scholarships and loan funds. Elton is the sixth graduate of the University of Texas School of Law to be honored as its Outstanding Alumnus. This was given to him in 1965 at the age of forty-five.

Mrs. Hyder, the former Martha Rowan, whose father founded the Rowan Drilling Company, is Fort Worth's dashing doyenne of board directors. Her great love has been the Van Cliburn International Piano Competition, headquartered in Fort Worth, and she has helped it grow into the most important piano competition in the world. As chairman from 1973 to 1977, she made numerous trips to Europe and the U.S.S.R. to help promote the competition and the careers of the two Russian winners, Vladimir Viardo and Lexso Toradze. Today she is the only member of the Cliburn who has served continuously since its first competition in 1962.

In 1983, Martha Hyder served as chairman of the 1983 Albert Schweitzer Music Award given to Van Cliburn at Carnegie Hall. She moved to New York for a few months to bring together all her New York and Texas friends to participate in this important musical event followed by a smashing dinner dance at the Plaza.

Besides being a dynamic director and chairman, Martha Hyder is also an accomplished decorator. In 1973, as a gift, she personally decorated and furnished two parlors and five offices at Sweetbriar College in Virginia, her alma mater. The Hyders' Fort Worth home and their villa in San Miguel de Allende, Mexico, are renowned for their gracious hospitality. To establish Forth Worth as home to the Van Cliburn International Quadrennial Piano Competition in 1962, Mrs. Hyder helped stage perhaps the most unusual roundup in Texas history. In two weeks her committee combed the town and corraled the 48 grand pianos so urgently needed by the piano contestants converging from all over the world.

THE DAVIS BROTHERS OF FORT WORTH

Sons of Ken Davis, Sr., T. Cullen, William Seldon and Kenneth W. Jr., are Fort Worth's "billionaire brothers." In 1969, each inherited 30 percent of their daddy's Kendavis Industries (oil field equipment, contract drilling, exploration and production, in all 84 companies worldwide, with revenues exceeding $2 billion). Cullen and Ken bought out younger brother Bill's interests in Kendavis for a reported $100 million, but Bill still runs Davoil Oil and Gas.

William and his wife, Mitzi, are important backers of the Fort Worth Symphony. They gave their local orchestra a Stradivarius, now called "The William and Mitzi Davis Stradivarius." He also donated a panoramic theater to the Museum of Science and History, to complete the Planetarium given by his father years ago.

ROBERT A. MOSBACHER

International oil magnate and master organizer Bob Mosbacher is also Texas's best-known yachtsman. His brother "Bus" won The America's Cup, apex of yachting. Mosbacher chairmanned President Ford's finance committee in his '76 campaign. He hangs his yachting cap in Houston.

DR. DENTON COOLEY

Houston native Denton Cooley is regarded as the world's supreme heart surgeon. He is the shining light of Texas Medical Center, a complex of 24 medical institutions. Besides presiding over St. Luke's Hospital, Texas Children's Hospital and the Texas Heart Institute, he amassed a fortune investing in Houston real estate.

MR. AND MRS. HARRIS MASTERSON III

Harris Masterson, trustee of Houston's impressive Museum of Fine Arts, is so impressive himself, garbed in his heavy gold "Lord Mayor's" chain and courtly dress, that he was once mistaken by an out-of-towner at Carnival as King Notsuoh (Houston spelled backward). He and his wife, the former Carroll Sterling, heiress to a Humble Oil fortune, live in sumptuous splendor at their Palladian mansion, Rienzi, named for his mother's father, Rienzi Melville Johnson. Their ballroom, added by architect Hugo Neuhaus in 1914, is perhaps the most lavish west of Buckingham Palace. Indeed, its pink-and-orange floor covering once belonged to the Duke of Buckingham. The Mastersons enjoy entertaining 200, or tea for two, surrounded by rare Chippendale, Adam mirrors, crystal chandeliers, first period Wooster porcelain and a priceless El Greco.

SYBIL HARRINGTON

Widow of Amarillo's oil baron Donald D. Harrington, Sybil Harrington is "the pet of the Met." New York's Metropolitan Opera, that is. She adores opera, and the Opera adores her. Like the Good Fairy of the West, she has waved her golden wand and, presto, the most lavish productions in the Opera's history have been made possible. Franco Zeffirelli. Placido Domingo. *La Bohème. La Traviata. Manon Lescaut. The Masked Ball.* All sumptuously staged. All underwritten by Sybil Harrington. Handsome is as handsome does, too. And handsome lives. Fifth Avenue duplex. Homes in Phoenix and Amarillo. But very private. Back home she's a strong supporter of the Amarillo Symphony. The Harrington String Quartet is her creation. She's president emeritus of the Harrington Foundation, established by her husband. The Foundation has given away millions, endowing such causes as the building of Amarillo Medical Center's Cancer Center and Discovery Center. Mrs. Harrington also founded the Costume Institute in the Panhandle Plains Historical Museum, and the Harrington Foundation was back of the Museum's $6-million petroleum wing.

MRS. BEN J. FORTSON

One of the world's handsomest art museums is presided over by one of Texas' handsomest ladies, Kay Carter Fortson. She is president of Fort Worth's Kimbell Art Museum, considered by many to be architect Louis Kahn's masterpiece. Built in memory of her uncle, the late Kay

Kimbell, it is a modern temple to beauty. Mr. Kimbell was a modest, re-tiring man, and a very wealthy one. With a fortune made in grain, insur-ance and oil, he and his wife, Vera, assembled an extraordinary collec-tion of fine eighteenth-century British and French paintings. Having no children of their own, they acquired a family of immortal sons and daughters in fine portraits by Gainsborough, Romney, Corot and the like. Shortly after World War II, their art dealer, Bert Newhouse of New York's noted Newhouse Gallery, came upon a stunning self-por-trait by the eighteenth-century French woman artist Vigée-Lebrun. It had been taken by Adolf Hitler from the Stringer-Rothschild family and given to a Vienna museum. After Germany fell, the painting was returned to its original owners. Newhouse obtained it from them, took it to Fort Worth, and sold it to the Kimbells. They were fascinated with its history. "Isn't it something!" marveled Mr. Kimbell. "A little fellow who used to sweep out his father's flour mill in a tiny town in Texas has brought the picture Hitler stole from the Rothschilds to Fort Worth." Mr. Newhouse agreed. It was, indeed, something. From then on, Kim-bell funds brought a lot of "somethings" to Fort Worth. They are now housed in glorious galleries paid for and supported by the Kay and Vera Kimbell Foundation.

THE HAYDEN HEADS

Corpus Christi's Hayden and Annie Blake Head are right up there in the South Texas social swim. He is considered one of Texas's top power brokers. A conservative lawyer for some of South Texas' major interests, he is sometimes referred to as "Mr. Republican."

Mrs. Head, soignée descendant of an old South Texas cotton family, always had others tend to her kitchen chores. Her husband's favorite story about his wife deals with his mother's first visit to them after their honeymoon. Since the cook was off for the afternoon, the new bride went up to her new mother-in-law's room to ask if she would like some-thing cool to drink. "Yes, dear," was the reply. "Iced tea would be just lovely." Unfortunately, Annie had never made iced tea. After searching to no avail through recipe books and on the tea package, she returned and

189

*Leading
Lights
in the
Lone Star
Galaxy*

admitted she didn't know how to make iced tea. "How *do* you make it?" Her mother-in-law threw her arms around her and whispered, "I haven't the slightest idea. Never made iced tea in my life." They were fast friends from then on.

THE ALGUR MEADOWS FAMILY

Visitors to the Dallas Museum of Fine Arts delight in seeing first-rate paintings by Impressionist and modern masters, as well as pre-Columbian rareties, all thanks to the family of oilman Algur Meadows. The city's Southern Methodist University has another Meadows' gift: Meadows Museum, devoted to Spanish paintings. Algur Meadows had a career as varied as his formidable art collections. Son of a Vidalia, Georgia, physician, he made his way to the top first as a security guard, then as traveling salesman, movie stunt man, lawyer and loan company partner before striking it rich in oil. By 1936, the company he helped form, General American Oil, had expanded into real estate development, mortgage banking and insurance. In the early sixties, he and his wife, the former Elizabeth Boggs Bartholow of New York, became avid art collectors. In 1967, the Meadows' collection caused quite a stir in the art world when 44 of their French Impressionist paintings, valued at $1,362,750, were found to be fakes. Several were by Hungarian forger Elmer de Hory, the subject of Clifford Irving's book *Fake.* Undaunted, Meadows then bought $2 million worth of paintings from New York's Wildenstein & Company, this time making positive his Gauguins, Monets, Degas were not only the real thing, but the finest available. Today, the Meadows family, headed by his son, Robert, are major stockholders of the vast General American oil empire . . . and they are still collecting—but only the best.

JAMES STORM

Jim Storm's success saga ranges from yucca to yacht. His family migrated to Corpus Christi two steps out of the Texas dust bowl. He worked as an oil roughneck, and learned the business well. Today Mr.

Storm personally owns more offshore drilling rigs than any individual anywhere and rents them to potentates everywhere. Each rig costs from 30 million dollars up. At last count, he owned 16. Jim Storm is most famous for his 112-foot yacht *Celika S.* Built for R. E. Olds, founder of Oldsmobile, the yacht was also once owned by racketeer Al Capone. Jim and his vivacious native Argentinian wife, Chela, reconditioned it lavishly and entertain their constant flow of international clients aboard. They can seat 26 for a formal dinner party. Jim heads Corpus Christi's prosperous part.

RICHARD AND HARRY BASS

No relation to the Fort Worth Perry Bass family. These are the Bass brothers of Dallas who have made millions developing resort properties. Vail, Colorado, for Harry; Snowbird, Utah, for Dick.

SIMON HENDERSON

The Hendersons loom large in Lufkin. Besides owning a major interest in Lufkin Industries and Lufkin Federal Savings & Loan, they have extensive real estate holdings in East Texas. Simon III is president of Lufkin Federal.

TOM BROWN

Not the *Tom Brown's School Days* Brown. He's Thomas C. Brown, of Midland. His Tom Brown, Inc. oil production company operates very profitable drilling rigs.

FRED HERVEY

Former mayor of El Paso and chairman of El Paso's American Bank of Commerce, Fred Hervey seems to have lassoed quite a lot of loot in a career that spans seventy years. Sun World Corporation, Circle K Corporation and a chain of food stores are not all his interests. He's a big owner of the four Rs: racehorses, real estate, radio stations, restaurants.

191

*Leading
Lights
in the
Lone Star
Galaxy*

W. E. FONDREN

Walter W. Fondren III's granddad, W. W., was a president and founder of Humble Oil (with Farish, Blaffer and Wiess). A former University of Texas football star, W. W. III runs Houston's very sizable Fondren Foundation with his sisters Ellanor Ann Fondren and Doris Fondren Allday.

THE DORNS

San Antonio's Dorn family fortune originated in the oil fields of Western Pennsylvania. With their father's Forest Oil Corporation. Heading the family clan from San Antonio is Dale Dorn. His younger brothers Clayton, David, Richard and John, as well as his sister, Martha Dorn Bird, no longer live in San Antonio, but haven't strayed too far away. You'll find these Dorns at the top of the social heap in Houston, Midland, Denver and Corpus Christi.

GEORGE PARKER

Patron of the arts George Parker is perhaps the most eligible bachelor in Texas. His late father, George, Sr., became the largest private stockholder of Texaco when he sold his family's drilling company to it. George Parker owns ranchland in Calgary, as well as homes in France, New York, San Antonio and Dallas.

HENRY TAUB

Henry Taub is patriarch of one of Houston's oldest and most prominent families. A major supporter of civic charities, he heads family interests started by his grandfather, Ben Taub, who was Jesse Jones' closest business partner. Taub interests include the Richmond Truck Car Company, real estate and tobacco.

LAURENCE SHEERIN

Larry Sheerin, San Antonio-Brownsville oilman, has done much for preserving the past, and polo. He and his brother, Robert, spurred on the sport with a family-sponsored polo team. Agriculturist, chef, collector of rare guns and art, his friends call him "a Renaissance man." He and his wife, Betty Lou, have transformed an historical 1893 vintage hotel in Rio Grande City into a charming restaurant and inn, La Borde House. It's now a favorite haunt of tourists heading for Mexico and South Padre Island, as well as birdsmen and hunters visiting the Falcon Dam Reservoir nearby.

OSCAR WYATT

Houston, Corpus Christi and Cap Ferrat are all part of Oscar Wyatt's world. Founder and chairman of Coastal States Gas, he's also husband of glamorous international hostess Lynn Sakowitz Wyatt. The Wyatts bought W. Somerset Maugham's famed Villa Mauresque on the French Riviera, where the late Princess Grace was a frequent guest.

B. J. MCCOMBS

Red McCombs owns car dealerships throughout Texas, a drive-in grocery chain and lots of longhorns. He is also partner in ranches, oil leases and San Antonio's pro basketball team, the Spurs.

Clients of John Staub— "The Court Architect"

J OHN FANZ STAUB was born in Knoxville, Tennessee, and was a graduate of M.I.T. Hugo "Baron" Neuhaus commissioned him to build his home in Houston and introduced Staub to leaders of Houston society. Several had bought property in Texaco chief J. S. Cullinian's exclusive Shadyside compound. For over 40 years, Staub's great taste and talent made him the architect to Texas aristocrats—and one of them.

1926   Stable for Mr. and Mrs. Robert D. Randolph (*destroyed*)
        South Post Oak Lane and Riverway
        Houston, Texas

1926   Bayou Bend for Miss Ima Hogg
        2940 Lazy Lane
        Houston, Texas
        (Birdsall P. Briscoe, associate architect; alterations by John F.
            Staub and by Staub, Rather & Howze)

1926	House for Judge and Mrs. Frederick C. Proctor 2950 Lazy Lane Houston, Texas (associate to Birdsall P. Briscoe, designing architect)
ca. 1926	House for Mr. and Mrs. Robert E. Powell (*project*) Baytown, Texas
1927	Penthouse for Mr. and Mrs. Jesse H. Jones Lamar Hotel, Lamar Avenue and Main Street Houston, Texas (Alfred C. Finn, associated architect; *dismantled*)
1927	House for Mr. and Mrs. Edwin E. Bewley Fort Worth, Texas
1927	River Oaks Community Center (*demolished*) 2506–2516 River Oaks Boulevard Houston, Texas
1927	De Pelchin Faith Home (*project*) Houston, Texas
1927	Alterations and additions to house of Dr. and Mrs. Edward Randall, Jr. (*project*) Galveston, Texas
1927	Bay house for Mr. and Mrs. Frank N. Bullock 311 Bayridge Road Morgan's Point, Texas
1928	House for Mr. and Mrs. John P. King 4926 Crestline Road Fort Worth, Texas
1928	House for Mr. and Mrs. William C. Helmbrecht 3815 Avenue P Galveston, Texas
1928	House for Dr. and Mrs. Edward Randall, Jr. 3502 Avenue P Galveston, Texas (additions by John F. Staub)
1928	House for Mr. and Mrs. Rudolph C. Kuldell 1400 South Boulevard Houston, Texas
1928	House for Mr. and Mrs. Amon G. Carter (*project*) Fort Worth, Texas
1928	Garage remodeling and greenhouse for Mr. and Mrs. Harry C. Wiess 2 Sunset Road Houston, Texas
ca. 1928	Alterations to house of Mr. and Mrs. Laurence S. Bosworth 1310 South Boulevard Houston, Texas

ca. 1928   Alterations to house of Mr. and Mrs. A. Sessums Cleveland
8 Courtlandt Place
Houston, Texas

1929   Lodge for Mr. and Mrs. W. T. Carter, Jr. (*altered*)
331 West Friar Tuck Lane
Houston, Texas

1929   Parish house for Palmer Memorial Church (*altered*)
6221 South Main Street
Houston, Texas

1929   House for Mr. and Mrs. Kemp S. Dargan
1317 North Boulevard
Houston, Texas

1929   Junior League building (*altered*)
500 Stuart Avenue
Houston, Texas

1929   House for Mr. and Mrs. Herman Gartner
Fort Worth, Texas
(additions by John F. Staub)

1929   Additions to house of Dr. and Mrs. Frederick Rice Lummis (*altered*)
3921 Yoakum Boulevard
Houston, Texas

ca. 1929   Gasoline service station for Humble Oil & Refining Company
(*Between 12 and 20 stations were constructed, several in Houston but most in West Texas. None are known to exist.*)

ca. 1929   Tejas Club
Petroleum building, 1314 Texas Avenue
Houston, Texas
(alterations by John F. Staub; *dismantled*)

1930   House for Mr. and Mrs. Harry C. Hanszen
2955 Lazy Lane
Houston, Texas

1930   The Stables for Mr. and Mrs. Harry C. Wiess
North Post Oak Lane
Houston, Texas
(alterations by Staub, Rather & Howze)

1930   House for Mr. and Mrs. John Sweeney Mellinger
3452 Del Monte Drive
Houston, Texas
(alterations by John F. Staub)

ca. 1930   Stable for Mr. and Mrs. Carl Detering (*project*)
Houston, Texas

ca. 1930   House for Mr. and Mrs. Eugene Yates (*project*)
Birmingham, Alabama

1931	House for Mr. and Mrs. Wallace E. Pratt (*demolished*) 2990 Lazy Lane Houston, Texas	
1931	House for Mr. and Mrs. George A. Hill, Jr. 1604 Kirby Drive Houston, Texas	
1931	Additions to house of Mr. and Mrs. George Thompson, Jr. 1300 Humble Street Fort Worth, Texas	
1931	House for Mr. and Mrs. J. Robert Neal 2960 Lazy Lane Houston, Texas	
1931	Lodge for Mr. and Mrs. Wallace E. Pratt Pratt Ranch Hudspeth County, Texas	
ca. 1931	House for Mr. and Mrs. Charles Roeser (*project*) Fort Worth, Texas	
ca. 1931	House for Mr. and Mrs. Eugene Yates (*project*) Fisher's Island, New York (Erard A. Matthiessen, associate architect)	
1932	House for Mr. and Mrs. Raymond H. Goodrich (*altered*) 300 Pinewold Drive Houston, Texas	
1933	Alterations to house of Mr. and Mrs. Heinrich Renfert 2602 Avenue O Galveston, Texas	
1933	Alterations and additions to house of Mr. and Mrs. J. V. Vandenberge 604 North Craig Street Victoria, Texas	
1933	House for Mr. and Mrs. Hugh Roy Cullen 1620 River Oaks Boulevard Houston, Texas	
1933	House for Mr. and Mrs. David D. Bruton 2923 Inwood Drive Houston, Texas	
1933	House for Mr. and Mrs. Clarence M. Frost (*altered*) 2110 River Oaks Boulevard Houston, Texas	
1933	Humble Tower 912 Dallas Avenue Houston, Texas (Kenneth Franzheim, associated architect)	

1933	Alterations to house of Mr. and Mrs. Kenneth E. Womack 8 Remington Lane Houston, Texas
ca. 1933	Mission Manufacturing Company building 5220 Jensen Drive Houston, Texas
1934	Florence Crittenton Rescue Home (*demolished*) 5009 Scotland Street Houston, Texas
1934	Ravenna for Mr. and Mrs. Stephen P. Farish 2995 Lazy Lane Houston, Texas
1934	Alterations and additions to house of Mr. and Mrs. Harry C. Wiess 2 Sunset Road Houston, Texas
1934	House for Mr. and Mrs. H. J. Lutcher Stark (*project*) Orange, Texas
1935	House for Mr. and Mrs. J. Cooke Wilson (*altered*) 2500 Ashley Avenue Beaumont, Texas
1935	House for Mr. and Mrs. William J. Crabb 2416 Pine Valley Drive Houston, Texas
1935	Alterations and additions to house of Dr. and Mrs. E. M. Arm- strong (*altered*) 1128 Bissonnet Avenue Houston, Texas
1935	Sweeny building (*demolished*) 4110 South Main Street Houston, Texas
1935	House for Mr. and Mrs. Robert Bowles 3015 Inwood Drive Houston, Texas (additions by Staub & Rather)
1935	Texas Memorial Museum 2401 San Jacinto Street University of Texas, Austin, Texas (Paul Philippe Cret, consulting architect. Only the central section of this building was constructed.)
1935	Mirabeau B. Lamar Senior High School 3325 Westheimer Road Houston, Texas (Kenneth Franzheim, associated architect; Lamar Q. Cato, Louis A. Glover, and Harry D. Payne, associate architects)

1935	House for Mr. and Mrs. George S. Heyer 2909 Inwood Drive Houston, Texas
ca. 1935	House for Mr. and Mrs. McDonald Meachum (*project*) Houston, Texas
1936	House for Mr. and Mrs. J. Coulter Means, Jr. 3904 South MacGregor Way Houston, Texas
1936	Oak Shadows for Mr. and Mrs. Ray L. Dudley 3371 Chevy Chase Drive Houston, Texas
1936	House for Mr. and Mrs. George V. Rotan 2300 Pine Valley Drive Houston, Texas
1936	Alterations to house of Mr. and Mrs. John W. Herbert, III 800 Rivercrest Road Fort Worth, Texas
1936	House for Mr. and Mrs. Tom Scurry (*altered*) 1912 Larchmont Road Houston, Texas
1936	Additions to Halliburton Oil Well Cementing Company building 7204 Navigation Boulevard Houston, Texas
1936	House for Mr. and Mrs. J. Meredith Tatton 601 West North Street Victoria, Texas
1936	House for Mr. and Mrs. Richard W. Neff (*project*) Houston, Texas
1936	Houston Building & Loan Association building 1114 Capitol Avenue Houston, Texas (Kenneth Franzheim, associated architect; *altered*)
1936	House for Mr. and Mrs. James L. Britton 1824 Larchmont Road Houston, Texas (alterations by John F. Staub; *altered*)
1936	Ranch house for Mr. and Mrs. Lamar Fleming, Jr. Fleming Ranch Kerr County, Texas
1936	House for Mr. and Mrs. Sellers J. Thomas (*altered*) 3304 South MacGregor Way Houston, Texas
1936	House for Mr. and Mrs. Alex C. Camp 8617 Garland Road Dallas, Texas

1936	Greenhouse for Mr. and Mrs. Hugh Roy Cullen 1620 River Oaks Boulevard Houston, Texas
ca. 1936	House for Mr. and Mrs. Lindsey H. Dunn (*project*) Houston, Texas
ca. 1936	Ridglea Country Club (*project*) Fort Worth, Texas
1937	House for Mr. and Mrs. Robert D. Straus 1814 Larchmont Road Houston, Texas (additions by John F. Staub and by Staub & Rather; *altered*)
1937	Standard Brass & Manufacturing Company building 2018 Franklin Avenue Houston, Texas
1937	House for Mr. and Mrs. Ernest Bel Fay 105 North Post Oak Lane Houston, Texas (additions by Staub & Rather)
1937	House for Mr. and Mrs. John M. Jennings (*altered*) 2212 Troon Road Houston, Texas
1937	House for Mr. and Mrs. W. L. Moody, III 5115 Avenue T Galveston, Texas
1937	House for Mr. and Mrs. L. Randolph Bryan, Jr. 3315 Ella Lee Lane Houston, Texas
1937	Pi Beta Phi Sorority House 2300 San Antonio Street Austin, Texas
1937	House for Mr. and Mrs. Alexander F. Weisberg (*destroyed*) 8726 Douglas Avenue Dallas, Texas
1938	Office building for Quintana Petroleum Company (*project*) Houston, Texas
1938	Alterations to house of Mr. and Mrs. Rudolph E. Kraus 2323 Shell Beach Drive Lake Charles, Louisiana
1938	House for Mr. and Mrs. Dan J. Harrison, Sr. 2975 Lazy Lane Houston, Texas
1938	Super service station for Humble Oil & Refining Company (*About 20 stations were constructed in different Texas towns, including Houston. None are known to exist.*)

1938	House for Mr. and Mrs. Andrew Jackson Wray 3 Remington Lane Houston, Texas
1938	House for Mr. and Mrs. Claud B. Hamill 2124 River Oaks Boulevard Houston, Texas (additions by Staub & Rather)
1938	House for Mr. and Mrs. Arthur A. Seeligson Olmos Park, Texas
1938	House for Mr. and Mrs. A. C. Glassell 6007 East Ridge Drive Shreveport, Louisiana
1938	House for Mrs. Anne Burnett Hall Windfohr (*altered*) 1900 Spanish Trail Westover Hills, Texas
1938	House for Mr. and Mrs. James O. Winston, Jr. 101 Carnarvon Drive Houston, Texas
1938	Houston Riding and Polo Club house (*demolished*) South Post Oak Road and Westheimer Road Houston, Texas
1938	Additions to Humble Building Dallas Avenue and Travis Street Houston, Texas (Kenneth Franzheim, associated architect)
1938	Bayou Club 8550 Memorial Drive Houston, Texas
1938	Alterations to Tall Timbers lodge for Mr. and Mrs. Ray W. Smith (project) Houston, Texas
1938	House for Mr. and Mrs. Alfred L. Bromberg (*project*) Dallas, Texas
1938	Alterations to Hurst for Mr. and Mrs. Laurence Williams 3 Garden Lane Metairie, Louisiana
1939	House for Mr. and Mrs. Albert Bel Fay 99 North Post Oak Lane Houston, Texas (alterations by Staub, Rather & Howze)
1939	Recreation house for Mr. and Mrs. Robert D. Straus 1814 Larchmont Road Houston, Texas
1939	House for Dr. and Mrs. F. M. Hight (*project*) Houston, Texas

1939   House for Mr. and Mrs. Ray J. O'Brien
6043 Gilbert Avenue
Shreveport, Louisiana

1939   Brannon-Welsh clinic
2715 Fannin Street
Houston, Texas

1939   House for Mr. and Mrs. Edgar G. Tobin (*project*)
San Antonio, Texas

1939   House for Mr. and Mrs. Edward H. Andrews
3637 Inwood Drive
Houston, Texas

1940   Bay house for Mr. and Mrs. Hugh Roy Cullen
Texas Corinthian Yacht Club
Kemah, Texas

1940   House for Mr. and Mrs. Thomas B. Slick, Jr. (*altered*)
606 Elizabeth Road
Terrell Hills, Texas

1940   House for Mr. and Mrs. Thomas H. Shartle
10600 Memorial Drive
Hunters Creek Village, Texas

1940   House for Mr. and Mrs. Percy Selden Straus, Jr. (*destroyed*)
11407 Memorial Drive
Piney Point Village, Texas

1940   House for Miss Eugenia Williams
4848 Lyons View Pike
Knoxville, Tennessee

1940   House for Mr. and Mrs. Hugo N. Dixon
4339 Park Avenue
Memphis, Tennessee

1940   House for Mr. and Mrs. Robert L. Ashe (*project*)
Knoxville, Tennessee

1940   Additions to Colonial Country Club
3735 Country Club Circle
Fort Worth, Texas

1940   House for Mr. and Mrs. Carl A. Mangold, Jr. (*project*)
Dallas, Texas

1940   House for Mrs. John Thomas Rather, Jr.
360 Blalock Road
Piney Point Village, Texas

1941   House for Dr. and Mrs. Allen McMurrey (*demolished*)
22 Briar Hollow Lane
Houston, Texas

1941   House for Mr. and Mrs. Don Q. Riddle
121 Radney Road
Piney Point Village, Texas

Staub & Rather

1945	Fondren Library Rice University Houston, Texas (William Ward Watkin, consulting architect; additions by Staub, Rather & Howze)
1945	President's House (*altered*) Rice University Houston, Texas
1946	M. D. Anderson Hall Rice University Houston, Texas (William Ward Watkin, consulting architect)
1947	Abercrombie Laboratory, Rice University Houston, Texas (William Ward Watkin, consulting architect; additions by Staub, Rather & Howze)
1947	Alterations to Shadyside for Governor and Mrs. William P. Hobby (*demolished*) 2 Remington Lane Houston, Texas
1947	Commercial building for Bonwit-Teller (*project*) Houston, Texas
1947	House for Mr. and Mrs. James A. Elkins, Jr. 3405 Meadow Lake Lane Houston, Texas (additions by Staub, Rather & Howze)
1947	Staub & Rather professional building 2814 Virginia Street Houston, Texas
ca. 1947	House for Mr. and Mrs. Richard M. Kleberg, Jr. (*project*) Kleberg County, Texas
1948	Burbank Junior High School 315 Berry Road Houston, Texas (Stayton Nunn, consulting architect)
1948	Harry C. Wiess Hall (Wiess College) Rice University Houston, Texas (additions by Staub, Rather & Howze; *altered*)
1948	Ranch House for Mr. and Mrs. Dan J. Harrison, Jr. Piloncillo Ranch Dimmit County, Texas

1949 House for Mr. and Mrs. Edwin B. McFarland (*destroyed*)
127 Iron Wood Road
Olmos Park, Texas

1949 Alterations and additions to Charles H. Milby Senior High
School
1601 Broadway
Houston, Texas
(Stayton Nunn, consulting architect)

1949 M. D. Anderson Memorial Library
University of Houston
Houston, Texas
(additions by Staub, Rather & Howze; *altered*)

1949 Additions to house of Mr. and Mrs. Thomas D. Anderson
3929 Del Monte Drive
Houston, Texas

1949 House for Mr. and Mrs. Percy Selden (Straus, Jr.)
11407 Memorial Drive
Piney Point Village, Texas

1949 St. Luke's Episcopal Hospital
6720 Bertner Avenue
Texas Medical Center
Houston, Texas
(Hiram A. Salisbury, associated architect; additions by Staub,
Rather & Howze)

1949 Batts Hall, Benedict Hall, *and* Mezes Hall
University of Texas
(Mark Lemmon, associated architect)

1949 House for Mr. and Mrs. John Flude
6 Shadder Way
Houston, Texas

ca. 1949 House for Mr. and Mrs. Dunbar Chambers (*altered*)
3990 Inverness Drive
Houston, Texas

ca. 1949 Alterations and additions to house of Mr. and Mrs. Carl Detering
10010 Memorial Drive
Houston, Texas
(additions by Staub, Rather & Howze)

1950 Petroleum Club (*dismantled*)
Rice Hotel
Texas Avenue and Main Street
Houston, Texas

1950 House for Mrs. Amy Staub Galyon
1841 Melrose Avenue
Knoxville, Tennessee

1950	Bay House for Mr. and Mrs. Ernest Bel Fay 103 Baycliff Drive Kemah, Texas
1950	House for Mr. and Mrs. William C. Helmbrecht 6810 Turtle Creek Boulevard University Park, Texas
1950	House for Mr. and Mrs. Seymour Sacks 703 South Post Oak Lane Houston, Texas
1950	Additions to house of Mr. and Mrs. Lloyd H. Smith Houston, Texas
ca. 1950	Employees' housing group, veterinary clinic, and barns Santa Gertrudis Division, King Ranch Kleberg County, Texas
ca. 1950	Lake Charles Public Library (Calcasieu Parish Public Library) 411 Pujo Street Lake Charles, Louisiana (William Ward Watkin, consulting architect)
ca. 1950	Heidi McFarlin mausoleum Mission Burial Park San Antonio, Texas
ca. 1950	Texas Medical Association building 1801 North Lamar Boulevard Austin, Texas
1951	Chapel of the Christ Child, Christ Church Cathedral 1101 Texas Avenue Houston, Texas
ca. 1951	Country house for Mr. and Mrs. Jacques F. Pryor Farm to Market Road 390 Washington County, Texas
ca. 1951	Stable for Mr. and Mrs. Edwin G. Bradley Bradley Farms Sedgewick County, Kansas

Staub, Rather & Howze

1952	Rienzi for Mr. and Mrs. Harris Masterson, III (*altered*) 1406 Kirby Drive Houston, Texas
1952	Alterations and additions to house of Mr. and Mrs. R. E. ("Bob") Smith 3208 Chevy Chase Drive Houston, Texas

1952   House for Mr. and Mrs. William C. Richardson
        1130 Thomas Road
        Beaumont, Texas

1952   Magnolia Hill for Mr. and Mrs. Charles F. Urschel
        330 Paseo Encinal
        Olmos Park, Texas

1952   House for Mr. and Mrs. Lewis J. Moorman, Jr. (*project*)
        San Antonio, Texas

1953   House for Mr. and Mrs. Robert P. Gregory
        8802 Memorial Drive
        Houston, Texas

1953   House for Mr. and Mrs. William N. Lehrer
        Garwood, Texas

1954   House for Mr. and Mrs. William L. Walker
        1840 South Live Oak Boulevard
        Wilmington, North Carolina
        (Leslie N. Boney, associate architect)

1955   Sealands for Mr. and Mrs. Harry E. Brants
        4164 Edgehill Road
        Fort Worth, Texas

1955   House for Mr. and Mrs. Joseph L. Hargrove
        524 Lloyd Lane
        Shreveport, Louisiana

1955   House for Mr. and Mrs. Hugh Sprunt
        4036 South Galloway Drive
        Memphis, Tennessee

1955   Alterations and additions to Museum of Fine Arts
        1001 Bissonnet Avenue
        Houston, Texas
        (associate to Ludwig Miës van der Rohe, designing architect; al-
            tered. Staub, Rather & Howze remodeled the existing mu-
            seum building while serving as associates for Miës' addition
            of Cullinan Hall.)

1956   House for Mr. and Mrs. George A. Peterkin, Jr.
        Hunters Creek Village, Texas

1956   House for Mr. and Mrs. Ben M. Anderson
        3740 Willowick Road
        Houston, Texas

1956   House for Mr. William S. Kilroy (*project*)
        Houston, Texas

1957   House for Mr. and Mrs. George A. Peterkin, Sr.
        2005 Claremont Lane
        Houston, Texas
        (additions by Staub, Rather & Howze)

1957	House for Mr. and Mrs. Irving M. Eisen 2990 Thomas Road Beaumont, Texas
1957	House for Miss Alma and Miss Lenora Detering 10002 Memorial Drive Houston, Texas
1958	Abercrombie country house Versailles, Kentucky
1958	House for Mr. and Mrs. James A. Elkins, Jr. Houston, Texas
1959	House for Mr. and Mrs. Lawrence S. Reed 107 North Post Oak Lane Houston, Texas
1959	House for Mr. and Mrs. Robert A. Mosbacher (*altered*) Houston, Texas
1959	United States Federal Office building 515 Rusk Avenue Houston, Texas (Rustay & Martin and Harvin C. Moore, associated architects)
1960	Houston Museum of Natural Science and Burke Baker Planetarium Hermann Park Houston, Texas (George Pierce-Abel B. Pierce, associated architects; additions by George Pierce-Abel B. Pierce and Staub, Rather & Howze)
1960	Bay house for Mr. and Mrs. Albert Bel Fay 1215 Kipp Road Kemah, Texas
1960	House for Mr. and Mrs. Hugh Brinkley 170 South Rose Road Memphis, Tennessee
1960	Rayzor Hall Rice University Houston, Texas
1960	House for Mr. and Mrs. Craig F. Cullinan, Jr. (*altered*) 215 Carnarvon Drive Houston, Texas
1962	House for Mr. and Mrs. Edward Randall, III (*altered*) 5135 Greentree Road Houston, Texas
1968	Restoration of Liendo and estate improvements for Mr. and Mrs. Carl Detering Liendo plantation Washington County, Texas

Constellations

THE GEORGE R. BROWN FAMILY

Houston's Brown & Root, one of this earth's largest construction companies, is George Brown's baby. Brown grew up in Belmont, Texas, one of seven children. After getting a mining engineer's degree in Colorado, he worked for Anaconda Copper there. When he was injured in a mine cave-in, he joined the construction firm his brother Herman had started with Herman's brother-in-law, Don Root. George Brown set up the company's Houston office in 1926 and became the power behind many a throne. His suite 8F in Houston's Lamar Hotel was the gathering spot for the city's master builders and power wielders. No one had more political clout than George himself. When Lyndon Johnson succeeded President John F. Kennedy, the word locally was "LBJ's in the

White House, but George Brown is President." The Browns gave important paintings and furnishings to the White House, including a Winslow Homer. He and his wife, Helen, often played host to presidents and kings of industry at their handsome Middleburg, Virginia, estate, Huntlands. Mr. Brown's great contributions to Houston include the vast Houston Center complex, a project of Texas Eastern Transmission Corporation, which he founded. The Browns' daughters, Mrs. Wallace Wilson of Houston and Nancy Brown Negley of San Antonio, quietly transform ugliness into beauty in their respective cities. Isabel Wilson with her mini-parks in Houston. Nancy with her Riverwalk and museum leadership in San Antonio. Say Texans: "The Browns have repaid Texas and the nation many times over for the prosperity they enjoyed." The Brown brothers' personal foundation has assets exceeding $100 million.

THE O'CONNORS

The O'Connor clan of Victoria is one of Texas' oldest and richest. Tom O'Connor started it all when he came over from Ireland four generations ago and became a cattle rancher. When oil was discovered on his property, he went into the oil business. Naturally, he had to have a bank to put his mounds of money in, so he became a banker, too. Dennis O'Connor is senior chairman of Victoria Bank & Trust Company, "the O'Connor family bank." Tom O'Connor, Jr., is the O'Connor patriarch, and the O'Connor relatives are legion.

THE DEALEYS OF DALLAS

George Bannerman Dealey, who died in 1946, left behind the *Dallas Morning News*, the "most prestigious newspaper in the Southwest." It was just a part of the family's A. H. Belo Corporation, which included WFAA-TV, Dallas' biggest station; two Dallas radio stations; a Beaumont radio-TV station; a chain of Dallas suburban daily newspapers; and Atlas Match Company of Dallas. Grandson Joseph M. Dealey took over as chairman of the board of A. H. Belo, and his son, Joe Jr., as vice-president and secretary.

THE MOODY BUNCH

At the head of Galveston's Moody family (cotton-insurance-banking-newspapers) is Mary Moody Northen. A childless widow in her nineties, she lives alone in the 30-room mansion built by her eccentric father, William Lewis Moody, Jr. Her daddy made a fortune in insurance thanks to a 1907 Texas law specifying that any insurance company doing business in Texas had to invest all its funds in Texas. Most national insurance companies picked up their policies and left the state rather than go along with it. Not W. L. Moody. He lassoed trained personnel from the agencies that had vacated and started American National Insurance with money he'd made as a cotton broker. It became one of the largest life insurance operations in the whole Southwest, with holdings of more than $300 million. He started Moody National Bank to handle all its deposits. In Galveston, Moodys don't speak to Moodys, except perhaps in court. Still suing each other over the inheritance are such prominent family members as William L. Moody, IV; Shearn Moody, Jr.; and Robert L. Moody of Austin.

THE BANKING OPPENHEIMERS

Brothers Dan and Herbert Oppenheimer run one of Texas' last private banks, D & A Oppenheimer. Their cousin, Frederick Oppenheimer, owns the San Antonio Bank & Trust. His wife, Dorothy, is from the Chittum ranching family. Frederick's brother, Jesse, didn't carry on the family tradition. He's an attorney, and a wealthy one at that.

THE FROSTS

First it was San Antonio's Frost Brothers Department Store which profited so, the Frost family started the Frost Bank. Then came ranchlands, cattle and oil. Pearl Frost, widow of Thomas C. Frost, is matriarch of the Frost family. Her son, Thomas, Jr., is chairman of the Frost Bank. A nephew, Joseph H. Frost, is a big investor in Datapoint Corporation (computers) and San Antonio's Plaza Nacional Hotel.

THE SEELIGSONS OF SAN ANTONIO

One of the richest oil and gas fields in South Texas belongs to the Seeligson family. Arthur, Jr., looks after the family's oil ranching and investments. His brother, Frates, an attorney, takes care of the legal part. Their mother, Ramona Frates Seeligson, is one of Texas' great *grandes dames*. Arthur is also a successful breeder of racing thoroughbreds. His horse, Avatar, won the Belmont Stakes in 1975.

THE MURCHISONS

The Murchisons and Hunts are Texas' wealthiest families. Both clans live in Dallas. The late Clint Murchison, Sr., son of an Athens, Texas, banking family, made it big in the oil field. He left his two children, John and Clint, Jr., hundreds of millions. Before he died in 1959, Murchison, Sr. (pronounced Merr-kiss-sun) controlled 115 companies ranging in everything from insurance to publishing. He told his sons "Money is a lot like manure. Pile it all in one place and it stinks like hell. Spread it around and it does a lot of good."

Spread it they did. John, graduate of Amherst and Yale, who died in 1979 at the age of fifty-seven, steered the company successfully into insurance, banking, publishing and the financial markets. His widow, Lupe, is the sister of Mrs. Stuart Hunt, whose father-in-law was H. L. Hunt's brother, Sherman.

Clint Murchison, Jr., is chief Murchison today—man and money behind such real estate ventures as the Trousdale Estates in Beverly Hills, the Racquet Club in Palm Springs and Vail Mountain Ski Lodge. But his biggest claim to fame worldwide is as big daddy of the Dallas Cowboys, the superstar team in the National Football League. He built the Cowboys' franchise from scratch in 1960 to its present worth of over $20 million.

Matriarch of the Murchison clan is the late Clint, Sr.'s, second wife, Virginia, now Mrs. Ed Linthicum of Dallas, La Jolla, Acapulco and Tampico, Mexico (when not at her two Texas ranches). Clint, Sr., had three brothers: John, who stayed in Athens; Frank, who moved to San Antonio; and Kenneth, of Dallas. Kenneth's daughter, Mary Murchison, made international news when she married Viscount Rothermere, owner of London's *Daily Mail* newspapers. Now divorced, Lady Rothermere divides her time between Newport, Palm Beach, Texas, New York and the Continent.

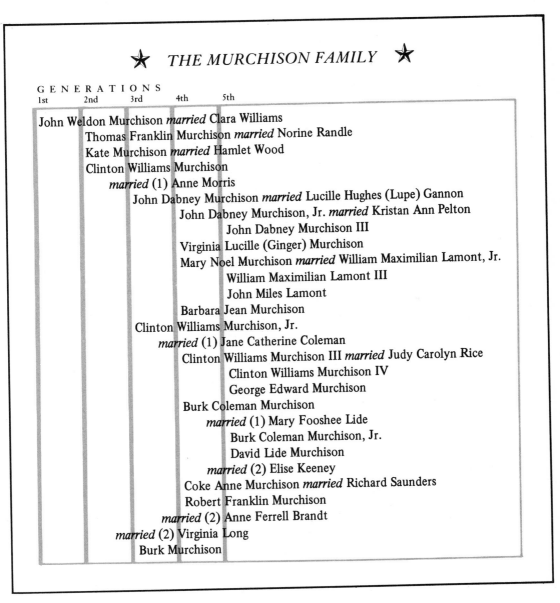

★ *THE MURCHISON FAMILY* ★

GENERATIONS
1st   2nd   3rd   4th   5th

John Weldon Murchison *married* Clara Williams
Thomas Franklin Murchison *married* Norine Randle
Kate Murchison *married* Hamlet Wood
Clinton Williams Murchison
    married (1) Anne Morris
        John Dabney Murchison *married* Lucille Hughes (Lupe) Gannon
        John Dabney Murchison, Jr. *married* Kristan Ann Pelton
            John Dabney Murchison III
        Virginia Lucille (Ginger) Murchison
        Mary Noel Murchison *married* William Maximilian Lamont, Jr.
            William Maximilian Lamont III
            John Miles Lamont
        Barbara Jean Murchison
      Clinton Williams Murchison, Jr.
        married (1) Jane Catherine Coleman
        Clinton Williams Murchison III *married* Judy Carolyn Rice
            Clinton Williams Murchison IV
            George Edward Murchison
        Burk Coleman Murchison
            married (1) Mary Fooshee Lide
                Burk Coleman Murchison, Jr.
                David Lide Murchison
            married (2) Elise Keeney
        Coke Anne Murchison *married* Richard Saunders
        Robert Franklin Murchison
        married (2) Anne Ferrell Brandt
    married (2) Virginia Long
    Burk Murchison

THE BENTSENS OF THE VALLEY

The Bentsen brothers, Lloyd, Sr., and Elmer, of McAllen, are the grandees of Texas' Rio Grande Valley. Raised in South Dakota, they came to the Valley after World War I, investing in real estate. After the 1929 stock market crash, they made a fortune in land, grapefruit groves, ranching and oil. Lloyd, Sr., chairmanned the family-owned Bank of McAllen. U. S. Senator Lloyd, Jr., served as president of the Bentsen-chartered Lincoln Life Insurance Company in Nebraska. It is now Lincoln Consolidated, a conglomerate covering everything from financing to funeral homes.

THE STARKS OF ORANGE

H. J. Lutcher Stark (1885–1965) built one of East Texas' largest fortunes with such enterprises as Lutcher and Moore Lumber Company, Vinton Petroleum and the First National Bank of Orange. His sons, Homer and William, oversee the Starks' $40 million-plus foundation, and a collection of art valued at $4 million. Ramona, a Stark daughter, married H. L. Hunt's grandson, John Bunker Sands, son of Carolyn Hunt Sands Schoellkopf.

AMARILLO'S MARSH FAMILY

Stanley Marsh 3, with his millions from natural gas, cattle, banking and TV stations, could easily be the richest man in the Texas Panhandle. And the most eccentric. He created "plains sculpture" by burying the noses of five fin-tailed Cadillacs in a field, giving an impression that they were all going to hell. His business meetings are memorable, too, thanks to the pet lion nesting at his feet. Mrs. Marsh was the former Wendy Bush, granddaughter of cattle king William Bush. Her mother was the daughter of Joseph Glidden, the inventor of barbed wire.

THE BUTTS OF HEB SUPERMARKETS

HEB Stores, founded by the late H. E. Butt, Sr., of Corpus Christi, employ 16,000 Texans. President of the statewide chain is H. E.'s younger son, Charles Butt, San Antonio bachelor, yachtsman and preservationist. H. E. Butt, Jr., is a national leader in lay church activities. Daughter Eleanor is wife of William H. Crook, former Ambassador to Australia. Matriarch of the Butts family is their mother, Mary, a moving force behind mental health and mental retardation programs. She is president of the H. E. Butt Foundation, organized in 1934 by her husband. One of its projects is a 2,000-acre camp in Texas Hill Country used by schools for the retarded, public and parochial institutions, mental hospitals, and as an ecumenical center for Christian learning. Among its many civic, health and spiritual projects, the H. E. Butt Foundation has given Corpus Christi a tennis center with 24 championship courts, scene of international tennis competitions. Charles Butt has preserved a Padre Island landmark, the pre-Civil War Aransas Pass Light Station, turning it into his private island retreat. He also recently restored a nineteenth-century architectural gem on San Antonio's King William Street for his town residence.

THE 7-ELEVEN THOMPSONS

Joe C. Thompson started as a Dallas iceman, heaving blocks of ice onto horse-drawn ice wagons while working his way through college. After graduating, he became an executive of an ice company, which in 1927 evolved into Southland Ice Corporation. Since his ice depots stayed open 16 hours a day, he discovered night customers often asked where they could buy butter, eggs or milk after grocery stores had closed for the day. To fill this need, Joe Thompson eventually converted his ice docks into mini-grocery stores. Open from 7 A.M. to 11 P.M., he named them 7-Eleven Stores, locating them in densely populated areas across the nation. Southland was a pioneer in "convenience" stores, expanding the operation into selling auto parts, too. There are now over 7,600 7-Elevens around the world (4,800 more than McDonald's). Annual sales exceed $3 billion. Joe's sons, John and Jere, are chairman and president, respectively. The vice-president is their younger brother, Joe, Jr.

THE ZALE FAMILY

Diamonds are a Zale's best friend, too. Morris B. Zale founded the Zale nationwide jewelry store chain, of which his brother-in-law, Ben Lipshy, is chairman. Son Donald Zale is vice-chairman. The founder's brother is William Zale. Another key personality in this Dallas diamond dynasty is the chairman's son, Bruce Lipshy.

MAVERICK

Samuel Maverick came to Texas in 1835, and just because he didn't do things the way other ranchers did, the Maverick name came to be synonymous with "a person who acts independently." Sam was different in that he didn't brand his cattle. When his herd stampeded and mixed with his neighbors' at roundup time, all unbranded stock was said to be "Maverick's." That's how the word entered our English language, and dictionary. Not only did Maverick contribute to our vocabulary, he also gave San Antonio the city's first big contributions to charity and religious institutions, as well as land for parks and a library. His progeny have been among San Antonio's most distinguished citizens—mayors, war heros, business and social leaders. Maury Maverick is the family's chief honcho today. To the world, Maverick may mean a free-spirited TV cowboy played by James Garner, or "nonconformist." To Texans, the name stands for Old San Antonio aristocracy.

STRAUSS

"Big D" to the Strauss clan means not only their hometown Dallas, but also Big Democrat. Lawyer Robert Schwarz Strauss is perhaps the party's most powerful mover-shaker in Lone Star land. He and his wife, the former Helen Jacobs, wield considerable political weight in Washington, too. Strauss served as Texas Democratic national committeeman, and in 1979 was the President's personal representative for Middle East negotiations. His brother, Ted Strauss, is chairman of both First City Bank of Dallas and Strauss Broadcasting Company. He is also a director of Houston's First City Bancorporation of Texas, Inc. Ted's wife, Annette, now on the Dallas City Council, has been deemed "the dynamo of Dallas fund-raising." Over three decades, she reportedly brought in $6 million for educational, cultural, business, medical and civic groups. In Big D, to drive behind the fund drive is usually . . . by Strauss.

S. MAURICE MCASHAN

Maurice and Susan McAshan are the largest stockholders of the giant conglomerate Anderson, Clayton & Company. Founded as a cotton merchant partnership by Susan's father, Will Clayton, in 1904, Anderson, Clayton expanded into food processing, life insurance and machinery manufacturing. The McAshans divide their time between Houston and Grandfather's Mountain in North Carolina.

JAKE HAMON

The Hamon hierarchy of Dallas has hobnobbed with U.S. presidents ever since William Howard Taft owned a Texas rancho. Jake Hamon, Jr., inherited his father's vast oil empire as well as his friendships in high places. During the Depression, Jake, Jr., made oil strikes himself in East Texas and today has operations in eight states. He's the only independent oilman ever elected president of the American Petroleum Institute. Certainly the only one once listed on the Best-Dressed List. He and his wife, Nancy, live on the grand scale, and for years had an annual New Year's Eve party, gathering together their friends from all over the world. Their wingding was held, not in Dallas, but Paris.

W. P. CLEMENTS

Bill Clements, first Republican governor of Texas since Reconstruction. Also served as Under Secretary of Defense under two presidents. He, his son, B. Gill, and daughter, Nancy Clements Seay, own one of today's biggest independent drilling operations, Sedco. Bill Clements started as a field roughneck during the Depression and became chairman of his company, with stock worth over $50 million. A hard-nosed, nuts and bolts businessman, he's quoted as saying, "Nothing is ever so bad that it can't be worse. Or better."

LAWRENCE WOOD
RICHARD WOOD

In 1834, John Howland Wood came down from Hyde Park to fight in the war between Texas and Mexico. After the Battle of San Jacinto, in which he participated, Wood went into ranching, buying up land in South Texas. He would send back to New York, get some money from his family, and trade his good cash for Texas scrip. Since Texas was a new republic without funds, he would trade the scrip for land, which was much more plentiful there than money. Today his heirs, Lawrence and Richard Wood, are turning part of their vast holdings in Refugio and Goliad counties into experimental farms, and creating entirely new industries on them. The Wood brothers have built the state's first legal distillery, Texas Spirit, capable of producing not only Scotch, bourbon, tequilla and vodka, but also alcohol and gasohol. All headquartered in their replica of a turn-of-the-century Texas country village which they call Sunshine Place. Banker-planter Lawrence Wood and his wife, the former Leonora Yturria, are two of Corpus Christi's most stylish hosts.

JOHN CONNALLY

John Bowden Connally, Jr., served three terms as governor of Texas; as Secretary of the Navy under John F. Kennedy; and as Secretary of the Treasury during the Nixon administration—a rather large leap after his initial entrance into the nation's capital to join the staff of freshman congressman Lyndon B. Johnson in 1939. During World War II, as a navy lieutenant, Connally was awarded the Legion of Merit. Afterward, he became attorney for Fort Worth oil king Sid Richardson, acquired oil property and made millions. Today he's a partner in Houston's biggest law firm, Vinson & Elkins, who represent over 8,000 clients. He and his vivacious wife, Nellie, live in an antique-filled house in Houston, and weekend on their 10,000-acre ranch outside San Antonio. Run by their daughter Sharon's husband, Robert Amman III, the Connally ranch has a 4,100-foot landing strip for private jets, a 40-foot swimming pool, a skeet range and two tennis courts. Their annual Santa Gertrudis cattle sale there is the place to be in July.

THE DUNN FAMILY

Patrick Dunn, one of South Texas' Irish empresarios, bought and ranched most of Padre Island in 1879. His son, Burton, sold Padre in the twenties, retaining part of the mineral rights for his daughters, Mrs. Hart Smith, Mrs. Blake Sweet, Mrs. Sam Seltzer and Mrs. Edwin Singer. Ed Singer, Corpus Christi oil-refining mogul, international financier, co-owner of the *International Herald Tribune,* and wife, the former Patsy Dunn, were the ones responsible for Corpus' celebrated Art Museum of South Texas, the architectural gem by Philip Johnson.

Until 1930, for five decades, most of Padre Island had belonged to Corpus Christi's Dunn family. Burton Dunn had inherited it from his father, Patrick, and was ranching on it when the "killer hurricane" hit. Despite the blinding storm, according to his granddaughter, Jennifer Singer, Dunn managed to lead his horse to the island's tallest dune almost by instinct. They hugged the sheltered side while the hurricane raged, and bit by bit, they were joined by Padre's animal kingdom—rattlesnakes, coachwhips, rats, bats, lizards, turtles, ground squirrels, gophers—all huddled together for survival. When the storm calmed down, each silently stole away.

DOMINIQUE SCHLUMBERGER DE MENIL

Mrs. Jean de Menil is Houston's one-woman art force. Her own $50-million private collection of modern art is bigger than that of many major museums'. So huge, and important, in fact, that she commissioned Renzo Piano, architect of Paris' famed Beaubourg museum of modern art, Georges Pompidou Centre, to design a building for it. Mrs. de Menil gave Houston's equivalent of Matisse's chapel at Vence in France. Her Rothko Chapel, dedicated in 1971, has a completely unconventional, octagonally shaped interior with 14 panels painted for it by U. S. abstractionist Mark Rothko, before his untimely death in 1970. It is open to all beliefs as a place of worship. Among the spiritual leaders who have conducted services there was the exiled Dalai Lama, in 1979. Dominique de Menil inherited a fortune from her father, the late Conrad Schlumberger, founder of gigantic Schlumberger, Ltd., the French oil-drilling-equipment conglomerate. Now in her seventies, mother of five, she is the widow of Baron Jean de Menil, who was Schlumberger's chairman from 1967 to 1970. They moved to Houston from France in 1941 and became American citizens in 1962. Houston hasn't been quite the same since.

CLARENCE SCHARBAUER

Clarence Scharbauer came to Midland in 1889. Before long he owned the hotel and the bank. West Texas, being bone-dry, made it necessary to provide his cattle with several acres each to keep them alive. So he bought more and more land. As it turned out, some of it included Permian Basin, one of America's richest oil producers. Now his heirs, the Clarence Scharbauer, Jrs., and their four children, are sitting pretty among some of the most valuable acres in Texas, or anywhere else.

ROSS PEROT

Ross Perot must be Texas' biggest Santa Claus. He had 28 tons of Christmas gifts airlifted to prisoners in North Vietnam during the war. That was after his failed $2-million mission of mercy to free them. Later, he also put up the money to get 11,000 prisoners released from a jail in Tehran. This superpatriot, son of a Dallas cotton broker, made his millions in the fledgling computer industry. During 1962, after working as a salesman with IBM, he started his very own Electronic Data Systems. In 1970, his company was flying so high on Wall Street that Perot's personal holdings, on his fortieth birthday, were estimated at $1½ billion.

In 1979, when two of his company's engineers were held hostage in Iran, jailed in a prison with 7,000 others, Perot personally went to their rescue. He secretly assembled a commando team, made of former Vietnam combat veterans working at his company. Even though Perot emphasized that their mission might cost their lives, every man he talked to volunteered. Perot himself flew to Iran, surveyed the high-security prison and had his company's commando-agents incite a Tehranian mob to storm the prison gates. In the melee, his two imprisoned engineers escaped and the Perot commandos spirited them out of the country.

Mission Impossible? Not when you have the millions, imagination, patriotism and perspicacity of Ross Perot.

JOANNE HERRING

Social queen of Texas? Joanne Johnson King Herring has been called just that. Her parties are legend. One, honoring Middle East oil potentates, had her French-rococo Houston home turned into a 1,000-and-one Nights sultan's palace. Widow of former Houston National Gas chairman Robert Herring, she's served as Texas' "official hostess," entertaining the VIPs of the world. Mrs. Herring is the only woman in America to hold dual consulate posts—for Pakistan and Morocco. She's also the first woman to represent either of these countries in a diplomatic position. Describing Joanne Herring, a friend said, "Gabor-glamour with a Southern accent."

HUNT

No worry about the Hunt dynasty disappearing. Billion-dollar oil magnate H. L. himself had 15 children, three families. H. L.'s "first family" produced lots of tots, too. Margaret Hunt Hill, the eldest, had three: Bunker, of Oil Bubble fame, has four children; Herbert, five; Caroline Hunt Schoellkopff, five; and Lamar, four. Lamar founded the American Football League, World Championship Tennis, Inc., and owns the Kansas City Chiefs professional football team to boot. Herbert manages such "first family" interests as Penrod Drilling, Hunt Energy and Placid Oil. And what is Bunker Hunt doing these days? Among other things, he's the world's leading breeder on the international thoroughbred scene. He owns over 1,000 bluebloods; a training center in Chantilly, France; a 700-acre horse stud farm in New Zealand; and Blue Grass Farm, five-farms big, deep in the heart of Kentucky.

Big doer in Big D is Ray Hunt. Whereas his half-brothers Bunker, Herbert and Lamar stay to themselves in their worlds of oil, commodities, pro sports and precious metals, Ray thrives on developing his community. His Reunion hotel complex in Dallas and Hyatt Regency Hotel in Fort Worth are now landmarks. CEO of Hunt Oil, chairman of Hunt

Investment, Woodbine Development and North Texas Commission, he may be the most powerful Hunt brother of them all. Ray Hunt is a board member of the American Petroleum Institute and Washington's Domestic Petroleum Council. He has also given Texas a batch of highly acclaimed magazines. His Southwest Media Corporation publishes *Texas Homes, D, Sport* and *Houston City.*

ALLAN SHIVERS, SR.

Austin's courtly elder statesman Allan Shivers served as governor of Texas longer than any other. When he left the governor's seat in 1957, Shivers became chairman of the University of Texas' Board of Regents, and has also been president of the U.S. Chamber of Commerce. A veteran attorney and banker, he was chairman of Austin Bancshares. When it was acquired by Texas' largest bank holding company, Inter First Corporation, Shivers became vice-chairman of that company. He and his wife, Mary Alice, are two of Austin's most esteemed citizens.

HAROLD FARB

Of Lone Star nobles, Harold Farb might be dubbed Lord Landlord. Mr. Farb reportedly owns over 23,000 apartment units dotted about the state. Besides a fortune from furniture and real estate, he owns *Ultra,* the magazine devoted to beautiful life-styles of Texas Beautiful People.

BETTY EWING

For more years than she cares to say, Betty Ewing has echoed Houston's high life through her avidly devoured social coverage in the *Houston Chronicle.*

Her reading public always saw her name in print, hence they pronounced it any way they chose. Eee-wing. A-wing. Uhwinge.

"I had a Scottish professor who called me, in class, Miss Urine," she confides. "This amused my family so much that they began to call me Pee-Pee. So thank God for the TV series *Dallas.* Playing in eighty-six

Houston's society columnist Betty Ewing greeting her wicked namesake, J.R. (Larry Hagman).

foreign countries, it put the Ewing name on the map internationally. At last, EVERYone knows how to pronounce it correctly. Now maybe my nephews will stop calling me Aunt Pee-Pee.

"When I was in London," she continues, "*Dallas* was the hottest series on TV there. Being a Ewing from Texas didn't hurt one little bit. They viewed me as a visiting celebrity, even interviewed me on TV talk shows. Quite a switch, for I'm usually the one doing the interviewing. The TV audience thought that I claimed no kin to the TV Ewings because J. R. is such an S.O.B. Even though I kept explaining that the TV Ewings are strictly fictitious, I'm sure those lovely Londoners still believe I'm right off the South Fork."

BARBARA JORDAN

Barbara Jordan is the first black woman ever to serve in the Texas Senate. Her skin is black and her tongue is platinum. In 1976, as a keynote speaker at the Democratic National Convention in New York City, her majestic oratory wowed the nation. Brilliant speechmaking runs in her family. Her father, an alumnus of Tuskegee Institute, was a Baptist minister. Her mother, daughter of a Baptist minister, ran circles around her contemporaries on the speaker's rostrum. As a student at Texas Southern University, Barbara soared into the public eye on the debating team, the only woman there to defeat such opponent teams as Harvard and Northwestern. After graduating summa cum laude, she went on to earn her L.L.B. from Boston University Law School. She was elected to the Texas Senate in 1966 and reelected in 1968. Voted the outstanding freshman legislator, she was the first freshman senator ever appointed to the research branch of the legislature. In 1972, Senator Jordan was elected president pro tempore, and when named governor for a day on June 10 of that year, she became the first black woman in American history to preside over a state legislative body. In 1972, she was the first black woman to serve in Congress. After retiring from Congress in 1979, she went on to the University of Texas, teaching intergovernmental relations and ethics to second-year graduate students at the Lyndon B. Johnson School of Public Affairs. Spaces in her class are the hot ticket on campus. When *Redbook* magazine polled its readers on "Women Who Could Be President," Texan Barbara Jordan headed the list.

MICHEL T. HALBOUTY

Michel T. Halbouty, son of a Lebanese immigrant, headed the first independent company to discover gas in Alaska. Not only has his Halbouty Alaska Oil Company made history, so has Halbouty, an oil expert, author and scholar. In 1925, he was water boy at Spindletop when it had its second "boom." Later, with Texas writer James Clark, he wrote two history books, *Spindletop* and *The Last Boom*. After his Spindletop experience, he enrolled at Texas A & M, earning a masters degree in geology and petroleum engineering. He went on to become chief geologist for Glenn McCarthy (1933–1937). Later, drilling on his own, he discovered nine new oil fields and made many millions. At the age of forty-seven, he returned to Texas A & M for another degree, in geological engineering. He has received about every honor the oil industry can bestow.

TOM LEA

Tom Lea, El Paso's supreme painter-writer, has murals in Texas public buildings, paintings in the leading museums and is author-illustrator of *The Brave Bulls, The Wonderful Country, Peleliu Landing, The Primal Yoke, The Hands of Cantú* and *A Picture Gallery*. The Kleberg family chose Tom Lea to write the approved family chronicles, *The King Ranch*, now a collector's item in two volumes. Baylor University honored him with a Litt. D. in 1967; Southern Methodist, an L.H.D. in 1970.

ISAAC HERBERT KEMPNER III

Isaac Herbert Kempner III is the Kempner you'll find at Houston's ultraexclusive clubs—Tjas, Bayou, Houston Country Club, as well as the Ace & Quail of Camden, Texas. Graduated from Choate and Stanford, married to the former Mary Carroll, he's one of the imperials of the Kempner family's Imperial Sugar Company of Sugarland, Texas. Imperial Sugar ranks among *Fortune*'s Top 1,000.

FAYEZ SAROPHIM

Fayez Sarophim and his wife, Louise, are two of Houston's most prominent art patrons. Her father was Herman Brown, a founder of Brown & Root, one of the world's largest construction companies. Fayez Sarophim came to the United States from his native Egypt in 1946 to attend Harvard Business School. After graduating, he moved to Houston to work for Anderson Clayton & Company, the giant international food conglomerate. There he met his bride-to-be, and in 1958 opened his own investment counseling business. He now handles well over $3 billion in pension and endowment fund investment portfolios for such clients as Rockwell International, Alcoa, Ford Motor and RCA. He brought Rice University's endowment from $65 million to $250 million in 15 years, emphasizing high-yield stocks. In the arts, the Sarophims are in the forefront. Their collection includes works by Picasso, Helen Frankenthaler, Hans Hofmann and Calder. The Houston Symphony Society, the Museum of Fine Arts and the Houston Ballet Foundation were quick to include both Sarophims in their inner circle and have consistently benefited from their panache and expertise.

TODDIE LEE WYNNE, JR.

Toddie Lee Wynne, Jr., and his wife, Jacquie, held the first Cattle Baron's Ball, the most tout-Texan of charity benefits, at their ranch near Big D. Beneficiary was the American Cancer Society. As with so many of their endeavors, they set the pace and it has been a must-attend event ever since. Toddie Lee is president of American Liberty Oil Company, which Wynne, Sr., bought from Amon Carter in 1957. The Wynnes are also involved in real estate development and amusement parks in the great Southwest. As one friend puts it: "Wynne, place and show."

WALTER M. MISCHER

Walter M. Mischer paved out a career for himself, literally. Raised on his family farm in Karnes County, Texas, he came to Houston shortly after World War II and started a road paving business. It was a period of massive real estate development, and his paving service was much in demand. As part of the contract, Walter Mischer became joint partner with many of his clients. Soon he was developing commercial properties on his own, financing one section at a time. Today he heads Houston's Mischer Corporation, and served as chairman of Allied Bancshares. Along with the Hunts, he is also a major stockholder in Marathon, manufacturer of offshore drilling rigs.

GERALD HINES

Gerald Hines, the master quality builder of Texas, has changed the face and skyline of cities from Chicago to China, but mainly his hometown of Houston. He developed its famed Galleria shopping mall-hotel-office complex; both One and Two Shell Plazas; the twin-towered Pennzoil Place, architected by Philip Johnson and John Burgee. They also collaborated on his Post Oak Central I and II. His El Paso tower in Houston, designed by I. M. Pei, is 75 stories, 1,049 feet high—the tallest building outside Chicago and New York. Around the country, Hines' projects include the Pillsbury Company's 1.5-million-square-foot headquarters in Minneapolis. Peking asked him to build its 3.5-million-square-foot foreign trade center. Financed and leased by American companies, its estimated cost is around $400 million. A native of Gary, Indiana, Hines came to Houston in 1948 as a young executive trainee. Houston hasn't *looked* the same since. He has built more of Houston's office space than anyone in its history, and he owns most of it.

Texas Quasars

Some Texan sons and daughters have cometed off and become quasars, shining in the heavens of Hollywood and other celebrity Valhallas. The diversity of their personalities is extraordinary. Compare:

Howard Hughes	Mean Joe Green
John Denver	Willie Nelson
Walter Cronkite	A. J. Foyt
Tommy Tune	

And those Texan ladies:

Mary Martin	Farrah Fawcett
Joan Crawford	Debbie Reynolds
Sissy Spacek	Shelly Duvall
Jaclyn Smith	Phyllis George

Perhaps the most powerful of all in the star wars is Sidney Sheinberg, the Corpus Christi boy who went on to become president of MCA Inc., that billion-dollar giant of the entertainment world. MCA includes films, video, records, music publishing, magazines, books, recreation services . . . with annual sales exceeding $1,328,988,000. As president and chief operating officer of Universal City Studios, Sidney Jay Sheinberg might well claim to be "E.T.'s grandfather." Sheinberg's own grandfather was a South Texas pioneer, one of the Grossman brothers who came over from Russia at the turn of the century. The Grossman family made their fortune first selling goods, then acquiring large holdings of real estate, oil, and starting Corpus Christi's department store, Grossman Brothers. Sid Sheinberg was born in 1935, the son of Corpus Christi's Harry and Tillie Grossman Sheinberg. After graduating from W. B. Ray High School, he attended Columbia College in New York, spent one year at the University of Texas Law School, then returned to Columbia, graduating from Columbia University School of Law. He taught for a year at UCLA Law School before joining MCA, starting there as #7 in its seven-man legal department. He was made president of MCA in 1973. Residing in Beverly Hills, he is married to literary agent Lorraine Gary, a former actress. Sheinberg is not only "E.T.'s grandfather," but also the father of two sons.

XVI

Peers of the Past

DAVID CROCKETT

King of the wild frontier Davy Crockett spent very little of his life in Texas . . . just enough to give his life at the Alamo. Born August 17, 1786, he was the son of a backwoods Tennessee innkeeper, John Crockett, native of Ireland and Revolutionary War hero. At his daddy's tavern, young Davy picked up his pugilist know-how and dreams of adventure. By the time he was twelve, he was off to conquer the world, working his way north on cattle drives. He became an Indian scout and hero of the War of 1812. Not only was he the Army's best shot, he was also unexcelled in hand-to-hand combat. Davy was elected to Congress and became a national celebrity for his opposition to President Andrew Jackson's Indian policy. "Be sure you are right, then go ahead" had been Davy's maxim as long as he lived. Which was not long after he opposed Jackson. The President saw that Crockett was defeated at the polls.

That's when Davy departed for Texas, to help in the struggle with Mexico. Here he could either retrieve his lost glory or die courageously in defense of freedom. In Texas he won both. On March 6, 1836, Colonel Crockett achieved immortality. At the Alamo, he and his men held out in a defense unsurpassed in history. He set an example of perseverance, honesty and courage that has been an inspiration for generations of Americans.

JAMES BOWIE

Jim Bowie first saw Texas as a boy when he and his brothers sneaked into Galveston to steal slaves from the pirate Lafitte. They led them through the woods to work their Louisiana plantation. Fighting was a way of life in those days, and Bowie's specialty was knife fighting. He designed the bowie knife and used it, spectacularly, sometimes dueling before crowds with his left wrist strapped to that of his opponent, or with both of their pants nailed to a log. He married into the famed Veramendi family of San Antonio. His wife, Ursula, was the daughter of Juan Martín de Veramendi, once vice-governor of Coahuila, Mexico. Bowie became a wealthy landowner and good businessman. But when his wife and two children died with her parents of cholera, he gave it all up and became a soldier in the cause of Texas. Fate put him back in the Texas town where he had met and married his great love—to San Antonio, and the Alamo.

JANE LONG

Jane Wilkinson was a socially prominent Natchez belle when she met her young surgeon, Dr. James Long, of the U. S. Army. They were married in 1815, when she was seventeen. Two years later, she accompanied him with her baby, Ann, and a servant girl, to Texas in the cause of freedom from the Spanish. Once there, Dr. Long left them in a mud fort on Galveston Bay, making Jane promise to remain there until he returned from battle. Jane waited, and waited, and although expecting another child, refused to leave when all soldiers and women had vacated the fort. Here she was to endure one of the bitterest winters in Texas history. Galveston Bay froze. Snow drifted over her hut. Hoping for rescue, she ran her red-flannel skirt up the fort's flagpole. She warded off bears and Indian cannibals, firing cannonballs with the fort's lone cannon. She kept campfires burning at night to make it appear the fort was fully manned. Four days before Christmas, 1821, Jane gave birth to her baby in a snowstorm. The young servant girl was ill, so Jane was alone, protecting her newborn by wrapping her in blankets. The next day she staggered onto the ice, gathering frozen fish, carrying them back in her skirt to her hungry brood. It wasn't until July one year later that friends found them, only to inform her that her husband had been captured and murdered by the Mexicans. Jane went back to Natchez with her friends, sold her home, and returned to help the Texas cause. She opened an inn at Brazoria and became a famous hostess to Texas nobs of the day. In appreciation, the Republic of Texas gave her land for a plantation near Richmond, Texas. She died there in 1880 at the age of eighty-two. They refer to Jane Long today as the "mother of Texas."

ELISABET NEY

Texas' first lady artist was eccentric. Born Elisabet Ney in Westphalia, Germany, in 1833, she early expressed the desire to become a sculptor. She didn't care if ladies didn't sculpt in those days. She did it anyway, becoming the most famous sculptor in Europe. Her likenesses of noted men and women now grace top museums all over the Continent. At the height of her fame, she married Dr. Edmund Montgomery and moved to Hempstead, Texas. No one knows why, for once there, she remained regally aloof from her neighbors, dressing in Grecian robes. When one of her children died of diptheria, she cremated the body in her living-room fireplace. Soon she tired of plantation life and mothering, moved to Austin, and set up a studio. The good doctor stayed behind caring for the children. Her earliest works were statues of Texas first citizens: Stephen Austin and Sam Houston. Today her studio in Austin is an art museum.

WILLIAM BARRET TRAVIS

William Travis was the martyr of the Alamo. An Alabama teacher and lawyer, young Travis came to Texas and became a leader in the Texas revolt against Mexico. He was made a lieutenant colonel and put in charge of the garrison at San Antonio. With 182 men, he fought off Santa Anna's overwhelming forces for 11 days before being burned and butchered with all of his brave band in the church-fortress known as the Alamo. His massacre was uppermost in the minds of Texans when they sought reprisal shouting: "Remember the Alamo." Only twenty-eight years old at his death, he became a symbol of bravery. Today his name is commemorated all over the state.

THE ALLEN BROTHERS

Everyone knows that Houston was named for General Sam. But it was founded by the Allen Brothers. Augustus C. Allen was a New York mathematics teacher who came to Texas three months after Texas became the world's newest independent nation. Seeking to make his fortune in real estate, he might be called Texas' first successful copywriter. Legend has it that while paddling up a small muddy creek called Buffalo Bayou, Augustus came to what he thought was an ideal site for a city. So he thereupon sat down on a stump, put his plug hat on his knees to use as a desk, and wrote this ad to attract settlers: "The town of Houston, situated at the head of navigation of Buffalo Bayou, is now for the first time brought to public notice. Houston is located at a point which must ever command the trade of the largest and richest portion of Texas. When the rich lands of this country shall be settled, trade will flow to it, making it, beyond doubt, the great indoor commercial emporium of Texas. Vessels from New Orleans and New York can sail without obstacle to this place, as the country shall improve, railroads will come in use and trade will make its way through this channel."

There was no town there at all. Not even a stake had been driven. Houston was no more than swamp fit only for alligators. In fact, alligators, a few Indians and several longhorns made up its entire population when Allen wrote the ad. Amazingly, everything envisioned in Allen's ad, which ran in newspapers throughout the North and East, came to pass. He and his brother, John, laid out what is the present-day Houston, the fourth largest city in America.

MIRABEAU BUONAPARTE LAMAR

The second president of Texas, Lamar came from one of Georgia's leading families. French Huguenots, the Lamars had first settled in Maryland during the late 1600s. After the American Revolution, they moved to Georgia, acquired vast acreage, and became one of the Deep South's richest plantation owners. Mirabeau, a poet-adventurer, flew the family nest and joined Sam Houston as a cavalry commander at San Jacinto. Impressed with Lamar's all-around ability, Houston appointed him secretary of war, then first vice-president of the Republic. He eventually succeeded Houston as president. A cultured man of courtly manners and aristocratic bearing, he later served as United States minister to Argentina. His nephew, Lucius Lamar, known as Dixie's Great Pacificator during the Civil War, was President Cleveland's secretary of the interior, and later served on the Supreme Court.

BENJAMIN MILAM

Benjamin Milam was one of the 26 original empresarios to first colonize Texas. When 300 men took San Antonio away from 1600 Mexicans, he was one of the two Texans killed in the foray. Before gathering his forces, Colonel Milam did a Paul Revere recruiting troops, asking "Who will go with old Ben Milam into San Antonio?" The saying and name has had a lot of mileage in Texas social circles ever since. For instance, in asking who was Mary Carter's family in Dallas, the answer would be "You mean Foxy Carter's wife? Why she was a Milam. So is Margaret McDermott. They're probably Milam cousins. Mary's family were cotton. And Margaret's husband, of course, founded Texas Instruments." Since Old Ben was killed before he took a wife, you can be sure their great-great granddad wasn't Ben.

J. PINCKNEY HENDERSON

J. Pinckney Henderson was the first governor of Texas after it became part of the United States. A Mississippian, his brilliance as an orator is credited for attracting hundreds of volunteers to aid in the Texas War for Independence. Henderson came to Texas in 1836, serving as attorney general during Houston's first term. Later he was the Republic's special minister to France and England, then minister to the United States. After the annexation of Texas, he was elected governor. Later he became a U. S. senator.

HOWARD HUGHES
WILLIAM MARSH RICE

Howard Hughes and William Marsh Rice were two Houstonians who had sensational demises. Almost everyone knows how Hughes, the eccentric billionaire, died. Drugs did him in.

But with Mr. Rice, Houston's wealthy investor-cotton trader, the butler did it. Accompanied, indeed, *directed*, by Rice's prominent Manhattan attorney. *The New York Times*, September 26, 1900, told of "Millionaire Rice's Mysterious Death." Rice, an eighty-four-year-old childless widower, was found dead in New York by his valet.

No one would have suspected foul play if the attorney hadn't immediately produced a newly signed will totally different from one in Houston that had been drafted by his long-time friend and lawyer, Captain James Baker. It was revealed later that Rice's valet-butler-secretary, Charles Jones, and the New York lawyer, Albert T. Patrick, had fed him arsenic, suffocated him, then forged his will, as well as some big checks. They would have gotten away with it, too, if Captain Baker hadn't rushed up in his private railroad car and proved murder most foul.

Captain Baker returned to Houston a hero, and Rice's fortune became the foundation of Rice University. The University named a building Baker Hall, and Baker later headed one of America's top 20 law firms, Baker & Botts. Captain Baker was also the first president, and a major stockholder, of Texas Commerce Bancshares. He started a dynasty of James Bakers, all Houston attorneys. Best known of them all is James A. Baker III, President Reagan's White House chief of staff.

As fate would have it, Mr. Rice's nephew, David Rice, married Mattie, the daughter of Captain Baker's law partner, Judge Walter Botts. Their daughter, Ella Rice, became the first wife of Howard Hughes.

★ *PART TWO*

The Peerage Listing

The First Families of the Republic of Texas

T EXAS IS HEROIC, and it is its heroic quality that makes it unique. Its vast size and even vaster wealth of natural resources are in the heroic mold, but what really made Texas heroic was its history and the quality of the men and women who made it. Texas began in a Heroic age of a soldiers' republic, in a context when often legends become bigger than the men, but some men were even bigger than the legends. Like many new nations, it had to fight for its existence, and its aristocracy emerged, like so many in a Heroic age, as the leaders in the fight. The founders of a peerage of a new nation are those who achieved purposes; this is as true of the armored Norman knights who won England at the Battle of Hastings and founded a peerage in the year 1066, as it is true of these "powder-stained buck-skinned people," as a Texan historian, William Ransom Hogan, called the soldiers and statesmen who won the freedom of Texas in 1836. The Heroic age of the Republic of Texas gave it its soul. A Heroic age is created by, and indeed creates, men who are larger than life, and it is the larger-than-life aspect of Texas that makes it different. It gives Texans their confidence and charm, the reassurance that comes from a belief that the Good Lord made Texas on the first day of Creation, and made the rest of the world afterward with what was left over. It not only gives Texans their undeniable good manners, but perhaps it gives them, too, what an English lady visiting the Republic called "the bump of invention" to enable them to cope with anything that is not, perhaps, larger than life.

The Heroic age of Texas is the period which transformed a Spanish and Mexican dominated wilderness into an independent republic. Spanish and French settlement began there as early as 1682, but little was achieved, and by 1800 there were only three towns—San Antonio, Nacogdoches and Goliad—with a population in the future republic and state of perhaps 7,000. "Anglo-American" settlement had begun with William Barr, whose land grant from the Spanish crown was made in 1798. Others followed him, first as subjects of Spain, and subsequently as subjects of Mexico when that country achieved its independence in 1821. That year Stephen Austin led the "Old Three Hundred," supposedly 300 families, to begin colonization of land granted by Mexico. This trickle turned to a flood, and by 1836 there were probably about 30,000 "Anglo-American" settlers.. Mexico tried to restrict, control, and (the last straw) to disarm the settlers. The first battle of the Texas Revolution, its Lexington, was at Gonzales on October 2, 1835. In December, San Antonio was captured and the Mexicans withdrew beyond the Rio Grande. However, it was the events of the first four months of the following year that created the Republic.

On February 23, 1836, the Mexican dictator, Santa Anna, recaptured San Antonio and besieged the Texan garrison there in the Alamo, a mission building within the town. While that siege was in progress, on March 2, Texans meeting at Washington-on-the-Brazos drew up the Declaration of Independence, and established the Republic. On March 6, Mexican troops stormed the Alamo, and the entire garrison of Texans were killed.

On March 19, a Texan force under Colonel James W. Fannin surrendered at Goliad, and on March 27, Santa Anna ordered the massacre of these 300 men. After days of retreat, the Texans utterly defeated Mexico at the battle of San Jacinto (near modern Houston) on April 21, in a battle that lasted for 20 minutes.

The new Republic's survival was assured, although the Mexican threat was not finally removed until the American-Mexican War of 1846–1848.

Texas is the only state of the Union to have been an independent republic, a nation in its own right until it was annexed by the United States on either December 29, 1845, or February 19, 1846 (you can argue the date on how you interpret the formalities). The Lone Star Republic was no ramshackle community, but had an established government with a congress, judiciary, treasury and taxation system. Its diplomats represented their nation in Washington and in Europe, and Texan consuls in six British and a number of continental European ports aided the flow of new settlers. The numerous German settlers entered into contracts sealed by Texan consuls in Antwerp and Hamburg, which assured them of their land before they left Europe.

Texas society was typical of the nineteenth century in general; bankers owned racehorses, and politicians seeking to impress voters rode around in four-wheeled carriages. Newspaper editors fought for causes, real-estate developers built cities and made or lost fortunes, and merchants traded across the world. It was a man's world: "Texas was a heaven for men and dogs but a hell for women and oxen."

President Lamar had dreams of a Texas reaching to the Pacific, but even the smaller boundaries of the modern state encompass an area larger than France, the largest country (in area) in Western Europe, and the "Anglo-American" nation-state could well have joined the British Empire if it had not been annexed by the United States.

"Anglo-American" is however a misnomer for the Texan nation; a significant proportion of the Spanish-Mexican settlers who had been there before the Declaration of Independence chose the freedom of the new republic, and Mexicans died at the Alamo and fought at San Jacinto for Texas. Two Germans, one Dane, and a black youth also died at the Alamo, but the majority were Americans of British origin, mostly from the southeastern states, which have contributed so much to Texan origins.

The Heroes of the Alamo included 28 natives of Texas, but an equal number were natives of the British Isles, and reflect the fact that only half of the inhabitants of the British Isles were Anglo-Saxons (or "English"). The rest were Celtic: Scots, Irish and Welsh, and of those who died at the Alamo there were 12 Englishmen, 10 Irish, 5 Scots and a Welshman. But many of the American-born heroes were of Scotch-Irish origins, descendants of the Scots and Ulstermen who had come to the East Coast states a century before and moved down the valleys of western Virginia to the western Carolinas, Kentucky, Tennessee and Georgia, settling the Piedmont and mountain country between the planters on the tidewater, and the Indians.

The Scotch-Irish who have contributed so much to Texan ancestry and character descend from Protestant settlers in Northern Ireland in the seventeenth century. Many of them were Scots, but some were English, and many of their descendants came to America. It has been estimated that 25 percent of the population of the United States in 1800 was of Scotch-Irish origin, as have been at least seven presidents.

As well as the naturally evolving peerage of the new nation, recognizable by their leadership, there were others, some genuine and some bogus. The French Marquis Harolde Augustus de Bourbel du Montpincon left Europe to escape his creditors and the courts (not a rare reason for emigration, nor indeed for many North Americans who left their homesteads "G.T.T.," Gone to Texas, for a new start). He had a genuine title and a 700-year-long Normandy pedigree, but changed his name and dropped his title when he came to Texas under the alias of Mr. Harold Bargue. By contrast, Philip Boegel fled from charges of embezzlement in Holland and adopted a title as "Baron" de Bastrop, to become Texas' first bogus baron, his title no doubt proving useful to his enormous influence, which made him a colonists' godfather to Moses and Stephen Austin. Sam Houston, too, sought to create the Order of Knights of San Jacinto. As he wrote on January 28, 1843, this was "to create some reward for the worthy, as we have no cash, to encourage gentlemen." But this appears to have got no further than naming three members of the order, and leaving some uncertainty about the color of the ribbon. (The Sons of the Republic of Texas have now revived this order, to honor services to Texas.) Robert Mills, nicknamed "the duke of

Brazoria," had no title, but had wealth equal to any real duke, until the War Between the States ruined him.

The following, then, are the First Families of Texas, the Heroes and Founders of the Republic. They are a mixture of all kinds: generals who won great battles, failures for whom nothing succeeded, ministers of religion, auctioneers of slaves, founders of great fortunes, men who died penniless, great educators, keepers of society brothels, editors of newspapers, Indian traders; they cover the whole range of human endeavors, and their endeavors made Texas. Many of them, such as the young bachelors who died at the Alamo, left no descendants; and there are others we know left descendants whom we are still tracing. We at Debrett's have been compiling peerages and peerage genealogies since 1769, and in our long experience we know that we can never hope to record every descendant in a world where, for example, Robert "King" Carter of Virginia has a reputed 50,000 descendants. Moreover, such an enterprise takes time; *Debrett's British Peerage*, for example, is complete and comprehensive because we have been compiling and updating our records for 200 years.

Texas has, of course, many sources of compiled genealogies, but more of ancestors than of descendants. While we invite descendants of the Heroes and Founders of the Republic to have their detailed descent formally recorded, particularly in our next edition, we have limited our objectives in the present edition. Where these are readily available, and verifiable, we have reported heads of families of recent generations; this should bring family connections within living memory. We are particularly grateful to the Daughters of the Republic of Texas.

In composing this roll of honor of the Lone Star Republic the effort has been made to include a Who Was Who of the notables and chief heroes of the decade of independent nationhood and of the events preceding it. No doubt we can add further interesting entries in future editions and include many more twentieth-century descendants than can be gleaned in a first clarion call. Within the brief biographies the reader may also glimpse the texture of the times in notes about such matters as dueling codes, medicinal quackery, drinking habits, religion, the making of Lone Star flags, the social round, tall talk, Texan poetry, and derring-do aplenty. Among our listings, the honor "county namer" frequently occurs. We have endeavored to include all those notables and heroes active in the Republic who had counties named in their honor, as sometimes was the case in their own lifetimes but in most cases was a posthumous distinction awarded to them. The majority and more of all Texas counties are named after Revolution and Republic figures.

HUGH PESKETT
Senior Genealogist
Debrett's Ancestry Research

The Signers of The Declaration of Independence

THE Texas Declaration of Independence, made at Washington-on-the-Brazos on March 2, 1836, was the culmination of a series of events. The 30,000 "Anglo-Americans" who lived in Texas were subjects of Mexico, and owed their land grants to Mexico, but a series of revolutions and military dictatorships in that country had led to oppression and abrogation of the Mexican Federal Constitution of 1824. This in particular had provided for each state to frame its own constitution, Texas being included with the state of Coahuila, and not separately. This was unsatisfactory, and the Texan Convention of 1833 proposed that Texas should be a separate state, but still within Mexico. When Stephen Austin took this petition to the capital, he was imprisoned. Santa Anna became the dictator, and in 1834 he declared that Mexico was not yet ready for democracy.

Oppression followed, and hostilities against the Mexican government had already begun when the Texans adopted the Declaration of November 7, 1835, made at San Felipe. This sought to justify the hostilities, and to reassure Mexican liberals that their aim was not secession, but to remain as a state within the Mexican Federal Constitution of 1824, although they held it their right to establish an independent government. However, this compromise failed in its purpose, and complete independence was the only solution.

The compromise Declaration of November 7, 1835, was superseded therefore by a new and outright Declaration of Independence framed at Washington-on-the-Brazos on March 2, 1836, as a result of a convention called by the provisional government. This began by reciting the nature of government, and that Mexico had failed to protect the lives, liberty and property of its subjects. It further stated that the government had changed from a federal republic to a military despotism which was ruling at the point of a bayonet and was failing to provide education, trial by jury, and freedom of religion. The Mexican government had thereby forfeited its right to govern them.

The original document is now housed in the capitol building in Austin, and the men who signed it are listed here in the order in which they signed. They began signing on March 3, 1836, but some delegates arrived late, Samuel Carson not arriving until March 10. His signature, as the last to arrive, was preceded by that of Thomas Barnett, the only member of the "Old Three Hundred" who signed it. Those with prior political experience were Richard Ellis (No. 1), Lorenzo de Zavala (No. 15), Robert Potter (No. 29), Sam Houston (No. 37), and Martin Parmer (No. 40).

The reluctance of Austin and his colony to be involved is understandable; they owed title of their land to Mexico, and had everything to lose, whereas many of the leaders of the independence movement were newcomers, with little to lose if they failed, but much to gain by success.

1. *RICHARD ELLIS*, Signer (Delegate from Pecan Point)

A politician, Ellis was a senator in the First, Second, Third and Fourth Congresses. He was elected chairman at the Convention when it met for its sessions in bitter weather in the house of a blacksmith named Noah T. Byars. Here were forged in the fire of their determination the

Declaration itself and the Constitution of the Republic, and an ad interim government was organized. Ellis was born in 1781. Married. Died in 1846. Probable namer of Ellis County.

Twentieth-century descendants include the families of James J. Cashion, Norfleet Dandridge Ellis, John Ross Johnston, Henry John Ellis, J. W. Dollarhide, Johnnie R. Johnston, Robert Eugene Galavin, Horace Seldon Crew. (DRT nos. 2401, 2411, 5555, 6861.)

2. *CHARLES B. STEWART*, Signer (Represented Austin)

A physician, Stewart was born in Charleston, South Carolina, in 1806. His second marriage was to Mrs. Elizabeth Antoinette (Nichols) Byrd. Nine children (two adopted). Died in 1885 at Montgomery.

Twentieth-century descendants include the families of Edmund Bellinger Stewart, George Conoly, Henry F. Lindley, Arthur O. Barclay, Marion T. Ford, Earl B. Wilcox. (DRT nos. 4538, 4868, 5502.)

3. *JAMES COLLINSWORTH*, Signer (Represented Brazoria)

Collinsworth was commended for his conduct at San Jacinto, where he served as aide-de-camp to Houston with the rank of major. At the 1836 Convention he nominated Houston for commander in chief of the Texas Army. He was a diplomat, politician and adjutant general of the Republic of 1839; chief justice and owner of a considerable law library; candidate for presidency against Lamar in 1838. Born in Tennessee, 1806. He jumped into Galveston Bay "under the influence of Ardent Spirits for at least a week beforehand" and drowned in 1838. (At least three challenges by Collinsworth to duels with people such as President Anson Jones were averted.)

4. *EDWIN WALLER*, Signer (Delegate from Brazoria)

During the war his ship ran the blockade at Velasco. As president of the board of land commissioners for Brazoria he was one of its first realtors. First Mayor of Austin (1840). Later a Secessionist. Born in Spotsylvania County, Virginia, 1800. Married Julia M. de Shields. Seven children. Died in Austin, 1881. Waller County is named in his honor.

Twentieth-century descendants include the families of Philip M. Curry, Hiram B. Waller, Edwin Waller, Jr. (DRT nos. 19, 496, 111.)

5. *ASA BRIGHAM*, Signer (Represented Brazoria)

Brigham was one of five individuals who contributed 500 acres of land each to pay for the first steamboat to navigate the Brazos River, its arrival being celebrated by a ball in 1834. The rivers became highways of commerce in early Texas, roads being useless. Politician, treasurer of the Republic, 1839. Mayor of Austin, 1842. Born in Massachusetts about 1790. Married Mrs. Ann (Johnson) Mather (second wife). Died in Washington, Texas, 1844.

6. *JOHN SMITH DAVENPORT BYROM*, Signer
(Represented Brazoria)

Born in Hancock, Georgia, about 1798. Byrom first married Nancy Fitzpatrick (divorced); second, Mary Anne Knott. Five children (three from first marriage). He died in 1837.

7. *JOSE FRANCISCO RUIZ*, Signer (Represented Bexar)

A revolutionary in 1813, Ruiz represented Bexar, and was unable to speak English at the Convention. Born in San Fernando de Bexar (San Antonio) in 1783. Died there in 1840.

Twentieth-century descendants include the families of José María Villareal, Juan Antonio Reyes. (DRT no. 5017.)

8. *JOSE ANTONIO NAVARRO*, Signer (Represented Bexar)

A liberal revolutionary as early as 1813 in the then Spanish Empire, Navarro became referred to later as an "Americanized Texan." Indeed, he is cited as having had a "pleasant friendship" with Stephen F. Austin until the latter's death. He was captured by Mexicans on the Santa Fe Expedition, to which he reluctantly accepted appointment as commissioner. Condemned to death, he was reprieved and eventually released on parole. He was a Secessionist. Born in 1795. Married. He had four sons, who fought for the Confederacy. Died in 1871 in San Antonio. Navarro County was named after him.

Twentieth-century descendants include the families of John C. Ross, Evander McIver Ross, Juan José Navarro, Arthur C. Ross, Carl Clifton Ross, H. W. D. Langston, Howard G. Sandel, Howard William Wilkins, Edgar E. Lackner. (DRT nos. 2150, 3040, 3446, 5829.)

9. *JESSE B. BADGETT*, Signer
(Elected a Delegate by Soldiers at the Alamo)

Badgett was under the command of Travis at the Alamo. He was born about 1807 in North Carolina. Returned home to Arkansas after the Convention.

10. *WILLIAM DEMETRIS LACEY*, Signer
(Delegate from Colorado)

Joined the Texas Army in Galveston. Born in Virginia in 1808. Married Mrs. Sarah Ann (Bright) McCrosky. Four children returned to Texas after his death. Died in 1848 in Paducah, Kentucky.

11. *WILLIAM MENEFEE*, Signer
(Delegate from the Colorado Municipality)

One of five commissioners who selected Austin as the capital of Texas. Politician, representing the Colorado District during the Republic. Vice-Presidential candidate. Born in Knox County, Tennessee, in 1796. Married the former Miss Agnes Sutherland. Eight children (the last, a daughter, was born in Texas). Died in 1875.

Twentieth-century descendants include the families of O. P. Basford, Edward Richardson, Charles Roy Hassel Crockett, John Edward Luty, Walter H. Wilcox, Charles Henry Cope, Thomas J. Hill, James C. Whittington. (DRT nos. 1418, 1666, 1679, 2618, 4103, 4230.)

12. *JOHN FISHER*, Signer (Represented Gonzales Municipality)

His brother, William S. Fisher, commanded the Mier Expedition. He was born in Virginia in 1800, and later returned there. He died in Charlotte, North Carolina, in 1865.

13. *MATHEW ("OLD PAINT") CALDWELL*, Signer
(Represented Gonzales Municipality)

Captured on the Santa Fe Expedition, Caldwell was released and later commanded the 200 men who defeated Adrian Woll in the Battle of Salado. Born about 1798 in Kentucky. He first married Mrs. H. Morrison; second, Mrs. Lily Lawley. Three children (at least). Died in 1842. Known as "Old Paint," Caldwell County was probably named after him.

14. *DR. JUNIUS WILLIAM MOTTLEY*, Signer
(Delegate from Goliad)

Aide-de-camp to Thomas J. Rusk at San Jacinto, Mottley was mortally wounded there. Dr. Mottley, as a surgeon, had earlier supplied the post at Goliad with surgical instruments worth at least $125. Born in Virginia about 1812. Heirs could not be located. Buried on the battlefield. Motley (sic) County was named in his honor.

15. *LORENZO DE ZAVALA*, Signer
(Represented Harrisburg Municipality)

Lorenzo de Zavala received an empresario contract from Mexico in 1829 to introduce 500 families into Texas, after a career as a liberal revolutionary. Appointed Mexican minister to France by Santa Anna. Appointed ad interim vice-president after the Convention (as a supporter of Texan independence). His home was used after the Battle of San Jacinto as a hospital for the wounded. Sent with Santa Anna to Mexico to negotiate a treaty. Became an author on Mexican politics. Born in 1789 in Yucatán. First married Teresa Correa; second, Emily West. Six children (three by each wife). He died in November 1836. Zavala County was named in his honor.

16. *GEORGE WASHINGTON SMYTH*, Signer
(Represented Bevil Municipality)

Smyth was a surveyor who went to Texas to join the Austin colony in 1830. He later became a U. S. congressman. Born in 1803 in North Carolina. Married Frances M. Grigsby. Seven children. Died in 1866 in Austin.

Twentieth-century descendants include the families of Edward Fitzgerald McFadden, Joseph Grigsby Smyth, Murray Green Smyth, Ramsey Clarke Armstrong, James Quay McCammon, Edward Fitzgerald McFaddin II, Almonte Byron Flanary, Richard Bush Shultz, Milton H. Johnson, Joseph Duncan Blades. (DRT nos. 2845, 5024, 5783, 7828.)

17. *STEPHEN HENDRICKSON ("DOCTOR") EVERITT*, Signer
(Represented Jasper)

Everitt joined the Lorenzo de Zavala colony. He was known as

"Doctor" Everitt, although he did not practice medicine in Texas. Senator Everitt was attacked in Congress by Surgeon General Ashbel Smith who repeatedly struck him with a buggy whip, which resulted in one of many memorable "severe fights" in Congress and in Smith's resignation. Born in 1807 in New York. Married Alta Zera Williams. Four children. Died in 1844 in New Orleans.

Twentieth-century descendants include the families of Patterson Windham Everitt, John Lucius Everitt, James Madison Everitt, John Wesley Laird, Wallace Paul Conring, August E. Krumm, Harold W. Kreeger. (DRT nos. 7132, 7199, 7299, 7300.)

18. *ELIJAH STAPP*, Signer (Represented Jackson Municipality)

Stapp was postmaster in Jackson County. Born about 1783 in Virginia, he came to Texas in 1830 with his wife and children. Nine children (three born in Texas). Buried in 1843 in Edna.

Twentieth-century descendants include the families of John Marion Stukes, Clem Arvel Jones. (DRT no. 1664.)

19. *CLAIBORNE WEST*, Signer (Represented Jefferson County)

West moved to Texas in 1831, becoming a county postmaster. He created Jefferson Municipality. Born about 1800 in Tennessee. His first wife was Anna Garner; his second, Mrs. Prudence Kimbell, in 1847; his third, Mrs. Florinda (McCulloch) Day. Nine children (by his first wife). Died in 1866. Probably buried in Seguin.

Twentieth-century descendants include the families of James Floyd Kimball, Joe Walker Martin, Bernard Eugene Ludeman, Thomas Jefferson West, George Washington Henry, Jr., Don O. Baird, DeWitt Morgan, Albert Brown Hall III. (DRT nos. 1983, 3196, 6878, 7785.)

20. *WILLIAM BENNET SCATES*, Signer
(Represented Jefferson County)

Scates was a soldier at Velasco and at the Siege of Bexar. He also was present at San Jacinto in Benjamin F. Bryant's company of Sabine Volunteers. Born in 1802. His first marriage was to Theodocia Clardy Smith; the second, to Sarah McMillan in 1850. Seven children (two by the first wife; five by the second). Died in 1882, Colorado County.

21. *MICHEL BRANAMOUR MENARD*, Signer
(Represented Liberty Municipality)

A trapper and Indian trader, Menard came to Texas in 1832. He organized the Galveston City Company with McKinney and Williams (see entry under Notables and Heroes of the Republic), representing Galveston for the Republic from 1840–1841. Menard paid $50,000 to the hard-up Republic, which no doubt assisted in the matter of an early law awarding him a large chunk of Galveston Island. Later a grand jury was to complain that "the bargain and sale to Mr. Menard was indeed a *bargain* by which the Government *chiselled* itself out of $2,000,000, Minus $50,000." Posterity has felt that the can-do of Menard, McKinney and Williams was more important to the future of Galveston than a matter of formalities. Menard was born of French parentage in 1805, near Montreal, Canada. He first married Marie Diana la Clère; second, Catherine Maxwell in 1837; third, Mary Jane Riddle; and fourth, Mrs. Rebecca Mary West in 1850. One child (from the last marriage). Died in 1856 in Galveston. Menard County was named in his honor.

Twentieth-century descendants include the families of James Steele Kerr and Clarence Walters Lokey. (DRT no. 4514.)

22. *AUGUSTINE BLACKBURN HARDIN*, Signer
(Represented Liberty)

Hardin arrived in Texas in 1825 with his three brothers, and helped put down the Fredonian Rebellion. He was born in 1797 in Franklin County, Georgia. First married Mary Garner; second, Mariah Hardin. At least six children (five by the second wife). Died in 1871. Hardin County was named for the "Hardins of Liberty."

Twentieth-century descendants include the families of Michael Rush Splane, Charles George Mahavier, William Blackburn Green, E. T. Cessna, Hamilton H. Young. (DRT nos. 2163, 2408, 2904, 3119.)

23. *JOHN WHEELER BUNTON*, Signer
(Represented Mina)

Bunton came to Texas in 1835, settling at Bastrop. He was at the Siege of Bexar, and fought with Jesse Billingsley's company at San Jacinto. He and his recently wed wife, Mary Howell, were captured at sea by the Mexicans. Later, Bunton became a rancher in Bastrop. Born in

1807 in Sumner County, Tennessee. Died in 1879.

Twentieth-century descendants include the families of J. W. Bundrett, Dr. Victor Oatman, J. W. Blakeslee, Desha Bunton. (DRT nos. 369, 1821.)

24. *DR. THOMAS JEFFERSON GAZLEY*, Signer
(Represented Mina)

Gazley came to Texas in 1829 and became a surgeon with the army, later a lawyer and leading Mason. He was a congressman for Harrisburg County. Born in 1801 in Dutchess County, New York. Died in 1853.

25. *ROBERT M. COLEMAN*, Signer (Represented Mina)

Coleman was aide-de-camp to Sam Houston at San Jacinto after service against the Indians, and at San Antonio. He raised a regiment of rangers as a colonel. Born about 1799 in Kentucky. Married. Six children. Drowned in 1837.

26. *STERLING CLACK ROBERTSON*, Signer
(Represented Viesca Municipality)

Soldier, colonizer and legislator. Assistant quartermaster general at New Orleans in 1812. Originally from Nashville, with Houston and others, he organized what was to be called the Robertson Colony of 800 colonists. It is doubtful he fought at San Jacinto. Represented the Milam District briefly before returning to settle the affairs of the colony. Born in 1785; died in 1842. Robertson County is named in his honor.

Twentieth-century descendants include the families of Maclin Robertson, James Phillip Sneed, James West, E. Sterling C. Robertson, Z. F. Fulmore, Colonel W. C. Harlee, Huling Parker Robertson, Dr. Henry Carroll Bailiff, Sterling Clack Robertson, James Archibald Gamel. (DRT nos. 897, 1247, 1402, 1537, 1795, 3843.)

27. *GEORGE CAMPBELL CHILDRESS*, Signer

The Declaration of Independence was written in Childress' own hand. Uncle of Sterling C. Robertson (see above Signer). Editor of the *National Banner and Nashville Advertiser*. Came to Texas in 1834, and settled there after the death of his wife, Margaret S. Nance, a year later.

Because of his "high character and patriotic enthusiasm" he was appointed to meet his friend President Andrew Jackson in order to seek recognition of Texas by the United States. Born in Nashville in 1804; committed suicide in 1841. Childress County was named in his honor.

Twentieth-century descendants include the family of Charles Stuart Childress, Jr. (DRT no. 4033.)

28. *BAILEY HARDEMAN*, Signer
(Represented Matagorda Municipality)

Hardeman was one of the five drafters. Arrived in Texas in 1835. A secretary of the treasury and a secretary of state, he signed the Treaty of Velasco with Santa Anna. Born in 1795 in Davidson County, Tennessee. Married Rebecca A. F. Wilson. Died in 1836. Hardeman County was named in honor of him and his brother, Thomas Jones Hardeman, an active Mason.

Twentieth-century descendants include the family of Sam Wilson Hardeman. (DRT no. 1021.)

29. *ROBERT POTTER*, Signer
(Represented Nacogdoches Municipality)

A midshipman convicted of maiming, Potter first appeared in Texas helping to equip the forces at the siege of Bexar. After the Convention he was appointed ad interim secretary of the Texas Navy, later being commissioned into it and given command of the port of Galveston. As a Regulator he came to a bad end in the Regulator-Moderator War on his return from the Sixth Congress in 1842. Potter County was named for him.

30. *THOMAS JEFFERSON RUSK*, Signer
(Represented Nacogdoches Municipality)

After his partners absconded with his money in a mining and land speculation enterprise, Rusk arrived in Texas and organized a company of Nacogdoches volunteers to join the Texan troops at San Antonio. At the Convention he was elected secretary of war and fought at San Jacinto, becoming brigadier general in command of the Texas Army thereafter. In 1845 his influence was exercised in favor of annexation to the United States, and he joined Houston as a Texan senator in Washington. Born in 1803 in the Pendleton District in South Carolina. Married Mary F. Cleveland, and committed suicide in 1857 following her death. Both Rusk County and the town of Rusk are named in his honor.

Twentieth-century descendants include the families of Dr. T. P. Davis, J. Richard Gray, John David Matthews, Warren Carroll Brewer, Commodore Washington Tunnell, Edwin A. Wilson, William Eugene Cotton. (DRT nos. 2031, 2043, 3902, 4069, 4843.)

31. *CHARLES STANFIELD TAYLOR*, Signer
(Represented Nacogdoches Municipality)

Taylor was in Texas around 1830 as a merchant. He became a lawyer after the revolution and a local leader. Born in 1808 in London, England. Married Anna Marie Ruoff, sister-in-law of Adolphus Sterne, a German immigrant to Texas and a Republic notable. Thirteen children. Died in 1865.

Twentieth-century descendants include the families of Lawrence Sterne Taylor, Carl Henry Rulfs, Richard Holbrook, Billy Jack Pearce, John Venable Hughes, John Dabney Murchison, Edward Nicholas Maher, Lester Joseph Newman, Edward James Gannon, Jr., John Stuart Hunt, William Christian Helmbrecht, Jr., William Dabney Campbell, Frank S. Schott, Howard Smith Motley, Carl Henry Rulfs, Robert Conrad Schindler, Benjamin Franklin Sharp, Allan A. Bailey, Stephen B. Tucker, Eugene Harmon Blount, James Lewis Caldwell McFaddin. (DRT nos. 2824, 3032, 3435, 3458, 3494, 3510, 3524, 4687, 4731, 4735, 4745, 4749, 4761, 7340.)

32. *JOHN S. ROBERTS*, Signer
(Represented Nacogdoches Municipality)

Roberts was attracted to Texas from Louisiana to become a junior officer prominent in military events prior to the Declaration of Independence. He became a merchant after the revolution. Born in Virginia in 1796. Died in 1871. Roberts County was named in his honor.

33. *ROBERT HAMILTON*, Signer
(One of Five Men Sent by Pecan Point)

Probably the wealthiest man to sign the Declaration of Independence, Robert Hamilton was a Scotsman who moved via business with his brothers in North Carolina to the Red River area. Sent to Washington with George C. Childress (see above) to negotiate recognition of independence in Washington and to establish commercial relations, an assignment his broad connections and personal affluence qualified him for. Thereafter he remained in Red River County. Born in 1783; died in 1843.

34. *COLLIN MCKINNEY*, Signer
(Represented Red River and Pecan Point)

McKinney represented Red River in the First, Second and Fourth Congresses, although his Texas citizenship was under challenge due to border vaguenesses with Arkansas. Born in 1766 in New Jersey. His first wife was Amy Moore; he married Betsey E. Coleman in 1805. Ten children (six by the second wife). Died in 1861. Historians agree that both Collin County and its county seat of McKinney are named after him.

Twentieth-century descendants include Michael Benjamin Ross, John Austin Hendrix, Frank Clifford Beard, Robert Batiste Lawrence, Jerome Cecil Sullivan, Collin Joe Milam, James William Norwood, William David Fields, Robert Lloyd Leggett, Joseph Hardie Lawrence, James Cary Gossett, Arthur Maxwell Thomas, Jr., Louis Garver, Dalton Scales, Captain Henry Haden Hopkins, Moran Kuykendall McDaniel, June Howell Thomas, Jr., Mason Wilkerson Riddle, Charles Troy Holmes, James Rhea Hill, Henry Slaughter, Thurman James Geer, William Davis Felder, William F. Neale, Samuel Leek McKinney, Gus W. Thomasson, Robert Ashley Milam, Leilam Milam, Benjamin R. Milam, P. T. Talbot, Walter C. Judd, Jesse Milam, Jefferson Milam Matthews, Wade Hampton, C. G. Watson, Robert J. Turner, John Malone Kelly, E. K. Taylor, John Hamilton Neill, Benjamin Franklin McKinney, Claud Greer McKinney, Lee Melton, Clark Purcell Lupton, Josiah Lauderdale Kelly, Dee Jay, Richard Reed Guice, Raymond Ferris, John Wilson Drye, Richard Acquilla Cole, J. L. Cantrell, Edward G. Beall, E. C. Bailey, Travis Malachi Dumas, Verna Josiah Dumas, S. M. Roach, Herbert Howard Lewin, Milton Steele, James Lafayette Greer, Newton Taylor.

(DRT nos. 338, 339, 1052, 1059, 1255, 1256, 1257, 1258, 1259, 1260, 1263, 1264, 1268, 1273, 1275, 1278, 1281, 1282, 1284, 1287, 1289, 1293, 1294, 1295, 1298, 1307, 1308, 1310, 1315, 1318, 1321, 1325, 1399, 1669, 1844, 1959, 2676, 1691, 3199, 3787, 3803, 3963, 4264, 4267, 4398, 4445, 4446, 4448, 4748, 5131, 5564, 6146.)

35. *ALBERT HAMILTON LATIMER*, Signer (Represented Red River and Pecan Point Area, Later Disputed as Part of Arkansas)

Latimer was a Unionist, but with sons fighting for the Confederacy. Born in Huntingdon, Tennessee, in 1808. Married to Elritta Smith first, and to Elizabeth Richey second (both before arrival in Texas). Later he married Mary Grattis. Nineteen children (four, eight and seven by successive marriages). Died in 1877.

Twentieth-century descendants include the families of Albert Hamilton Latimer, Jr., James S. Brooks, Wade Monroe Parks. (DRT nos. 326, 2123, 4685.)

36. *JAMES POWER*, Signer (Represented Refugio)

Power was in business and mining in New Orleans and Mexico. In 1826, he founded the Power and Hewetson Colony. His influence seated Houston at the Convention of 1836, and he became representative at the Second Congress for Refugio. Born in 1788 in the vicinity of Ballygarret, County Wexford, Ireland. Married Dolores Portilla first; her sister Tomasita second. Seven children (two to the first sister and five to the second). Died in 1852.

Twentieth-century descendants include the families of James Hamilton Fleming, James Roger Fleming, Francis Benjamin Shelton, Philip Power, Joseph Daniel Shay, Howard E. Fish, John James Welder, Robert Earl Cliburn, James Power, Jr., Louis H. Woodworth, Cooper Baron Walker, John Park Boyd, James F. Power, Carl F. Baumgartner, Phil Power, Edward LeGrand Dunlap. (DRT nos. 567, 568, 600, 723, 733, 1990, 2061, 2192, 3058, 6262, 6623, 7120.)

37. *SAM HOUSTON* ("The Raven"), Signer (As a Member of the Refugio Delegation)

Houston was the greatest hero of the Republic of Texas. His father was a veteran of the American Revolution. As a teenager he ran away to join the Cherokee Indians, learning their language. After the War of 1812, he went to Nashville, and in due course was elected governor of Tennessee. He then rejoined the Cherokee, taking citizenship, and named by them "The Raven," also the title of a celebrated American biography by Marquis James. He went to Texas in the early 1830s and quickly embroiled himself in the ferment for independence, being elected in 1835 major general of the Texan Army.

After the Alamo and the controversial Runaway Scrape caused by his retreat before Santa Anna's overwhelming forces, he attacked the Mexican Army at San Jacinto and routed them in 20 minutes for the loss of nine Texan lives in one of the most decisive battles of world history, and perhaps one of the most romantic episodes of the nineteenth century. Wounded in the ankle, he lay under an oak tree below which he received the surrender of Santa Anna, and then turned to write to his lady love: "From the field of San Jacinto. . . ." He was elected president of the Republic in 1836 in honor of the great victory, which established the independent nation of Texas. He was elected to a second term in 1841. He claimed at one point that no less than 24 men were challenging him to duels, a result often of such insults as his calling "Wetumka," his name for President Burnet, a "hog thief"! After joining the Union he went to Washington as senator of Texas with Thomas Rusk. At secession, he held that Texas had reverted to independence as a state and so shortly became superseded as governor. Born in Rockbridge County, Virginia, in 1793. Married Eliza H. Allen in Nashville, who left him; second, Tiana Rogers, an Indian; and third, Margaret Moffette Lea. Eight children by the third wife. Died in 1863. The city of Houston and Houston County are named in his honor.

Twentieth-century descendants include the families of Roy White Hearne, Clarence Eugene Thornall, William Joseph Burch, Charles Stanley Roberts, Ivol Edwin Burnham, Gordon W. Johnson, Joseph Clay Stiles Morrow, Davia Evan Decker, Edward Allen Everitt, Robert Alexander John, Franklin Thomas, Joseph C. S. Morrow, Governor Price Daniel, Temple Lea Houston, William Carrol Henderson, Dudley Bryan Foy, Robert E. McDonald, Andrew Jackson Houston, Augustus David Paulus, John Pritchett Smith, J. Randolph Sanders, Franklin Weston Williams, W. R. Bringhurst. (DRT nos. 117, 191, 1697, 1708, 1816, 2152, 2464, 3821, 4270, 4511, 4571, 4815, 4864, 5570, 7068.)

38. *DAVID THOMAS*, Signer (Represented Refugio Municipality)
Thomas was elected ad interim adjutant general and then made acting secretary of war when Rusk left to join the army. Mortally wounded in an accident on the ship *Cayuga*, he may have reached the battlefield of San Jacinto before dying. Born in 1801.

39. *EDWARD CONRAD*, Signer (As One of Four Refugio Delegates)
Conrad was born in Philadelphia, April 1811. He applied for land in Stephen Austin's colony in early 1836. He was sent as a junior officer to recruit men in New Orleans, where he died in July 1836.

40. *MARTIN PARMER* ("The Ring-tailed Panther"), Signer (Represented San Augustine Municipality)
A hunter and trapper in Missouri, Parmer was elected to that state's senate before coming to Texas after 1825, where he participated in the Fredonian Rebellion, serving as a president of that briefly lived republic called Fredonia. Later he was chief justice to Jasper County. Tradition knows him by one of the more eccentric appellations of Texicana as the "Ring-tailed Panther." Born in Virginia in 1778, he was married four or five times, the legality of his splicings often being controversial. First, he was married to Sarah Hardwick (nine children); by 1835 he was living with a second wife, Sevina Lorna; third, a Mrs. Margaret Neal; and fourth, Zina Kelly, who survived him. A possibly bigamous marriage (on the uxorial side at the altar) was to Candace Midkiff. The extent of "Panther" progeny by the four other marriages is not clear. (See entries under Jasper County, Carriage Trade of the Republic, where two sons, Isham and William, are listed.) He died in 1850. Parmer County was named in his honor. (The name used in his lifetime and by his children was Palmer. "Parmer" originates from the apparent spelling on the Declaration. It is used on his tombstone.)
Twentieth-century descendants include the families of Edward Ernst, Walter Everett McRee, Robert Bruce Shearer, Byron Campbell, Duff McMillan, Homer Richard Stewart, Douglas Hall, Napoleon Bonaparte Roark, John Russel Roark, Hector McKenzie, Green McDuff McMillian, Joseph A. Zielinski, Alfred William Morris, Edmund Byrd Parsons, Joe F. Myers, John Walker Morris, H. Thad Childre, James Obediah Driscoll, Allen Brown Farris, Antoon Hubert Strybos, John

Andrew Werner, W. J. Werner, Guy Hooker Morris, Lynne Peter Atmar, Phil H. Stricker. (DRT nos. 1958, 2481, 2517, 2547, 2570, 2600, 6316, 6364, 6377, 6768, 6769, 7093, 7743.)

41. *EDWIN OSWALD LEGRAND*, Signer
(Represented San Augustine Municipality)

He was at the siege of Bexar and also participated at San Jacinto. Afterward he became a notable in San Augustine County. Born in North Carolina in 1803. Unmarried. Died in 1861.

42. *STEPHEN WILLIAM BLOUNT*, Signer
(The Third Representative from San Augustine)

Blount missed San Jacinto by a day. Afterward he became a local official. Born in 1808 in Burke County, Georgia. Married Mrs. Mary (Landon) Lacy. (They lived in a fine Greek Revival house in San Augustine.) He died in February of 1890.

Twentieth-century descendants include the families of Thomas William Blount, John Franklin Blount, Capt. Thomas William Blount, Ben Harwit, Edwin B. Wilson, William Stephen Moss, Stephen W. Blount, Edward S. Blount, Charles B. Wallace, Hubert Franklin Blount, John Merton Hassenflu, Edward Augustus Blount, Guy Arthur Blount, Dewey Raymond Griffin, Eugene Harmon Blount, James Lewis Caldwell McFaddin, Archibald Clark Holmes, T. Markham Sleeper, A. Clarence Holmes, Henry Earl Huffor, Robert Conrad Shindler. (DRT nos. 321, 696, 962, 2066, 2336, 2369, 3032, 3490, 3601, 3865, 3952, 4011, 4068, 7878.)

43. *JAMES GAINES*, Signer (Represented Sabine Municipality)

Gaines came to Texas as early as 1812 and joined the Gutiérrez-Magee Expedition, but left after seeing Mexicans execute Spanish leaders after the Rosalis battle. He was first judge of Sabine, representing it as senator in the Fourth, Fifth and Sixth Congresses. Left Texas for the California gold rush in 1856 as a comparatively old man. Born in 1776 in Culpeper County, Virginia. Married Susanna Morris. Five children. He died in November 1856. Gaines County is named in his honor.

Twentieth-century descendants include the family of Thaddeus C. Sparks. (DRT no. 1347.)

44. *WILLIAM CLARK, JR.*, Signer
(Represented Sabine Municipality)

He came to Texas in 1835, represented Sabine in a single Congress, and later moved to Nacogdoches where he was a merchant. Born in North Carolina in 1798. Married Martha B. Wall. Four children. Died in 1859.

Twentieth-century descendants include the families of William Henry Harris, Ernest William Pinkston, John Edward Scherer Van Cronkhite, Frank Sebastian Schott, Howard Motley. (DRT nos. 3510, 4989.)

45. *SYDNEY O. PENINGTON*, Signer
(Represented Shelby Municipality)

Penington came to Texas from Arkansas, and a year or two later was fighting at the siege of Bexar. He represented Shelby in the First Congress, but died in 1837. He was born in 1809.

46. *WILLIAM CARROL CRAWFORD*, Signer
(Represented Shelby Municipality)

The last surviving signer of the Declaration of Independence, ironically, Crawford immigrated to Texas in late 1834 because of ill health. He was related to Charles Carrol, the last surviving signer of the United States Declaration of Independence. He moved from Shelby to Camp County in 1859. Born in North Carolina in 1804. Married Rhoda Jackson. Nine children. Died in 1895.

Twentieth-century descendants include the families of Stanley W. Sotcher, Benjamin Blanton Moore, John Carrol Crawford, Leone Sanders Thompson, Blanton Benjamin Moore. (DRT nos. 1818, 1965, 2440, 7229.)

47. *JOHN TURNER*, Signer (Represented San Patricio)

Turner moved to Texas in 1834 from Tennessee. After the Convention he ranged the settlements procuring horses and supplies. In the

First Congress, he later moved to Houston and became bankrupt. Born in North Carolina about 1802; died in Houston, Texas, in 1844.

48. *DR. BENJAMIN B. GOODRICH*, Signer
(Represented Washington Municipality)

At the Convention, Dr. Goodrich polled signers for their age, place of birth and originating state or country. He was born in Brunswick County, Virginia, in 1799. Married Serena Corrothers of Kentucky. Nine children. Died in Anderson, Grimes County, in 1860.

Twentieth-century descendants include the families of Delbert Leggett, John D. Covert, James Hines Muldrow, J. E. Clarke. (DRT nos. 371, 937, 1340, 2661.)

49. *DR. GEORGE WASHINGTON BARNETT*, Signer
(Represented Washington Municipality)

Shortly after arriving in Texas, Barnett was commissioned as a junior officer, fought Indians and participated at Bexar. He served as a senator in six congresses. Born in 1793 in South Carolina. Married Eliza Patton in Tennessee. Six children. He was killed by Indians while hunting deer in 1838.

50. *JAMES GIBSON SWISHER*, Signer (Represented Washington Municipality)

A veteran of the War of 1812, Swisher participated at the siege of Bexar and helped arrange the terms of Mexican surrender. His son Harvie Swisher fought as a first lieutenant at San Jacinto. He moved to Austin in 1846. Born near Franklin, Tennessee, in 1794. Married Elizabeth Boyd. Three children. Died in 1864. Swisher County was named in his honor.

Twentieth-century descendants include the families of Richard Newton Lane, John R. Blocker, John Milton Swisher, Jr., John S. Hoover. (DRT nos. 283, 1364, 1996.)

51. *JESSE GRIMES*, Signer (Represented Washington Municipality)

Grimes settled in Grimes County in 1827 and held various offices under the Mexican regime. He was a senator of the Republic for various counties. Born in present Duplin County, North Carolina, in 1788. His first wife was Martha Smith, who died before he went to Texas; he then married Mrs. Rosanna Ward Britton a year before immigrating. Fifteen children (six by the second wife). Died in 1866. Grimes County was named in his honor.

Twentieth-century descendants include the families of James McDonald, Jr., Frederick Leonard Schumpert, W. C. Preston, B. G. Harris. (DRT nos. 530, 544, 1691, 6584.)

52. *SAMUEL RHOADS FISHER*, Signer (Represented Matagorda Municipality)

Fisher came to Texas and settled in Matagorda County in 1830. After the Convention he was appointed secretary of the Texas Navy, a vitally important force for ensuring the safety of incoming settlers, who mostly at that time arrived by sea from New Orleans. The Texas Navy consisted initially of the four schooners *Liberty, Invincible, Independence* and *Brutus*. Fisher was born in Pennsylvania in 1794. Married Ann Pleasants. Three children. Died in 1839. Fisher County was named in his honor.

Twentieth-century descendants include the families of John Woods Harris, Walter Howard Meyers, John Harris Meyers, Wilmer Dallam Masterson, Mason Webster, Jr. (DRT nos. 3123, 5864.)

53. *SAMUEL AUGUSTUS MAVERICK* (And First Maverick of That Ilk), Signer (Represented Bexar)

Shortly after arriving in Texas a graduate of Yale, Maverick was captured by Mexicans following the Goliad Massacre. During the siege of Bexar he had served as a guide. He was captured again in the Adrian Woll Raid. Ranched in Matagorda, serving in the Texan Congress. Unlike many settlers, the Mavericks moved to a more healthy locality near San Antonio where mosquitoes did not represent the menace they did to lowland and riverbank settlers. He told his son: "Of what use is all the lands of Texas or the figurs (sic) on a Bank book to a dead man."

The word maverick entered the English language as a result of unbranded cattle becoming known in Texas as "Maverick's." Unlike his more bureaucratic-minded neighbors, Maverick failed to brand all of his cattle, which tended to roam in the free-spirited, independent manner mavericks of both the cattle and human kingdoms will. Maverick was born in Pendleton, South Carolina, in 1803. Married Mary Ann Adams, 1836. Seven children. Died in San Antonio in 1870. Maverick County is named in his honor. The Mavericks are descended from The Reverend John Maverick of the Dorchester Colony, Massachusetts, a Puritan minister.

Twentieth-century descendants include the families of Albert Maverick, Robert McGarraugh, Albert Maverick, Jr., William Blair McMillan, James Thomas Padgitt, Norval John Welsh, Jr., Fred Weicker, Samuel Maverick, John Frost Maverick, Everett E. Weaver, Robert B. Green. (DRT nos. 725, 746, 1165, 2525, 2549, 5001, 5870, 6141, 6210, 6235.)

54. *JOHN WHITE BOWER*, Signer (One of Two Representatives from San Patricio)

Bower moved from Arkansas just as the revolution began. Represented Refugio in congresses from 1841 to 1843. Born in Talbotton, Georgia, in 1808. Married Bridget O'Brien.

55. *JAMES B. WOODS*, Signer (Represented Liberty Municipality)

James Woods arrived in Texas in 1830 and was alcalde of Liberty by 1834. Born in Kentucky in 1802. Served with Captain Franklin Hardin's Liberty Volunteers in late 1836. Married Mary A. White in Texas. Three children. One descendant was Bessy Rowland James, who aided husband Marquis James on research for *The Raven*, the Pulitzer Prize-winning biography of Sam Houston. According to descendants, James B. Woods was "a suicide from remorse."

Twentieth-century descendants include the families of Hammond Starks, D. A. Pruter (DRT no. 2124) Marquis James, John H. Norwood, Jr., Marquis James Norwood.

56. *JOHN W. MOORE*, Signer (Delegate from Harrisburg)

Moore settled in Harrisburg in 1830, and was elected *comisario* of the precinct of San Jacinto in 1831. A friend of William B. Travis of Alamo fame, he was with Travis at the capture of Anahuac Fort. After the Convention, he was elected contractor for the army. Held local offices. Married Eliza Belknap of Houston in 1839 after the death of his first wife. Born in Pennsylvania about 1797. Died there in 1846.

57. *ANDREW BRISCOE*

Andrew Briscoe attended the Convention, but rushed off to his command as captain of Company A, Infantry Regulars, at San Jacinto. He was a merchant, judge, railroad promoter and banker. Captained the Liberty Volunteers earlier at Concepción and in the siege of Bexar. Appointed chief justice of Harrisburg by Houston. After the Republic, he engaged in banking and brokerage in New Orleans. Born on the Briscoe Plantation in Mississippi in 1810. He married Mary Jane Harris. Five children. Died in 1849. Briscoe County is named in his honor.

Twentieth-century descendants include the families of Joseph Milton Howe, Knox Briscoe Howe, Thomas Perrin West, Major Michael Looscan. (DRT nos. 16, 59, 74, 202, 364, 5844.)

58. *THOMAS BARNETT*, Signer (Delegate from Austin Municipality)

Thomas Barnett was the only signer from Stephen Austin's "Old Three Hundred." In 1828, he was elected *comisario* for the district of Victoria. After the Convention, he was appointed by Houston as chief justice of Austin. Represented Fort Bend County in the Third and Fourth Congresses. Born in Kentucky in 1798. Married Mrs. Nancy Spencer, whose first husband was killed in a fight with Karankawa Indians. Six children. Died before 1845; his widow marrying Thomas M. Gray with a son, Robert M. Gray, by that marriage.

Twentieth-century descendants include the families of John M. Moore, Seth M. Little, John M. Moon. (DRT nos. 483, 1199.)

59. *SAMUEL PRICE CARSON*, Signer (One of Five Delegates from Pecan Point and Red River)

Carson was a member of the North Carolina Senate. After being defeated for another term, he purchased land on the Red River in 1835. He arrived at the Convention some days after the document was signed. He was the last to do so. Elected secretary of state, he was sent to Washington, D. C., to represent Texan interests. He spent liberally from his fortune in the cause of Texas, being forced in 1837 to mortgage many slaves in New Orleans for $10,000. Born in Pleasant Gardens, North Carolina, in 1798. Married the former Catherine Wilson. Two daughters (one adopted). Died in 1838. Carson County was named in his honor.

III

The Heroes
of the Alamo

THE ALAMO was a former Franciscan mission chapel, first used for military purposes by the Spanish and then the Mexican Army, and it is situated in modern downtown San Antonio. Texan forces captured it from the Mexicans in December 1835, and the Texan garrison of probably 152 men was besieged by Santa Anna's forces from February 24 to March 6, 1836. Thirty-two men from Gonzales answered a message for help and got through to reinforce them. The joint commanders were Travis and Bowie, but due to Bowie's illness, Travis took sole command, refused Santa Anna's call to surrender, and wrote his famous letter "To the People of Texas and all Americans in the world." That letter, and the tradition of the line he drew, inviting those willing to remain and defend the Alamo against overwhelming odds to step across the line, are very much part of the Heroic tradition of Texas. By March 4, the entire Mexican force of some 5,000 men had arrived, and on March 6, 1836, they stormed the Alamo, killing all the defenders. Some 15 noncombatants survived, including, in particular, the widow of Almaron Dickenson, who brought the news of the massacre to Sam Houston.

The defenders' sacrifice cost the Mexicans losses of 1,544 or more men, and also delayed their advance east, both of which were important factors in the subsequent victory at San Jacinto.

Santa Anna ordered the bodies of the defenders to be burned, and the questions of the exact number and identity of some of the defenders are the subject of debate. Many were young unmarried men, and little more than a dozen have left descendants, but the list reported here includes the most recent research, although it is probably not the last word on the subject. It is now generally accepted that the list inscribed on the Alamo cenotaph is not entirely accurate, although it is probable that final and conclusive answers to all of the debated points will never be known.

Nonetheless, the Alamo presaged the Heroic age of the Republic of Texas, and was Texas' Thermopylae.

JUAN ABAMILIO, born in Texas.

R. ALLEN, born in Texas.

MILES DE FOREST ANDROSS, born in Texas.

MICAJAH AUTRY, born in Sampson County, North Carolina, in 1794 or 1795. Wounded in the War of 1812. Married Mrs. Martha Wyche (Putney) Wilkinson. Practiced law in Jackson, Tennessee; came to Texas in 1835. Enlisted in the Tennessee Mounted Volunteers. Twentieth-century descendants include the families of Arthur Claude Hamilton, James Madison Greer, Henry Lee Holman, Hal Wyche Greer, Frank Taylor Higgins, Robert Autry Greer, James G. G. Scarborough. (DRT nos. 1167, 2585, 2900, 4780, 6083.)

JUAN A. BADILLO, born in Texas.

PETER JAMES BAILEY, born in Kentucky. Bailey County is named in his honor.

ISAAC G. BAKER, born in Arkansas.

WILLIAM CHARLES M. BAKER, born in Mississippi.

JOHN J. BALLENTINE, born in Texas.

ROBERT W. BALLENTINE, born in Scotland.

JOHN J. BAUGH, born about 1803 in Virginia; came to Texas before the Revolution. Auxiliary captain in the Volunteers; assumed command of the Alamo after Travis' death.

JOSEPH BAYLISS, born in Tennessee.

JOHN BLAIR, born in Tennessee.

SAMUEL C. BLAIR, born in Tennessee.

WILLIAM BLAZEBY, born in England.

JAMES BUTLER BONHAM, born at Red Banks, South Carolina, in 1807. School classmate of William B. Travis; practiced law at Pendleton, South Carolina, and later at Montgomery, Alabama. Joined the Mobile Greys and came to Texas in 1835; twice got out of the Alamo to get aid, but returned to the defenders.

DANIEL BOURNE, born in England.

JAMES ("JIM") BOWIE, born at Elliot Springs, Tennessee, in 1795. Settled in Rapides Parish, Louisiana, and came to Texas in 1828, having designed the knife which bears his name, and spent time searching for a lost mine on the San Saba River. He became a colonel of the Texas Rangers in 1830. He married Ursula María de Veramendi in 1831 (she and their two children died of cholera in 1833). He joined the Texas Revolution in 1835, and led the volunteers at San Antonio before the arrival of Travis and the regular army. He was bedridden by illness and was killed by the Mexicans in his cot. Bowie County is named in his honor.

JESSE B. BOWMAN, born in Texas.

GEORGE BROWN, born in England.

JAMES BROWN, born in Pennsylvania.

JAMES BUCHANAN, born in 1811 in Alabama. Twentieth-century descendants include the families of James Curtis Buchanan and Perry Veazey Allen. (DRT no. 4811.)

SAMUEL E. BURNS, born in Ireland.

GEORGE D. BUTLER, born in Missouri.

ROBERT CAMPBELL, born in Tennessee.

JOHN CANE, born in Pennsylvania.

WILLIAM R. CAREY, born in Virginia.

CHARLES HENRY CLARK, born in Missouri.

M. B. CLARK, born in Mississippi.

DANIEL WILLIAM CLOUD, born in Kentucky.

ROBERT COCHRAN, born in New Jersey, and came to Brazoria, Texas, in 1835. Joined the Army of Texas as a private in February 1836. Cochran County was named in his honor.

GEORGE WASHINGTON COTTLE, born in Tennessee about 1798. He came to Texas from Missouri in 1832 and joined the volunteers from Gonzales at the Alamo. Cottle County is named in his honor.

HENRY COURTMAN, born in Germany.

LEMUEL CRAWFORD, born in South Carolina.

DAVID ("DAVY") CROCKETT, born in 1786 in Limestone, Tennessee. Many legends grew around this homespun country boy from the Tennessee backwoods, including that his first wife, Polly Finley, was descended from Macbeth. Other stories throve on his prowess as a hunter, including that he killed 105 bears in less than a year by his own claim. Such foraging made him a useful soldier in the Andrew Jackson campaigns. After a spell in the Tennessee legislature, he served three terms in the United States Congress. After failing to be elected for a fourth term, he took his savaged pride to Texas and found a world big enough to hold him, briefly. He and his "Tennessee Boys" joined Travis at San Antonio, where they all died defending the position they held in the Alamo. His second marriage was to Mrs. Elizabeth Patton. Crockett County is named in his honor. Texas myth has it that Davy survived the battle of the Alamo and will rise to save Texas again.

Twentieth-century descendants include the families of Walter Preston Crockett, Samuel Caldwell Johnston, George Newton Ledlow, George W. Atkins, Jr., William McKinley Holdbrook, Burwell W. Humphrey, Jr., Jasper Leon House, Jr., Milton Parks, Charles F. Peveler, Jules G. Hexter, Ashley Wilson Crockett, Raymond H. Hendricks, David Finley Flowers, and William Andrew Lester. (DRT nos. 1003, 2348, 4258, 4343, 4527, 5850, 6574.)

ROBERT CROSSMAN, born in Pennsylvania.

DAVID P. CUMMINGS, born in Georgia.

ROBERT CUNNINGHAM, born in Tennessee.

SQUIRE DAMON, born in Tennessee.

JACOB C. DARST, born in Kentucky; settled in Guadaloupe County, Texas, in 1831. Twentieth-century descendants include the families of George N. Lamkin, James D. Darst, M. W. Hoopingarner, W. E. Caperton, M. H. Davenport, D. W. Hendricks and Stephen B. Springs. (DRT nos. 440, 2656, 4505, 5226, 7249.)

JOHN DAVIS, born in Kentucky.

FREEMAN H. K. DAY, born in Texas.

JERRY C. DAY, born in Missouri.

WILLIAM DEARDUFF, born in Tennessee.

STEPHEN DENNISON, born in England.

CHARLES DESPALLIER, born in Louisiana.

ALMARON DICKENSON, born in Tennessee, where he married Suzanna A. Wilkinson when she was aged fifteen. He came to Gonzales, Texas, in 1835, and was a captain of artillery at the Alamo. His widow (who had been at the siege with their infant daughter) brought the news of the massacre to Gonzales. Twentieth-century descendants include the families of Almaron Dickinson Griffith, Ernest Howard Griffith, and W. F. Gustafson. (DRT no. 6751.)

JAMES H. DILLARD, born in Tennessee.

JAMES DIMPKINS, born in England.

LEWIS DUEL, born in New York.

ANDREW DUVALT, born in Ireland.

CARLOS ESPALIER, born in Texas.

GREGORIO ESPARZA, born in Texas.

ROBERT EVANS, born in Ireland.

SAMUEL B. EVANS, born in New York.

JAMES L. EWING, born in Tennessee.

WILLIAM FISHBAUGH, born in Texas.

JOHN FLANDERS, born in Massachusetts.

DOLPHIN WARD FLOYD, born in 1807 in Texas. Lived at Gonzales, Texas, and went from there with other men to the Alamo. Floyd County is named in his honor. Twentieth-century descendants include the families of Berry Arthur Floyd and Joe Guy Stringer. (DRT no. 5543.)

JOHN HUBBARD FORSYTH, born in New York.

ANTONIO FUENTES, born in Texas.

GALBA FUQUA, born in Alabama.

WILLIAM H. FURTLEROY, alias Fontlroy, born in Kentucky.

WILLIAM GARNETT, born in Tennessee.

JAMES W. GARRAND, born in Louisiana.

JAMES GIRARD GARRETT, born in Tennessee.

JOHN E. GARVIN, born in Texas.

JOHN E. GASTON, born in Texas.

JAMES WILLIAM GEORGE, born in 1802 in Thornberry, Virginia. Married Elizabeth Deardroph in 1822 and came to Gonzales, Texas, and was one of the men of Gonzales who went to the aid of the Alamo. Twentieth-century descendants include the families of Charles William Hood, John D. Speer, Earl Elliot Hood, Lester Joe Smith, Harry Richard Baker, William Edward Martin, Ancil R. Hopp, Hubert A. Bernard. (DRT nos. 1881, 7158, 7305, 7306, 7467.)

JOHN CALVIN GOODRICH, born about 1809 in Tennessee and resident there in 1826. Came to Texas in 1834 with his brother Benjamin (a Signer of the Declaration of Independence), and joined the Army of Texas as a private.

ALFRED CALVIN GRIMES, born in Georgia.

JOSE MARIA GUERRERO, born in Texas.

JAMES C. GWIN alias Gwynne, born in England.

JAMES HANNUM, born in Texas.

JOHN HARRIS, born in Kentucky.

ANDREW JACKSON HARRISON

WILLIAM B. HARRISON, born in Ohio.

CHARLES M. HASKELL, born in 1817 near Nashville, Tennessee.

JOSEPH HAWKINS, born in Ireland.

JOHN M. HAYS, born in Tennessee.

PATRICK HENRY HERNDON, born in Virginia in 1802. Married Parmelee Smith, and settled at Navidad, Texas. He served as a private under David Crockett at the Alamo.

WILLIAM HERSEE, born in England.

TAPLEY HOLLAND, born in Texas.

SAMUEL HOLLOWAY, born in Pennsylvania.

WILLIAM D. HOWELL, born in Massachusetts.

THOMAS JACKSON, born in Ireland; married Louise Cottle and left four children.

WILLIAM D. JACKSON, born in Ireland.

GREEN B. JAMESON, born in Kentucky about 1807; was practicing law at San Felipe de Austin in 1830, and went to the Alamo as chief engineer under James Bowie.

GORDON C. JENNINGS, born in Pennsylvania.

LEWIS JOHNSON, born in Wales.

WILLIAM JOHNSON, born in Pennsylvania.

JOHN JONES, born in New York.

JOHN BENJAMIN KELLOGG, born about 1817 in Gonzales, Texas; married Sidney Gaston in 1834. Twentieth-century descendants include the families of William Crockett Kellogg and Mrs. Ola Kellogg Glover. (DRT no. 4588.)

JAMES KENNEY, born in Virginia.

ANDREW KENT, probably born in 1797 in Madison County, Kentucky, and came to Texas from Missouri in 1828. He was one of the residents of Gonzales who went to the aid of Travis at the Alamo. He left a wife, Elizabeth Zumwalt, and children. Kent County is named in his honor. Twentieth-century descendants include the families of Crawford Burnett, Jr., William Thomas Robinson, Hodge P. Lord, Morris Gydeson, Joseph Byas, Adkinson D. DuBose, Robert Otis Bierschwale, Chester P. Wilkes, James Warren Robinson, Clarence E. Lamb, Ralph W. Gemmer, Billy Gene Caves. (DRT nos. 3947, 5005, 6245, 6516, 7206, 7251, 7252.)

JOSEPH KERR, born in Louisiana.

GEORGE C. KIMBLE, born in Pennsylvania. He was one of 32 Gonzales citizens who broke through Mexican lines on March 1, 1836, to strengthen Travis and his defenders. Kimble County is named in honor of Lieutenant Kimble.

WILLIAM P. KING, born in Texas, he went to the Alamo from Gonzales. He was about twenty-four at the time of his death, and the son of John G. King senior. King County in West Texas is named in his honor.

WILLIAM IRVINE LEWIS, born in Virginia.

WILLIAM J. LIGHTFOOT, born in Virginia.

JONATHAN L. LINDLEY, born in Illinois.

WILLIAM LINN, born in Massachusetts.

TORIBIO D. LOSOYA, born in Texas.

EDWARD MCCAFFERTY, born in Texas.

JESSE MCCOY, born in Tennessee.

WILLIAM MCDOWELL, born in Pennsylvania.

JAMES MCGEE, born in Ireland.

JOHN MCGREGOR, born in Scotland.

ROBERT MCKINNEY, born in Tennessee.

GEORGE WASHINGTON MAIN, born in Virginia.

WILLIAM T. MALONE, born in 1817 at Athens, Georgia; came to Texas in 1835 and enlisted in an artillery company. He had heirs who inherited his bounty land.

WILLIAM MARSHALL, born in Tennessee.

ALBERT MARTIN, born in Rhode Island about 1806; he was the messenger sent by Travis to Gonzales for reinforcements, and led them back to the Alamo.

ELIEL MELTON, born in Georgia.

THOMAS R. MILLER, born in Tennessee about 1795; came to Texas in 1830 and settled at Gonzales. He was one of the men from Gonzales who went to the aid of Travis at the Alamo.

WILLIAM MILLS, born in Chattanooga, Tennessee, 1815; married Martha Lee Adams and settled in Texas in 1833. He enlisted in the Army of Texas in 1836. Twentieth-century descendants include the families of William Henry Sebastian, James Luther Staton I, Randolph Paul Leube, Jr., James Luther Staton II. (DRT nos. 2370, 2437, 7116.)

ISAAC MILLSAPS, born in Mississippi about 1795, and later settled in Gonzales, Texas; he was one of the men from there who joined Travis at the Alamo. He left a blind widow and six children. Twentieth-century descendants include the families of William Jasper Millsaps and Claude P. Hull. (DRT no. 903.)

EDWARD F. MITCHASSON, was a doctor born in Virginia about 1807, and came to Texas from Missouri in early 1836; he went to San Antonio with the Army of Texas.

EDWIN T. MITCHELL, born in Georgia.

NAPOLEON B. MITCHELL, born in Texas.

ROBERT B. MOORE, born in Virginia.

WILLIS A. MOORE, born in Arkansas.

ROBERT MUSSELMAN, born in Ohio.

ANDRES NAVA, born in Texas.

GEORGE NEGGAN, born in South Carolina.

ANDREW M. NELSON, born in Tennessee.

EDWARD NELSON, born in South Carolina.

GEORGE NELSON, born in South Carolina.

JAMES NORTHCROSS, born in Virginia.

JAMES NOWLAN, born in England.

GEORGE PAGAN, born in Mississippi.

CHRISTOPHER A. PARKER, born in Mississippi.

WILLIAM PARKS, born in North Carolina.

RICHARDSON PERRY, born in Texas.

AMOS POLLARD, born in 1803 in Ashburnham, Massachusetts, and trained as a doctor in New York; settled at Gonzales, Texas, in 1834, and was appointed surgeon of the Texas volunteer army in 1835.

JOHN PURDY REYNOLDS, born in Pennsylvania.

THOMAS H. ROBERTS

JAMES ROBERTSON, born in Tennessee.

ISAAC ROBINSON, born in Scotland.

JAMES M. ROSE, born in Ohio.

JACKSON J. RUSK, born in Ireland.

JOSEPH RUTHERFORD, born in Kentucky.

ISAAC RYAN, born in Louisiana.

MIAL SCURLOCK, born in 1809 in Chatham County, North Carolina; settled at San Augustine, Texas, with his brother William in 1834; he volunteered as a private in the Army of Texas in 1835.

MARCUS L. SEWELL, born in England.

MANSON SHIED, born in Georgia.

CLEVELAND KINLOCH SIMMONS, born in South Carolina.

ANDREW H. SMITH, born in Tennessee.

CHARLES S. SMITH, born in Maryland.

JOSHUA G. SMITH, born in North Carolina about 1808, he settled near Bastrop, Texas, in 1835, and died at the Alamo as a volunteer. He was unmarried.

WILLIAM H. SMITH, born in Texas.

RICHARD STARR, born in England.

JAMES E. STEWART

RICHARD L. STOCKTON, born in Louisa County, Virginia.

A. SPAIN SUMMERLIN, born in Tennessee.

WILLIAM E. SUMMERS, born in Tennessee.

WILLIAM D. SUTHERLAND, born in Tennessee.

EDWARD TAYLOR, born in Texas.

GEORGE TAYLOR, born in Texas.

JAMES TAYLOR, born in Texas.

WILLIAM TAYLOR, born in Tennessee.

B. ARCHER M. THOMAS, born in Kentucky.

HENRY THOMAS, born in Germany.

JESSE G. THOMPSON, born in Arkansas.

JOHN W. THOMSON, born in Louisa County, Virginia.

JOHN M. THRUSTON, born in Pennsylvania.

BURKE TRAMMEL, born in Ireland.

WILLIAM BARRET TRAVIS, born in 1809 in Edgefield County, South Carolina; his family moved to Alabama, where he was admitted to the bar and practiced as a lawyer. He married Rosanna Cato in 1828, but separated in 1831 and divorced in 1835, leaving two children. His career in Texas was partly as a lawyer but largely military, and he was in command of the Alamo with the rank of lieutenant colonel. Travis County is named in his honor.

Twentieth-century descendants include the families of Thomas Green Davidson, Jr., John Huffman Turbeville, and R. L. Kincaid. (DRT nos. 210, 4151.)

GEORGE W. TUMLINSON, born in Missouri.

ASA WALKER, born in Tennessee.

JACOB WALKER, born in May 1799 in Tennessee; moved to Nacogdoches where he married Sara Anne Vauchere in 1827. It was reported that he was the last man killed at the Alamo.

WILLIAM B. WARD, born in Ireland.

HENRY WARNELL, born in Arkansas.

JOSEPH G. WASHINGTON, born in Tennessee.

THOMAS WATERS, born in England.

WILLIAM WELLS, born in Georgia.

ISAAC WHITE, born in Kentucky.

ROBERT W. WHITE, born in Texas.

HIRAM J. WILLIAMSON, born in Pennsylvania.

DAVID L. WILSON, born in Scotland.

JOHN WILSON, born in Scotland.

ANTHONY WOLFE, born in England.

CLAIBORNE WRIGHT, born in North Carolina.

CHARLES ZANCO, born in Denmark.

JOHN, a Black slave boy of Francis de Sauque.

The Senior Officers at the Battle of San Jacinto

DETAILS OF the Battle of San Jacinto are not generally agreed upon, and one Texas historian has described it as "the most controversial event in all of Texas history." However, its outcome was both certain and ultimately conclusive, because it assured the survival of the new Republic by the total defeat of the Mexican Army. Indeed, it was as decisive and formative for Texas as was the Battle of Hastings for England in 1066. Just as England acquired a new landed warrior aristocracy of the leaders of the Norman and Breton army at Hastings, so Texas acquired a new landed soldier-peerage from the leaders of their victorious army. This is how all new landed peerages begin.

The Texan army had retreated from Gonzales as the Mexicans advanced until they were in the vicinity of what is now the city of Houston. After some maneuvering and minor skirmishes, Sam Houston, with just over 900 men, was facing Santa Anna with some 1500 men. The

Texans launched a surprise attack during the Mexicans' siesta, and achieved a total victory in about 20 minutes. Mexican losses were 600 or more killed and some 200 wounded. By the following day a further 700 or so had been captured, and barely a dozen Mexicans escaped for the loss of nine Texans killed and 30 wounded. In practical terms, this was conclusive, although minor military actions continued along and near the Rio Grande for a decade and more. It was not until shortly after the annexation of Texas into the Union that full-scale war was renewed in April 1846. Some 8,000 Texans enlisted in the American army, including many veterans of San Jacinto. By the Treaty of Guadaloupe Hidalgo of 1848, Mexico finally abandoned all claims to Texas, and ceded to the United States a vast area westward to and including California, which fulfilled the dreams of Mirabeau Buonaparte Lamar. This treaty was the final consequence of the Battle of San Jacinto, and as an inscription on the battleground memorial claims, nearly a million square miles of the territory of the United States was acquired as a result of that victory.

The following are the senior officers in the army at the battle, with the rank of captain or above. Erastus "Deaf" Smith calls for some comment, as he was a man of many parts. Originally a scout, Houston put him in command of a company (i.e., with the rank of captain), but his destruction of Vince's Bridge, which played an important part in the battle, was additional to his other duties.

1. SAM HOUSTON, Commander in Chief

(See under Signers of the Declaration of Independence, entry No. 37.)

2. JOHN A. WHARTON, Adjutant General

Five months before the battle, Houston appointed Wharton "Texas Agent" in New Orleans charged with buying supplies. Later, in attempting to rescue his statesman and diplomat brother, William Harris Wharton, from capture, he was imprisoned himself by the Mexicans. He represented Brazoria twice in Congress. Born in Nashville in 1806; he trained there as a lawyer. At his funeral in 1838, President Burnet described him as "the keenest blade of San Jacinto." Wharton County is named in honor of the brothers.

3. GEORGE WASHINGTON HOCKLEY, Inspector General

At San Jacinto, Hockley was in charge of the two cannon called the "Twin Sisters." In his capacity as commander of artillery, the cannon played a major role in the victory. He began his career in the War Department in Washington where he met Houston who persuaded him to move to Nashville. He followed Houston to Texas and was made chief of staff on Houston's appointment as commander in chief. The friendship continued when he was made secretary of war in 1838 by Houston. Born in Philadelphia in 1802. He died in Corpus Christi in 1854. Hockley County was named in his honor.

4. JOHN FORBES, Commissary General

In his capacity as logistics chief, Forbes played a major role in supplying the victorious forces and was put in charge of the spoils of battle, which included the sword of Santa Anna, which he duly retained in his possession. He and Houston signed a preemptive treaty earlier in the year with the Cherokee Indians. Later he was mayor of Nacogdoches County. He was born in Cork, Ireland, in 1797. He married Sophie Emily Sisson in 1818. He died in Nacogdoches in 1880.

5. WILLIAM G. COOKE, Adjutant Inspector General

Cooke is listed in the archives as having fought at San Jacinto. His military career began at the siege of Bexar and ended in 1837 when he went into the pharmacy business. He returned as quartermaster general of the Republic and laid the military road from Brazos to Red River. He was captured on the Santa Fe Expedition. Born in Fredericksburg, Virginia, in 1808. Married José Antonio Navarro's niece, Angela. Died in 1847. Two years later, Cooke County was organized and named in his honor.

6. ALEXANDER HORTON, Aide-de-Camp to Sam Houston

Horton was left in charge of a family cabin on the Attoyac River in Texas at age thirteen when he and his widowed mother and her family moved to Texas in 1823. He fought in the early battles of the Revolution, and later became mayor of San Augustine during the Republic. He also helped arrest the leaders of the Regulator-Moderator War. Died in 1894 as one of the oldest survivors of the battle. (See also entry under Carriage Trade of the Republic.)

Twentieth-century descendants include the families of Robert S. Greer, M. M. Overby, Felix P. Murphy, Ben E. Woods, Sam Houston Murphy, James W. Burlingame, Joseph W. Richey, Joseph W. Richey, Jr., Rodney Craig Litton. (DRT nos. 901, 1125, 1132, 3750, 3907, 7233, 7645.)

7. *LORENZO DE ZAVALA, JR.*, Aide-de-Camp

Following the battle, the Zavala home nearby was used as a hospital for wounded Texans and later for wounded Mexicans. He was the son of Lorenzo de Zavala, Sr. (See under Signers of the Declaration of Independence, entry No. 15.)

8. *WILLIAM H. PATTON*, Aide-de-Camp

Patton participated in the siege of Bexar and was appointed to aid Houston at San Jacinto, later being one of the group to accompany Santa Anna to Washington. He was born in Hopkinsville, Kentucky, and then settled in Brazoria after 1828. He later became a surveyor, settling in San Antonio. Murdered by Mexicans in 1842.

9. *JAMES COLLINSWORTH*, Aide-de-Camp

(See under Signers of the Declaration of Independence, entry No. 3.)

10. *JAMES HAZARD PERRY*, Volunteer Aide

A critic of Houston before and after the battle, Perry was arrested and released only in order to participate on the field of battle. Born in New York State in 1811. Died of apoplexy fighting for the North in 1862.

11. *ROBERT EDEN HANDY*, Volunteer Aide

A cofounder with William Lusk of the town of Richmond, Handy was a businessman in real estate before and after the Revolution. He assisted Houston at San Jacinto. With Deaf Smith he was one of the first to hear of the fall of the Alamo. Born in Philadelphia in 1807. He came to Texas from Pennsylvania in 1834. Died in 1838.

Twentieth-century descendants include the families of James Allee Handy, Walter P. Schuster, Robert Eden Handy, James Hutchins Handy, Joe Ramirez III. (DRT nos. 6600, 6612.)

12. ROBERT M. COLEMAN, Volunteer Aide
(See entry No. 25 under Signers of the Declaration of Independence.)

13. THOMAS JEFFERSON RUSK, Secretary of War
(See under Signers of the Declaration of Independence, entry No. 30.)

14. JUNIUS WILLIAM MOTTLEY, Aide-de-Camp to Rusk
(See under Signers of the Declaration of Independence, entry No. 14.)

15. MOSES AUSTIN BRYAN, Aide-de-Camp to Rusk
From third sergeant in Moseley Baker's company, Bryan was transferred to the staff of the secretary of war as aide-de-camp at the battle. He served as interpreter at the conference between Houston and Santa Anna. President Lamar later posted him to the legation in Washington with Anson Jones. Bryan's father-in-law was Stephen F. Austin. He worked in his store after 1831 and accompanied Austin to Mexico as secretary. He joined the Somervell Expedition in 1842. Born in Missouri in 1817. His first marriage was to Adeline Lamothe of Louisiana; his second, to Ira Randolph Lewis' daughter, Cora. Five children (by the second wife). Died in 1895.

Twentieth-century descendants include the families of Lewis Randolph Bryan, Charles Chester McRae. (DRT no. 5933.)

16. EDWARD BURLESON, Colonel
Burleson commanded the center of the line in the battle. He was elected colonel of the 1st Regiment of Texas Volunteers and was one of the six officers consulted at noon on the day of battle by Houston in the council of war in which the options to attack or to defend were discussed. He arrived in Texas in 1830 and joined the Austin second colony. As a leading officer of the Republic he was prominent in Indian wars before being elected vice-president of the Republic in 1841, running against Anson Jones for the presi-

dency unsuccessfully in 1844. Born in Buncombe County, North Carolina, in 1793. Married Sarah G. Owen of Alabama. Six children survived. Died in 1851 in Austin. Burleson County was named in his honor.

Twentieth-century descendants include the families of James Marshall Hubbs, Rufus L. Holt, Albert Smith, Oscar Owen, Frank DeGress Posey, Jack Winfield Perkins, Darrell Wade Butler, James Green Burleson, George W. MacDonnell, Carlos Bee. (DRT nos. 606, 706, 1542, 2592, 4306, 4503, 7066, 7101.)

17. SIDNEY SHERMAN, Colonel

Sherman opened the attack at San Jacinto. The battle cry "Remember the Alamo" has been attributed to him. His wife designed the battle flag. Houston had put him in charge of the left wing of the Texas Army. He was one of the six officers partaking in the council of war preceding the battle that day. He had brought 52 Kentucky volunteers to the Texas revolution a year before. Later he was sent East to raise more troops, and he returned with his wife to settle on the bluff overlooking the battlefield. Born in Marlboro, Massachusetts, in 1805. Married Catherine Isabel Cox, who was reported as "lovely in bouffant white velvet" at Houston's San Jacinto Ball in 1837. Died in poverty in 1873. Sherman County and Sherman in Grayson County are named in his honor.

Twentieth-century descendants include the families of Sidney Sherman Brady, James Anthony Walsh, Ernest Bassett Latham, Malcolm M. Graham, William Escrage Kendall, Joseph Marie Odin Menard, Frederick Eugene LeCand, William Earl Kendall, William Theodore Kendall, Sidney Sherman Kendall, John A. Williams, Albert Sidney Williams, John Warwick McCullough, Edward Downing Futch, Clovis Auteene Brown, James Kleiber Vaughan, Charles Jack Bean, Charles Donovan Williamson, Leonard Wiles Craig, Sr., Leonard Wiles Craig, Jr., Sidney Sherman Walsh, Widmer Sperry Hunt, Andrew Silvestre Barada, Jr., D. Scott Keene, John Duddy Griggs. (DRT nos. 429, 1037, 1129, 1638, 1661, 3867, 5897, 5925, 6136, 6180, 6181, 6201, 6203, 6320, 7804.)

18. JAMES CLINTON NEILL, Lieutenant Colonel, Artillery

Commanding the artillery, Neill was wounded in the skirmish of April

20, which preceded the main action on the following day. Earlier he had been in command of the Alamo and its area, but on becoming sick, left the fort in the charge of Travis. Born in North Carolina in 1790, he moved to Milam County in Texas with his wife and three children in 1831. Died in Navarro County in 1845.

Twentieth-century descendants include the families of Frances D'Grass Posey, Robert Lee Posey and Eugene Ford Posey, Mack Madison Mullican. (DRT no. 6897.)

19. HENRY MILLARD, Lieutenant Colonel

Millard commanded the right flank of the Texan army at the battle and partook in the war council summoned by Houston before the Texan attack on the Mexicans. After the battle he was one of the group who tried to arrest President Burnet for favoring the freeing of the captured Santa Anna. Later appointed by Houston to treat with the Indians. Born in Natchez, Mississippi, in 1807. Married Mary Warren Beaumont, in whose name he founded a town. Died in Galveston in 1844.

Twentieth-century descendants include the families of Frederick Sipe Millard, Jr., Joseph P. Adams, George Franklin Rader, Howard Elwood Preece, Henry Haley Millard, Edward Jerome Dunfee, Roy Charles Jones, Daniel Gene Keidatz, Jr., Max Kyle Omberg, Marvin Hugh Ferrell, Laymon Larry Bruce, Joel Theodore Carlson. (DRT nos. 5695, 5731, 5732, 5733, 5734, 5735, 5736, 5737, 5738, 5739, 5740, 5742, 7364.)

20. ALEXANDER SOMERVELL, Lieutenant Colonel

Somervell was one of six senior officers summoned to the noon war council by Houston, at which the decision to attack or to defend was argued. He commanded the 1st Regiment of Texas Volunteers. He was appointed secretary of war by President Burnet later. In 1842, Houston appointed him leader of the Somervell Expedition. Born in Maryland in 1796, he was granted land in Stephen Austin's second colony after 1832. Died mysteriously in 1854. Somervell County is named in his honor.

21. JOSEPH L. BENNETT, Lieutenant Colonel

Bennett was one of the six officers summoned to the council of war preceding the battle. He commanded the 2nd Regiment of Texas Volunteers. He raised a battalion for the Somervell Expedition in 1842. He came to Texas in 1834; died in 1843.

(N.B. Another and more colorfully recorded Bennet was the six-foot-tall Valentine Bennet, quartermaster of the Texas Army, who supplied the army with good beef before San Jacinto. Asked in later years what uniform the Texans wore at San Jacinto, he replied: "Rags, sir, just rags; nine out of every ten soldiers who fought in the Texas Revolution wore this same uniform, and sire, it was a fighting uniform.")

22. *MIRABEAU BUONAPARTE LAMAR*, Commander of the Cavalry

Elected president of the Republic in 1838, and previously its first elected vice-president, Lamar was an expert horseman, accomplished fencer, prolific poet, gifted orator, a publisher, painter in oils, and one of the great heroes of the Republic. After news of the Alamo and Goliad, he rushed to join the army as a private. As such, he rescued Houston and Rusk in the fighting at San Jacinto on the first day, while they were surrounded by Mexicans. He was verbally appointed commander of the cavalry on the field of battle. Ten days later he was appointed secretary of war by President Burnet. An ambitiously imaginative president, he favored extending Texas to the Pacific, and drove the Cherokees into Arkansas. At his suggestion, Austin was made the new capital. His vision in creating a public education system, financed by public land endowments, earned him the title "Father of Education" in Texas. The poet-president's phrase, "Cultivated mind is the guardian genius of democracy," is the motto of the University of Texas. Born near Louisville, Georgia, in 1798. His first marriage was to Tabitha Jordan, by whom he had a daughter, Rebecca Ann. His second marriage was to Henrietta Maffitt, by whom he had a daughter, Loretto Evalina. Died in 1859. Lamar County is named in his honor.

Twentieth-century descendants include the families of Ethelbert H. J. Andrews, Samuel Douglas Calder. (DRT nos. 655, 1156.)

23. *LYSANDER WELLS*, Major

Placed in charge of a detachment of cavalry, Wells was one of the six officers summoned at noon on the day of the battle for a war council held to decide whether to attack or to defend. Three days before the battle he had distinguished himself in an engagement. He commanded cavalry at the Council House fight later in the war, but was killed following a duel with William D. Redd who had refused to give battle to a Comanche chieftain at San Antonio in 1840. He was born in Middletown, Connecticut, and came to Texas for the revolution from Kentucky.

24. JOHN M. ALLEN, Acting Major

Allen was a recruiter and later first mayor of Galveston. Born in Ireland in 1780. Died in 1847.

25. ISAAC N. MORELAND, Captain of Artillery

Moreland came to Texas in the fall of 1834 and commanded the regular artillery at San Jacinto. A lawyer, he was associated in practice with David G. Burnet. He was chief justice of Harris County until his death in 1842.

26. HENRY WAX KARNES, Captain of Cavalry

Karnes came from Arkansas to Texas and fought in most of the early battles of the revolution and was with Deaf Smith on the scouting patrol to Harrisburg before the Battle of San Jacinto. He was later deputed to exchange prisoners with the Mexicans, but ended up a prisoner himself. (See also entry No. 29, Henry Teal.) Raised companies to fight Comanches. Born in Tennessee in 1812; died in 1840. Karnes County is named in his honor.

27. WILLIAM H. SMITH, Captain of Cavalry

28. ANDREW BRISCOE, Captain

Captain of Company A, Infantry Regulars. (See under Signers of the Declaration of Independence, entry No. 57.)

29. HENRY TEAL, Captain

Teal was sick, and did not fight during the battle. He recruited a company of about 40 men in East Texas after the siege of Bexar and brought them to San Jacinto, recovering in time to accompany Karnes to negotiate with General Urrea, who had them both detained for their knowledge of his preparations for a fresh invasion, warning of which was apprised to Rusk with "The Whip-Handle Dispatch." Teal, Karnes and others wrote the message and gave it to a Mexican concealed in a hollow whip handle. Teal escaped later and was promoted to command a regiment. He was murdered in his tent by a man called Schultz in 1837. Teal came to Texas before 1826 and settled in the San Augustine area.

30. AMASA TURNER, Captain

Turner led a company at San Jacinto; later he was promoted to colonel. In later years he thwarted the attempt at a coup d'etat in Velasco aimed at overthrowing President Burnet. Plantation owner in Lavaca County. Born in Massachusetts in 1800; died in 1877.

31. RICHARD ROMAN, Captain

Roman won personal distinction in the battle, where he led the company formed by John Hart. In the summer he became an aide-de-camp to General Rusk. He served in Congress; became a Texas Ranger; joined the gold rush. Born in Fayette County, Kentucky, in 1811, he came to Texas via the Black Hawk War. Died in San Francisco in 1875.

32. WILLIAM S. FISHER, Captain

Fisher reinforced Houston at San Jacinto with Company I, 1st Regiment of Texas Volunteers, which he had raised. Prominent later in actions against the Mexicans, he was leader of the ill-fated Mier Expedition and was captured and imprisoned in Mexico until released in 1844. Came to Texas from Virginia in 1834. Died in Jackson County in 1845.

33. WILLIAM WOOD, Captain

34. JESSE BILLINGSLEY, Captain

Billingsley commanded Company C, 1st Regiment of Texas Volunteers, at San Jacinto, where he was wounded. Born in Rutherford County, Tennessee in, 1810. Married Eliza Ann Wimers. Three children. Died in 1880.

Twentieth-century descendants include the families of Harrell M. Hatter, Francis Marion Billingsley, Thomas William Gordon, Harrell Mattice Hatter, James Edward Prestbo, Lonnie M. Beckham, Oswaldo F. Hernandez Campos. (DRT nos. 2333, 2362, 4430, 5656.)

35. *MOSELEY BAKER*, Captain

Baker raised troops in East Texas. During the Runaway Scrape, he refused to retreat eastward of his hometown of San Felipe, motivating him later to attempt the impeachment of Sam Houston who ordered San Felipe burned during the retreat. But at San Jacinto he commanded Company D, 1st Regiment of Texas Volunteers. After the revolution he was a planter and lawyer in Houston with periods as a senior officer in actions against Mexicans and Indians. Born in Norfolk, Virginia, in 1802. A fashion reporter covering the San Jacinto ball in 1837 noted that Mrs. Mosely (sic) Baker (possibly the former Eliza Ward) was attired in white satin with a black-lace overdress. Guests at these galas often rode 50 miles on horse in order to attend. Baker died of yellow fever in 1848.

36. *WILLIAM J. E. HEARD*, Captain

Commanded Company F, 1st Regiment of Texas Volunteers.

37. *WILLIAM W. HILL*, Captain

Hill's company was Company H of the 1st Regiment of Texas Volunteers. He was on the sick list during the battle.

Twentieth-century descendants include the families of Charles H. Heimsath, James West. (DRT nos. 577, 1788.)

38. *ROBERT STEPHENSON*, Acting Captain (in the place of William W. Hill, who was on the sick list)

39. *HAYDEN ARNOLD*, Captain

Arnold commanded 6th Company, 2nnd Regiment of Texas Volunteers. Born in 1805; died in 1839.

Twentieth-century descendants include the families of James

Joshua King, George Hayden King, Ralph Hayden King, George Maurice Wunderlick. (DRT no. 5645.)

40. WILLIAM WARE, Captain

Ware raised the 2nd Company, 2nd Regiment. He was also at the siege of Bexar. Born in Kentucky in 1800. Settled in Montgomery County at Ware's Creek, which is named after him. His second marriage was to Ann Crane in 1836. Eight children (three by the first marriage). Died in Wareville in 1853.

Twentieth-century descendants include the families of Joseph M. Kincaid, James E. Webb, Joel D. Fenley, John Crane Ware. (DRT nos. 751, 786, 839, 4332.)

41. WILLIAM M. LOGAN, Captain

Logan commanded the 3rd Company, 2nd Regiment. His impressment of slaves had contributed to the Anahuac disturbances of 1832. He was sheriff of Liberty County until his death in 1839.

42. WILLIAM MCINTIRE, Captain

43. JAMES GILLASPIE, Captain

Gillaspie commanded the 6th Company, 2nd Regiment of Texas Volunteers. He later was superintendent of the state penitentiary in Huntsville. Born in Vermont in 1805. Died in 1867.

44. BENJAMIN FRANKLIN BRYANT, Captain

Company commander. Born in Georgia in 1800. His second marriage was to Roxana Price. Died in 1857, after a life spent protecting the frontier from Indians in a fort called Bryant Station named after him.

Twentieth-century descendants include the families of Hugh Gibson, Sam Mewhinney, Leo Sunseri, LaFitte Bryant, Harmon Duncan Bryant, Paul E. Denney, Emzy Theodore Jones, Jr., Raymond Gilbert Bryant, Mitchell M. V. Grossman, Elie P. Bryant, Francis Marion Blankenship, Jess

Blankenship, Albert J. McKay, J. Fred Cooke, Charlie Mack Galaznick. (DRT nos. 2041, 2104, 2171, 3576, 4855, 5880, 6174.)

45. *WILLIAM KIMBOROUGH* (or *KIMBROO*) Captain

Kimborough commanded the 8th Company, 2nd Regiment of Texas Volunteers. A native of Bedford County, Tennessee, he settled with his wife and one child in David G. Burnet's coloney after 1831. Died in Anderson County in 1856.

46. *JUAN NEPOMUCENA SEGUIN* (Mexican), Captain

A Mexican-Texan hero of independence, Seguin came into early contact with Anglo-Americans in the 1820s. As political chief of San Antonio, he is credited with the "first strictly revolutionary meeting in Texas." He brought his recruits to join Austin, fought with Jim Bowie at Concepción, and partook in the siege of Bexar, where he joined William B. Travis in pursuit of the enemy. He came out through the Mexican lines at the Alamo with a plea for reinforcements. He commanded the rear guard in the retreat of Texans, giving Houston valuable time by repulsing Santa Anna's attempt to cross the Brazos near San Felipe. He joined Houston in time for the battle, and with Karnes led the pursuit.

He returned to San Antonio where he gave military burial to the ashes of the Alamo heroes. Later, in the Senate, he worked for amity between Mexican-Texans and Anglo-Texans. In 1840 he returned from Mexico with warning of Mexican intentions of reconquering Texas. His role in the Woll raid by Mexicans has been controversial. He argued against annexation by the United States in 1845 in the belief that security could be achieved by Mexican recognition of Texan independence. In 1848 he returned to Texas. Born in San Fernando de Bexar (San Antonio) in 1806. Died in 1889.

(N.B. Juan was the son of Erasmo Seguin, who was a source of immense help to the early settlers in Texas.)

47. *ERASTUS* (*DEAF*) *SMITH*, Master Scout

"Deaf" Smith was a man of few words, cool in the face of danger, and knowledgeable about the land in which he lived. He scouted for Fannin and

Bowie before the Battle of Concepción, brought on the Grass Fight, and guided Francis Johnson to Ben Milam in San Antonio. He was sent by Houston to obtain news of events at the Alamo, returning with Mrs. Almeron Dickenson and her baby. By destroying Vince's Bridge, he prevented further reinforcements from reaching the Mexicans before the Battle of San Jacinto, where he further distinguished himself. He married Guadalupe Ruiz Duran in 1822. Four children. Born in Dutchess County, New York, in 1787. Died at Richmond in Fort Bend County in 1837. Deaf Smith County is named in his honor.

Twentieth-century descendants include the families of William Christian Kroeger, Joe N. Sanderson, Charles Sykes Broadbent, Lloyd Eldon Mellor, Duane Elliott Mellor, Robert Arthur Wood, Juan Smith Tarin, Carlos Flores, William R. Deuvall, Ben Sappington, Irvin F. Gorner, Frank P. McCarty, Henry Rollins Wofford, Otes Moore Farnsworth, Oran Gould Kirkpatrick, Simpson Kroeger, John Q. Wall, Henry Roach. (DRT nos. 43, 349, 467, 559, 713, 753, 811, 1220, 1283, 1323, 1433, 2311, 2354, 2908, 3018, 5800, 7085, 8101.)

Other Notables
and Heroes
of the Republic

E VEN A SOLDIERS' REPUBLIC needs more than soldiers to create and maintain it. Once the battles were won, civilian life had to go on, and develop. It takes a great many people with a great many different talents to make a new nation, and they all play a part, including the soldiers themselves. Some of the larger-than-life people portrayed here had a great many talents, and used them all in the making of Texas.

It should not be thought from these examples that all Texan Methodist ministers died leading cavalry charges, that all colonels were also "doctors" and many physicians "majors," nor that all Indian fighters were Princeton graduates, but in this section our readers will find the first Texan millionaire; real-estate developers, of whom some founded the city of Houston while others founded nothing; and planter grandees bankrupted by the War Between the States. Graduates from Oxford and Yale; a surveyor from Vienna; a divorce lawyer who was the Patrick

Henry of Texas; and a German lawyer who fought at San Jacinto and then married the heiress of the King Ranch. All appear in the company of the slave auctioneer who brought his house from Virginia with him, the designer of the Colt revolver and the inventor of the bowie knife. There is Abraham Lincoln's former partner on a flatboat, a selection of newspaper owners and editors (including one who wore a wooden leg and, so equipped, fought in the cavalry), and among the ladies, the white wife and mother of Indian chiefs, and the owner-hotelier of what was probably (reading between the lines) the contemporary best whorehouse in Texas, among other things.

Real and bogus honors include the genuine aristocrat who pretended to be a commoner, and the commoner who pretended to be an aristocrat (both of them Europeans fleeing from the law); the only three knights of Sam Houston's Order of San Jacinto; and the permanent memorials of those in whose honor a county is named—for place-names are remarkably persistent—most of the counties of Texas being named after notables and heroes of the Republic, and a remarkable cross-sectioned peerage of them that role of honor is.

These are some of the people who made Texas, remarkable, larger-than-life, but nonetheless human characters. They could almost compete with the characters of Texas' "tall talk," such as Davy Crockett's uncle who lived ". . . at the jumping off part of the western country. He is celebrated in that part of the *world* for the following peculiarities: he shaves himself with sheet lightning, and eats pickled thunderbolts for his breakfast, and hail stone life pills when he's sick, picks his teeth with a pitchfork, combs his hair with a rake, fans himself with a hurricane, wears a *cast iron* shirt, and drinks nothing but kreosote and aquafortis."

But while the Crockett legends have grown, it has been suggested that the reason why the Sam Houston legend failed to outstrip the facts was due to the sheer difficulty in elaborating upon the startling truth. Indeed, in many ways there are parallels between Sam Houston and his soldier politicians and those champions of earlier great causes, King Arthur and the constantly dueling knights of the Round Table. Sam Houston was cast in an Arthurian mold. Here are some of his knights, and not a few of his enemies (if not already treated in our preceding sections under Signers of the Declaration of Independence and The Senior Officers at San Jacinto).

AUGUSTUS CHAPMAN ALLEN AND JOHN K. ALLEN
(Founders of Houston)

There were six Allen brothers, all active for several decades in Texan social and economic affairs. Augustus (a professor of mathematics) and John were the most prominent. They fitted out and equipped the schooner *Brutus* during the Revolution, in order to safeguard the all-important sea route for supplies and reinforcements, later selling the ship to the Texas Navy at actual cost. Upon buying a half league of land on the Buffalo Bayou, they picked a site so perfect, that they decided to found a town there named after Sam Houston.* Due to the absence of big hotels in those early Texan days, they put up for free all visitors in search of lodging, such that it was testified they spent $3,000 a year on the investment of hospitality on behalf of the future of the leading city of Texas today. Following the death of John Allen, estate problems arose between Augustus and his wife, Charlotte (Baldwin) Allen, whose fortune had financed the beginnings of their business empire. Augustus Allen left for Mexico to build a new business, and died in 1864. The Allens were born in New York.

MARTIN ALLEN (Old Three Hundred and Carriage Trade)

Old Three Hundred settler Martin Allen was granted the right to operate a ferry across Buffalo Bayou opposite Harrisburg in 1830. He appears to have been wealthy enough to own a racehorse (see entry under Carriage Trade of the Republic). The horse is recorded in the tax return of 1840, although Allen died in Washington County a couple of years earlier, suggesting that his stable had housed more than one racehorse. He was born in Ireland in 1780.

* Their message to settlers included the following copy:
"The town of Houston, situated at the head of navigation of Buffalo Bayou, is now for the first time brought to public notice. Houston is located at a point which must ever command the trade of the largest and richest portion of Texas. When the rich lands of this country shall be settled, trade will follow to it, making it, beyond doubt, the great indoor commercial emporium of Texas. Vessels from New Orleans and New York can sail without obstacle to this place, as the country shall improve, railroads will come in use and trade will make its way through this channel." The success, however, of their city is owed to John Kirby Allen's proposal to the Texas Congress to build a capitol building at the Allen brothers' expense, providing that the new nation would accept their site as the national capital, although they were careful to stipulate that the building would revert to them in the case of the capital being moved, as it later was to Austin.

Twentieth-century descendants include the families of Martin Robert Allen, Addison Dwight Rogers, James B. Allen, John Preston Buck, William Henry Ray, Jerry C. Smyth, George K. Spangler, Miles Johnston Allen, Miles Newton Allen, Harry George Harrison. (DRT nos. 1616, 2005, 2133, 2173, 2466, 7112, 7968.)

HORACE (HORATIO) ALSBURY (Old Three Hundred Patriot)

A native of Kentucky, Alsbury took part in the siege of Bexar and fought with Karnes as a private at San Jacinto. His wife was the sister of Declaration of Independence signer José Antonio Navarro, and may have been one of the women evacuated from the Alamo, where tradition has it she nursed James Bowie during the early stages of the siege. As a child she had been placed under the guardianship of Bowie's mother-in-law.

KENNETH L. ANDERSON (Vice-President)

Vice-President of the Republic in 1844, and formerly speaker in Congress, Anderson was one of the greatest lawyers and orators of the Republic. He settled in San Augustine in 1837. He was born in North Carolina in 1805; buried in 1845 in the county later named after him.

RICHARD ("BIG DICK") ANDREWS (County Namer)

Huge in weight and mighty in muscle, Andrews was an Indian fighter known as "Big Dick" who joined the Revolution's forces. Wounded at Gonzales, the Texan Lexington, he died fighting alongside Bowie and Fannin at the Battle of Concepción in 1835. He settled with his family in the Fort Bend area. Andrews County in the Panhandle is named in his honor.

DR. BRANCH TANNER ("THE OLD ROMAN") ARCHER (Vice-President)

Archer was president at the Consultation held to discuss action following the usurpation by Santa Anna of control of the Mexican government. By declaring the Texans' loyalty to the liberal Mexican Constitution of 1824, and by rejecting Santa Anna, the Consultation provided a motive for the war, which had already actually started. Archer himself fought at the battle of Gonzalez. Archer, Stephen Austin and William H. Wharton were then appointed commissioners to obtain help from the United States. He and Collinsworth founded The Texas Railroad, Navigation and Banking Company, which collapsed in the Panic of 1837. "The Old Roman," as he was often called, was one of the most talented of men in the Texan art of swearing, which led a British observer to note of Texan oaths that they were such that "the genius of Depravity herself had tasked her utmost powers to produce them for the especial use of this rising State." Born in Fauquier County, Virginia, in 1790. Died in 1856. Archer County is named in his honor.

JAMES ELIJAH BROWN AUSTIN (Brother of Stephen Austin)

James Austin came with the Old Three Hundred, bringing 300 Spanish horses to Texas. In 1832 he helped put down the Fredonian Rebellion. Born in Missouri in 1803. Married Eliza Martha Westall in 1828. Died in 1829.

MOSES AUSTIN (Father of Stephen F. Austin)

Moses Austin never lived to settle his 300 families of colonists in the promised land of Texas. Instead his son, Stephen F. Austin, took up the mantle as the Joshua of Texas. Lead mining was the attraction that had first brought Moses to Mexico. His lucky encounter with "Baron" de Bastrop in San Antonio in 1820 eventually secured a grant for the settlement of his "Old Three Hundred" on 200,000 acres. His death in 1821 left the legacy to be fulfilled by his twenty-eight-year-old son, Stephen. Moses was born around 1761 from a Connecticut family going back in America to 1638. Married Maria Brown. (See entries in this section for his children, Stephen, James and Emily Austin Bryan Perry.)

The many twentieth-century descendants include the families of Edward Wheler Parker, Guy Morrison Bryan II, Stuart Sherar, William Joel Bryan, Erin Bryan, Charles W. Shaver, Frank A. Hervey, James Thomas Stratton, Fred A. Brock, Guy Webb Adriance, James Franklin Perry, Henry Austin Perry, Jr., John Ward Beretta, Alvord Rutherford, Walter Klingman, John S. Caldwell, E. G. Helm, Jr., Lewis Randolph Bryan, Charles Chester McRae. (DRT nos. 176, 1645, 1681, 2313, 2457, 2583, 2812, 3129, 3462, 3552, 5644, 5769, 5933, 8091.)

STEPHEN FULLER AUSTIN
(The Most Celebrated Founding Father of Texas Colonies)

A master colonist of endless patience, resource, moderation, and with indefatigable managing skills, Austin sincerely desired Texas to be a viable Mexican state even after the Mexicans forbade further United States' colonization in 1830. He also went so far as to discourage the Consultation held in 1835 to consider declaring independence. Nonetheless, as one of three commissioners appointed to seek aid for the colonists in the United States, he eventually helped to materialize independence. After the death of his father, Moses Austin, in 1821, he took up his father's grant of lands that had been previously negotiated with the assistance of "Baron" de Bastrop of San Antonio. After endless difficulties, he finally located his famous Old Three Hundred colonists. By 1832, various more colonies of Austin's were peopling Texas to the number of 8,000 persons or more. His imprisonment in Mexico following a visit to Saltillo began a series of steps leading to Austin's disillusionment with Mexico. Defeated in the election for president in 1836, he was made secretary of state by his opponent President Burnet, but died in harness within a few months. Born in southwest Virginia in 1793. The state capital of Austin and Austin County are named in his honor.

For twentieth-century descendants of the Austin clan, see entry under his father, Moses Austin.

RICHARD BACHE (The Last Independent Texan)

A Pennsylvanian born in 1784, and a grandson of Benjamin Franklin, Richard Bache's was the single name voting for continued independence of the Lone Star Republic at the Convention of 1845 and against annexation by the United States. Yet he helped draw up the new state's constitution. During the war he had served in the Texas Navy. During the Republic he represented Galveston, where he was an import inspector. He died in Austin in 1848.

JAMES B. ("BRIT") BAILEY (Old Three Hundred Eccentric)

Bailey was another of the early Texas settlers who attracted "tall talk" stories. It was said that he would join any fight with gleeful shouts of "Free fight, boys" as he waded in hurling punches despite a lame leg and weak appearance. He also asked "to have my remains inter'd erect with my face fronting the west . . ." along with "[my] whisky jug, powder horn, rifle and ammunition." However, none of these freewheeling habits prevented him from acquiring enough property to distinguish him among the Old Three Hundred. Indeed, he had one of the first brick houses in the colony. Respect went with his general frontiersman integrity. He was born in North Carolina in 1770. His wife's name was Nancy. He died about 1833.

Twentieth-century descendants include the families of Abner Hubbard Polley, Sterling Hilmer Polley, Tom Moore Featherstone. (DRT no. 5544.)

"BARON" FELIPE ENRIQUE NERI DE BASTROP
(First Bogus Baron of Texas)

"Baron" de Bastrop was influential in helping sow the first seed of the nation called Texas by aiding Moses Austin in securing a land grant and in smoothing the path for the venture of Stephen E. Austin. He first arrived in Texas from the then Spanish territory of Louisiana in 1805, following the momentous Louisiana Purchase. He settled in San Antonio. As a representative at the capital of Saltillo he sought legislation helpful to the cause of immigration. His origins were controversial, as would be his noble title. Previously advanced theories on that include that he was a Prussian soldier of Frederick the Great, a French nobleman, an adventurer from the United States, and by his own last testament, that he was born in Holland the son of a Baron de Bastrop in about 1766. More recently it has been established that he was born Philip Hendrik Nering Boegel in Paramaribo, Dutch Guiana, in 1796. While no doubt responsive to the cause and company of aristocracy, it seems he fled Holland to escape charges of embezzlement of tax funds. Rewards offered for his arrest led him to adapt the noble cover of "Baron" de Bastrop. He died in 1827. Cities in Louisiana and Texas bear his name, as does Bastrop County, Texas.

BERNARD E. BEE (County Namer)

Secretary of war under Houston and secretary of state under President Mirabeau Lamar, he was one of three commissioners sent to accompany Santa Anna to Washington after the capture of the Mexican dictator, having joined the Texas Army under Thomas J. Rusk. Born in

Charleston, South Carolina, in 1787. Died in 1853. Bee County is named in his honor.

PETER HANSBOROUGH BELL (County Namer)

Bell fought as a cavalry private with Karnes at San Jacinto, having left Virginia to fight for independence, and receiving land for his services. Later he joined the Texas Rangers under Zachary Taylor and Jack Hill, becoming a battalion commander. Born in Spotsylvania County, Virginia, in 1812. Twice elected governor of Texas after annexation. Married Mrs. Ella Reeves Eaton Dickens in 1857. Bell County is named in his honor.

THOMAS B. BELL (Old Three Hundred Patriot)

Thomas Bell was the bearer of the Lone Star flag at the battle of Concepción in 1835. His wife's name was Prudencio. Three children. A Thomas Bell family was living in Austin County in 1844.

GAIL BORDEN, JOHN P. BORDEN, PASCHAL PAVOLO BORDEN and THOMAS HENRY BORDEN

Borden County is named in the honor of Gail Borden, a prolific inventor in the agricultural and transportation fields, who began his career as surveyor to Stephen Austin. He also founded a Texan newspaper as early as 1835. He married three times and had seven children.

John fought at San Jacinto as a lieutenant in Moseley Baker's Company. He and Gail laid out the town of Houston in late 1836. Houston named John first commissioner of the General Land Office when he was twenty-four. He had nine children by his second wife, Susan Hatch.

Paschal also fought alongside his brother at San Jacinto, but as a private. By his second wife, Martha Ann Stafford, he had three sons.

Thomas was one of the Old Three Hundred. He worked on the newspaper of his brother Gail and also was interested in inventing. He had two sons by his first marriage to Demis Woodword. The four brothers were all born in Norwich, New York. Their father was Gail Borden, Sr. (Also, seen entry under Fort Bend County in the Carriage Trade of the Republic.)

Twentieth-century descendants of Gail Borden, Sr., include the families of S. G. Borden, Robert J. Davis, Joseph Louis Lockett, James

Cockran Borden, Gail Borden Johnson, Robert M. Sias, Reverend Robert Knox. (DRT nos. 659, 660, 661, 622, 1344, 1381, 1663, 2170, 3610.)

LE MARQUIS HAROLDE AUGUSTUS DE BOURBEL DU MONTPINCON (Alias "Harold Bargue")

Descended from an ancient Norman line going back to a Guillaume de Bourbel alive in 1110, this French nobleman arrived in New Orleans around 1840 under the alias of "Mr. Harold Bargue," a fugitive of Napoleonic conspiracies, and from a money fraud by some accounts engineered to raise funds for the abortive coups d'etat in 1835 and 1840 of the future Emperor Napoleon III, who in his last years was to speak of the "great sacrifice" of his friend. The son of a prominent Bonapartist, the young Marquis de Bourbel's friendship with the Emperor-to-be grew during their days in Italy as fellow Carbonari, the first revolutionaries of Italian independence. In New Orleans he set up a "factory" in liquor distilling, which was pilfered by employees when he caught the yellow fever.

Seeking his fortune in Texas, he arrived in Galveston in 1842, having bought 640 acres of land near Austin. A widower, he wrote in 1842 to the guardian of his children in England: "People here, by the bye, believe me a military man. I can't guess why, except a drunken one having said so, and since everyone repeated it—with my being silent on the subject. I might make you laugh with the details of my secret interview with the Minister of War, a great talker, to whom I so constantly nodded assent to all his *notions* that at last he nodded to me my commission as chief . . . at any rate I am no coward, & leading independent rough men, only I guess requires management and going ahead, but does not require those manoeuvres or tactics which would have puzzled me, had they given me regular troops. My undertaking is a secret. Each man has his horse and rifle and bowie knife. I have obtained some powder and an order for pack mules, and a few provisions to be given me on the frontier; and then I will have the frontier prairie to get through & creep in Mexico which way I will think fit." No more word was heard from him and he is believed to have joined the 1848 gold rush to California and married again there.

Twentieth-century descendants include the families of John de Bourbel Stansfeld, Jacques Heugel, Bayard de Bourbel, Philippe Heugel, Francois Heugel, John R. W. Stansfeld, Henri Heugel.

REZIN P. BOWIE (Of Bowie Knife Fame)

According to some sources, Rezin Bowie designed the bowie knife for his brother, James Bowie, the Alamo hero and leader. It became the great throwing knife, as copied in Texas, the South and Southwest, while having a variety of other practical uses, including the picking of teeth, making it "as handy as a shirt pocket." Legends grew up around its use by James Bowie. As a weapon it was only finally rendered obsolete by the six-shooter. Bowie knives were a frequent weapon chosen for duels among the lower orders of Texan chivalry, such as in feud-ridden Shelby County. He was born in Tennessee in 1793. He married Frances Neville in Nachitoches in 1812; they had five children. He died in New Orleans in 1841.

HENRY PERCY BREWSTER (County Namer)

Born in 1816 in South Carolina, Brewster heard of the Texas Revolution while on a trip to Alabama. At age twenty he joined Andrew Briscoe's Company as a private, serving as private secretary to Houston. He fought at San Jacinto; he became secretary of war during the Republic; and fought as a Confederate colonel in the War Between the States. He married Ann Elizabeth Royall. In later years he was a lawyer in San Antonio, and died there in 1884. Brewster County is named in his honor.

JOHN NEELY BRYAN (The First Family of Dallas)

Bryan had the distinction of being the first settler in Dallas. From his cabin there he plowed the land in his buckskin suit with a bois d'arc fork and crossed the river in a cottonwood dugout. His home was the first post office and courtroom in Dallas. He became a lawyer and served as a Dallas alderman. Born in Fayetteville, Tennessee, in 1810. Married Margaret Beeman, one of the first settlers in Dallas, where he had a family. Died in Austin in 1877.

Twentieth-century descendants include the families of Alexander Luther Bryan, Robert Alexander Warner, Ross Willard Brown, Minor Lafayette Woolley, Samuel Gayle Deatherage, Jasper Clark Box. (DRT nos. 5464, 5581, 5758.)

AYLETT C. ("STRAP") BUCKNER
(The Gilgamesh of Texas Tall Talk)

Heroic ages tend to prompt legends of folk who fight like the Mesopotamian Gilgamesh, with giant black bulls and best the Devil in combat. Such stuff was part of the tall talk about Strap Buckner. Another is that he "knocked down Stephen Austin's colony at least three times over." As a settler, he was a predecessor to the Old Three Hundred, which he joined. He quarreled with Austin over an extended period. In point of fact, his quite frequent challenges to duels were often easily requited by being laughed off, although perhaps there was no other recourse, given this giant man's martial skills and known ferocity. He began adventuring in Texas on the Gutiérrez-Magee Expedition of 1811, which first stimulated the idea of a Texas as part of the United States. He returned on the Mina Expedition, and again with Dr. James Long, claiming to have been the first colonist to settle and build on the Colorado River. He was already acknowledged by 1839 in *Harper's Magazine* to be one of the "three heroic figures of American folklore" along with Johnny Appleseed and Paul Bunyan. He was killed in the Battle of Velasco in 1832, one of the earliest martyrs of Texan independence.

DAVID GOUVERNEUR BURNET
(First President of the Republic of Texas)

Burnet fired the first shot in the struggle for South American independence in 1806 from the launch he commanded as a volunteer with Francisco de Miranda's expedition to free Venezuela from Spain. On falling ill in upriver Colorado he was nursed by Comanches, with whom he lived for two years. He married Hannah Estes of New York, and they settled across the San Jacinto river from the Lynchburg ferry. At the 1836 Convention after the Declaration of Independence he was elected ad interim president of the newborn Republic. His conservatism made him unpopular with the unruly Texas soldiery, so at the 1838 election Sam Houston was elected second president. Later Burnet returned as secretary of state. At his farm he experimented in agriculture. He was born the youngest of eight children in Newark, New Jersey, in 1788. He had sons. Burnet County was named in his honor.

JAMES HUGHES CALLAHAN
(Goliad Survivor and County Namer)

As a young soldier, Callahan fought at Coleto and was captured with Fannin at the Goliad, but escaped the massacre to become a noted Indian fighter and leader of the Callahan Expedition of Texas Rangers sent in pursuit of Apaches and other Indians. Born in Marion County, Georgia, in 1814. Married Sarah Medisa Day. Killed in 1856. Callahan County is named in his honor.

EWEN CAMERON (And the 17 Black Beans)

The leader of the mass escape from Salado of the captured men from the Mier Expedition of late 1842 was this Scottish Highlander-turned-leader-of-cowboys. He was a volunteer among the Kentuckians during the San Jacinto campaign. When Santa Anna ordered the recaptured escapees massacred, the local commander modified the order to every tenth man. Each prisoner was invited to select a bean from a pouch. Cameron drew a white bean, but was executed anyway as leader of the escape. Those who drew the fated 17 black beans were as follows:

L. L. CASH	JAMES OGDEN
JAMES D. COCKE	CHARLES ROBERTS
ROBERT DUNHAM	WILLIAM ROWAN
WILLIAM M. EASTLAND	J. L. SHEPARD
EDWARD ESTE	J. M. N. THOMPSON
ROBERT HARRIS	JAMES N. TORREY
THOMAS L. JONES	JAMES TURNBULL
PATRICK MAHAN	M. C. WING
HENRY WHALING	

Each one was then blindfolded and shot by firing squad. The rest suffered imprisonment in the ghastly Perote Prison until they escaped or were finally released in 1844. Cameron was born in his distant bonnie glens in 1811. Cameron County was named in his honor.

JOHN CARTWRIGHT (First Cotton Ginner)

Cartwright was a carpenter and ironsmith who became active in San Augustine (see Carriage Trade of the Republic) in the construction business. In the Redlands he is believed to have built the first cotton gin in Texas. Born in North Carolina in 1787. Married in 1806 to Mary Crutchfield. Died in 1841.

Twentieth-century descendants include the families of Robert Lee Warren, Summerfield G. Roberts, William B. Lupe, James Lane Taylor, Columbus Cartwright, William Garrett Sharpe, Philip Smith, Robert Burnis Hall, Robert G. Cartwright, Otto Clinton Woods, Glenn H. Fankhauser, Robert Lane Cartwright, James Cole Williams, Levy Thompson Clark, J. S. Laurence, Richard Fendall Slaughter, Charles Polk Slaughter, Walter Theodore Norman, Jr., Charlie Slaughter, Thomas Evans Stone. (DRT nos. 1435, 1443, 2543, 2991, 3166, 4866, 5007, 5335, 5337, 7538, 7551, 7588.)

HENRI CASTRO (Of Castro's Colony Fame)

Castro was a descendant of Portuguese nobility who entered into an empresario contract with Texas in 1842, eventually setting sail after many delays with 27 ships containing over 1,000 French settlers. He has been compared to Stephen Austin for his fine qualities of leadership and humanity as an empresario of Texas and deserves his place in the Republic hall of fame, despite his late arrival in Texas. Born in France in 1786; died in 1865. His many interests were carried on by his son, Lorenzo. Castro County is named in his honor.

THOMAS JEFFERSON CHAMBERS (County Namer)

Chambers worked with the Mexican Juan Antonio Padilla as Mexican surveyor general to help with the colonization program. He later became a state attorney, and was granted 30 leagues of land in several counties. He was active in the events leading up to the Revolution, providing his lands as security for the raising of troops, and was active in finance and politics under the Republic. In 1837 he "posted" former President David G. Burnet publicly as being "mean-spirited and cowardly" for refusing a duel, Burnet having "conscientious scruples" on such matters. Born in Virginia in 1802. Married Abbie Chubb of Galveston in 1850. Two daughters. Died in 1865 in Galveston. Chambers County is named in his honor.

Twentieth-century descendants include the family of F. K. Sturgis. (DRT no. 262.)

NESTOR CLAY (The "Master Spirit" of the Convention of 1832)

Born in Kentucky in 1799, Clay settled in Washington County, in

Texas, in 1824, where his son's "Clay Castle" plantation house had a glassed-in ballroom on its third floor. A constitutionalist, he was known as the "Master Spirit" of the 1832 Convention. Married Nancy Johnson. Died in 1835.

Twentieth-century descendants include the family of T. J. Thornhill. (DRT no. 1572.)

JAMES CORYELL (County Namer)

Coryell was in San Antonio in 1831 and joined the Bowie brothers in search of a silver mine. He settled in Coryell country where he was killed by Indians in 1837. Born in Ohio in 1801. Coryell County is named in his honor.

WILLIAM HENRY DAINGERFIELD
(Knight of the Order of San Jacinto)

Daingerfield came to Texas in 1837 and within a year or so was elected mayor of San Jacinto. He resigned as secretary of the treasury to become a diplomat for the Republic in the Netherlands. Houston appointed him one of the only three Knights of the Order of San Jacinto, with the proposal, "This I have a right to create. . . . The Ensign of the order is a Green Ribbon, on the left breast, or Button hold (sic) of the coat opposite the heart." Blue or red ribbons were suggested as alternatives. Born in Alexandria, Virginia, in 1808. Ambition and his Texan title brought him to the District of Columbia to practice as a lawyer, where he died in 1878.

JAMES WILMER DALLAM (Author of the "Lawyer's Bible")

Dallam moved to Matagorda in 1838. A Brown University graduate, he studied law in Baltimore. In Washington, D. C., he wrote his *Digest of the Laws of Texas*, which has been called the "lawyer's bible." He returned to Texas a newspaperman, and there wrote two short romances, *The Lone Star, a Tale of Texas* and *The Deaf Spy*. Born in Baltimore. Married Annie Fisher, daughter of Samuel Rhoads Fisher (Fisher County was named after him). One daughter, born in 1847. Dallam County was named in his honor.

Twentieth-century descendants include the families of Wilmer Dallam Masterson, Mason Webster, Jr., Branch T. Masterson. (DRT nos. 2594, 3123.)

THE DALLAS BROTHERS (Old Three Hundred)

The two brothers Walter R. Dallas and James L. Dallas, who were among Stephen Austin's original Old Three Hundred, were reputedly nephews of United States Vice-President George M. Dallas, whose brother was Commodore A. J. Dallas of the U. S. Navy, their father being Alexander James Dallas, a secretary of the treasury in the U. S. government. It has been suggested that any one of them may have had something to do with the naming of the great city of Dallas. Old Three Hundred historian Worth S. Ray has stated that the county and city of Dallas were named in honor of the vice-president, others that it is not clear for whom they are named. Certainly a Joseph Dallas was a settler near the future city in 1843. But the settlement (see entry in this section for the Allen Brothers) appears to have been named Dallas from its very start. Walter and James Dallas both served in the Texas Army, Walter being a veteran of San Jacinto.

Twentieth-century descendants include the family of William E. Dwyer. (DRT no. 1797.)

NICHOLAS HENRY DARNELL

(Last Most Worshipful Grand Master in the Republic)

Darnell helped organize the Masonic lodge at San Augustine and held all offices of the Grand Lodge of Texas, being most Worshipful Grand Master in 1844. The establishment of a Masonic lodge in any population center usually marked its success by increasing population and prosperity, the lodge also exercising strong influence on social affairs. He settled in San Augustine (see entry under Carriage Trade of the Republic) in 1838, and was elected speaker of the house in congress. A true gentleman, he declined to accept office as lieutenant-governor when declared the winner by a few votes, until all the votes had been returned, when his rival was declared elected. Later he moved to Dallas. Born in Williamson County, Tennessee, in 1807. Married Isabella Cozart. Seven children. Died in 1885.

Twentieth-century descendants include the families of Frank B. Daniel and Charles C. Rockenbaugh. (DRT no. 2541.)

NICHOLAS MOSBY DAWSON (Martyr at Salado)

Captain Dawson and his men were cut off by Mexicans and most were killed during the raid on San Antonio by General Woll, one of two such attacks that came six years after the Battle of San Jacinto, in which Dawson had participated as a second lieutenant. These actions eventually helped force opinion in Texas further in the direction of annexation by the United States. Dawson was born in Woodford County, Kentucky, in 1808. His remains were reinterred on "Monument Hill," near Brenham, alongside those of his men and of the victims of the Mier Expedition, including those who drew the infamous Black Beans. Dawson County is named in his honor.

JOHN B. DENTON (County Namer)

Denton was a deckhand on a flatboat in Arkansas as a boy. His wife, Mary Greenlee Stewart of Louisiana, taught him to read and write, and he became a Methodist preacher. For a better living, he taught himself law and went into practice. As a captain in Indian fighting, he died in a cavalry charge he led near Fort Worth in 1841. Born in Tennessee in 1806. Denton County is named in his honor.

GREEN C. DEWITT (County Namer)

In 1825, DeWitt won a grant to settle 400 families, which he did on the Guadalupe, Lavaca and San Marcos rivers. He hired James Kerr to lay out for him there the town of Gonzales, where he settled with his family, later representing Gonzales at the 1833 Convention. For a time Gonzales had been abandoned as a result of Indian raids, but the settlers returned to this early "Anglo-American" colony, which is regarded as having been the most successful colony after Austin's. DeWitt was born in Kentucky in 1787. He married and had six children. He died in 1835. DeWitt County is named in his honor.

Twentieth-century descendants include the families of Green DeWitt, C. P. Whittington, Christopher Columbus DeWitt, Jr., Alexander J. Johnson, Anton R. Simon, Dr. Cleburne Williamson, Lucien Chenault, Edward Harby Frank, Herbert S. Green, George Edward Baker. (DRT nos. 1985, 2035, 2553, 4461, 4665.)

PHILIP DIMMIT (County Namer)

Dimmit and Ira Ingram shared in the framing of the premature Goliad Declaration of Independence in 1835. As a prisoner in Mexico, he killed himself when told he would be shot if escaped prisoners did not return. He came to Texas in 1832 as a frontier trader, and was running a merchant's business in Corpus Christi Bay when seized. Born in Kentucky about 1801. Married María Louisa Lazo. Dimmit County is named in his honor.

SARAH RANDOLPH BRADLEY DODSON
(First Lone Star Flagger)

Old Three Hundred settler Edward R. Bradley died delinquent, but his daughter, Sarah Dodson, goes down in Texas history as the designer of the first Lone Star flag of Texas (See also entry in this section for Johanna Troutman). The flag was made of equal squares of blue, red and white calico. She presented it to the company of her soldier-husband, Archelaus Bynum Dodson. It was flown over San Antonio and again over Washington-on-the-Brazos, March 2, 1836, the day the Declaration of Independence was presented to the Convention. She was born in 1812; died in 1848.

Twentieth-century descendants include the families of Samuel J. Watson, Albert Allen Dinn, Frank M. McKinney. (DRT no. 6979.)

JOHN DURST (A Texan Paul Revere)

Durst was an Indian trader and army officer who learned of the invasion plans of Santa Anna in 1835 and rode with the news to East Texas in twelve and a half days to give warning. (See the Carriage Trade of the Republic, where he is listed under Nacogdoches County.)

Twentieth-century descendants include the families of Robert E. Moss, John S. Durst, William Putegnat, Thomas Walter Blake, John Walter Blake, Barlow Lee Jones, Wilbourn Sandford, Horatio Durst, James Pinkney Hall, Simmons Sutherland Hopkins, Eugene Erastus Bateman, George Gordon Lewis, C. Raymond Ulmer, L. L. Moore. (DRT nos. 396, 3207, 3593, 4256, 4465, 5493.)

THE DUVALS OF GOLIAD (County Namers)

Burr H. Duval, a captain in command of Volunteers of the 1st Regiment of the Texas Army, was killed at the Goliad Massacre. His brother John Crittenden Duval (called "Texas John") escaped to become a surveyor and a Texas Ranger, dying in 1891 at a ripe old age with a reputation as the first Texas man of letters, which included a celebrated account of his remarkable escape from Goliad and the adventures of Bigfoot Wallace, who yarned to his pal with great gusto. Brother Thomas Howard Duval was a Texas official holding a number of offices. The Duvals came from Kentucky, where their father, William Pope Duval, had moved from Mount Comfort, Virginia, before becoming governor of Florida. He later practiced law in Galveston, and Sam Houston was one of his clients. Duval County was named in honor of this family.

Twentieth-century descendants include the families of Paul Randolph Stalnaker, Edward Sidney Bock, Jr. (DRT no. 6694.)

WILLIAM MOSBY EASTLAND (First "Black Bean")

Eastland was a 1st Lieutenant in Thomas J. Robb's Company at San Jacinto, and a Texas Ranger until 1838. In the Somervell and Mier expeditions, Eastland was executed by the Mexicans in 1843, being the first of the prisoners to draw one of the infamous black beans. Born in Woodford County, Kentucky, in 1806. He first married Florence Yellowly; his second marriage was to Louisa M. M. Smith. Eastland County was named in his honor.

MRS. ANGELINA BELLE EBERLY
(Of Austin Cannon Firing Fame)

Mrs. Eberly fired a cannon at the departing forces under Thomas I. Smith, who were dispatched by President Houston to carry away with them the nation's archives when their destruction was threatened by Mexican invasion in 1842. A posse of Austin citizens sent to catch up and return the archives to the capital succeeded later that day. The citizens of Austin felt their capital was preserved as a result. Mrs. Eberly was a prominent hotelier. She and her first husband, Alexander G. Peyton, ran a hotel in San Felipe de Austin before the Revolution, which was burned down by Mexicans during the Runaway Scrape. Until then, it served as the rendezvous for the heroes and notables of the Republic-to-be. In 1836 she married Captain Jacob Eberly, eventually founding Eberly House in Austin in 1839. In 1847 she purchased the Tavern House in Galveston, where she died in 1860.

BENJAMIN EDWARDS (Founder of the Republic of Fredonia)

But for Stephen Austin, Texas might be called Fredonia today. How? The phenomenon in the early nineteenth century of adventurers founding settler states was more common than is supposed. In the case of the Boers of South Africa and of the Texans it worked. The most eccentric case of the reverse was the Frenchman who briefly established himself with South American Indians as Emperor of Araucania and Patagonia (a pretender still exists) in a Kiplingesque kingdom at the end of the world. Indeed, the notion of such states was so familiar then that it was possible during the 1830s for British swindlers to sell land grants in the name of the bogus "King of the Mosquito Shore and Nation," which "country" they demurely named as "Poyais" (one may still buy "title" to 100 acres of Poyaisian land for about $300 at auctions of old stock and bond certificates). The attempt by Benjamin Edwards four years before the Texan Declaration of Independence, along with 30 followers, to proclaim the independent Republic of Fredonia (a future signer of the Texan Declaration, familiarly known as "The Ring-tailed Panther," was a president), might well have been successful but for the disapproval of his own brother, the failure to make good on a treaty to divide Texas with the Indians, and the combined forces of the Mexicans and of Stephen Austin, who together put the Fredonian Rebellion down. The Fredonians then fled across the Sabine River. Edwards himself remained in Mississippi and was active in recruitment there for Texas during the Revolution. He died in 1837. Born in Stafford County, Virginia, in 1771.

HADEN EDWARDS (Of Edwards Colony Fame)

Edwards secured an empresario contract from Mexico in 1825 to settle 800 families, which he located in the Nacogdoches area, one of the oldest of the settled areas. While absent, his hot-headed brother helped launch the Fredonian Rebellion aimed at dividing Texas between the Indians and the Republic of Fredonia. The Indians missed the opportunity presented, and the Fredonians fled across the Sabine River pursued by Mexican militia. Born in Stafford County, Virginia, in 1771. Married Susanna Beall. Six children (survived). Died in Nacogdoches in 1849. Edwards County is named in his honor.

Twentieth-century descendants include the families of George A. Darden, Joseph Warren Speight, Louis O. Durst. (DRT nos. 376, 2467.)

GEORGE B. ERATH (County Namer)

An Austrian from Vienna, Erath came to Texas as a qualified surveyor in 1833. He fought at San Jacinto in the volunteer group of Jesse

Billingsley. Later he was active in the legislature of the Republic. Born in 1813. Died in Waco in 1891. Erath County is named in his honor.

DR. ALEXANDER WRAY EWING (Chief Surgeon at San Jacinto)

Ewing was appointed chief surgeon to the Texas Army. He was later active in railroads. Born in Londonderry, Northern Ireland, in 1809. He was given a grant in Austin's fifth colony. He studied medicine at Edinburgh University. He married Mrs. Susan Henrietta (Smiley) Reid first; Elizabeth Graham second. Two children (by his second wife). Died in 1853.

Twentieth-century descendants include the families of McWillie Martin, Hubert Elmer Gotcher, Samuel Dock Gupton. (DRT no. 349.)

JAMES WALKER FANNIN, JR. (Goliad Leader)

One of the great heroes of the Texan Revolution and leader in the Goliad campaign, Colonel Fannin was wounded in the Coleto battle. He was executed in his bed at the mission on the day of the massacre of prisoners following the surrender. Three hundred and forty-two men are believed to have been marched out of the fort, divided into three groups and shot by firing squads, only 28 making good their escape. Twenty doctors, nurses, interpreters and other noncombatants, however, were saved by Francisca Alvarez ("The Angel of Goliad"), wife of an enemy officer. Some she saved by hiding them on the fort's parapet. Like the battle cry "Remember the Alamo," so also was "Remember the Goliad" reputedly heard in the charge to victory at San Jacinto later in that crucible year of 1836. As soon as Fannin arrived in Texas in 1834 he became an agitator. He participated at the Battle of Gonzales and led the Texan forces in the battle of Concepción. Born in Georgia in 1804. Married Minerva Fort. Two daughters. Fannin County is named in his honor.

REBECCA JANE FISHER
("Mother of Texas" and Republic Orphan)

The only woman ever elected to the Texas Veterans Association and its last surviving member, Rebecca Fisher was also honored for many years by the legislature with requests to open its sessions with prayers. She was born to Philadelphian parents, Mary and Johnson Gilleland, who were killed by Indians on their ranch in 1840 when she was nine years old. She herself was captured by Indians but rescued by that romantic senior officer of the Republic and Confederacy, Albert Sidney Johnston. At thirteen, the orphan beauty rejected the marriage suit of a German nobleman, marrying at seventeen a Methodist minister named Orceneth Fisher, who was also a publisher of religious periodicals and tracts. There were six children. She joined her husband in his pastoral work, making arduous journeys across the West, particularly to Oregon. In her last 32 years she was president of the Daughters of the Republic of Texas, and helped implement Clara Driscoll's efforts to save the Alamo. She died in 1926 in Austin at the age of ninety-five. Although a child during the Republic, we include Rebecca Fisher to represent the brave and talented children of that nation.

Twentieth-century descendants include the families of Seth J. Mabry, Henry Morrow Little, Benjamin Fletcher Wright, Lena Simpson, John D. Brown, John Bernard Johnson, James Vernon Gibson, Robert L. Lamb, Robert William Brown, Dr. Patrick H. McKay, Josiah Creg Davidson, Edward Earnest Graf, Sterling Fisher, John Roger Langford. (DRT nos. 274, 907, 942, 1848, 3086, 3161, 3980, 4515, 5113, 7886.)

MAÑUEL FLORES (San Jacinto and The Carriage Trade)
Flores fought at San Jacinto with the Spanish-Texans in the company of his fellow San Antonian Juan N. Seguin as Seguin's first sergeant. He settled in Gonzales on the Guadalupe, taking up ranching (see entry under The Carriage Trade of the Republic). Married twice; the second marriage to Margarita Garza. He was killed at the Battle of San Gabriel in 1868.

BENJAMIN CROMWELL FRANKLIN (Messenger of Victory)
Franklin bore the good tidings of the victory at San Jacinto to President Burnet on Galveston Island. He took part in the battle as a private, after first having tried for a command as captain. He was the first to hold a judicial post in the Republic as a result of the urgent need to adjudicate on the matter of the capture of a brig owned by a U.S. citizen by the Texas Navy, without causing a diplomatic incident through delay. In 1836 he was appointed by Houston to the Supreme Court. He represented Galveston County in three of the legislatures. (See Carriage

Trade of the Republic entry.) He was born in Georgia in 1805. Married Eliza Carter Brantley first; Estelle B. Maxwell second. Two children (by the first wife). Died in Galveston in 1873. It is generally accepted that Franklin County was named after him.

Twentieth-century descendants include the families of Charles Milton Kemp, Hedley Vicars Jackson, Franklin Buchanan Kemp, James Milton Carnes, Robert Edwin Kemp, Charles Sumner Rudloff. (DRT nos. 68, 1662, 6142, 7205.)

BENJAMIN FRANKLIN FRY (The "Fighting Parson")

Fry was a Baptist Minister who is said to have preached under five of the "Six Flags over Texas," becoming known as the "Fighting Parson." He was at the siege of Bexar, at San Jacinto, and fought later in the Mexican War. He was born in Wilkes County, Georgia, in 1800. Married Nancy Carter in 1829. He preached his final sermon* on the day of his death in Jeddo, Bastrop County, 1872.

Twentieth-century descendants include the families of Samuel H. Hopkins, Joseph Harmon Grant. (DRT no. 2504.)

GEORGE WASHINGTON GLASSCOCK
(Abraham Lincoln's Fellow Flatboater)

Glasscock opened the first flour mill in West Texas, an early pioneer in wheat growing in Texas. He was a partner of Abraham Lincoln in flatboating on the Sangamon River. He moved to Texas to partake in the Grass Fight and the siege of Bexar. After annexation, he helped manage the Austin lunatic asylum. Born in Hardin County, Kentucky, in 1810. Married Cynthia C. Knight in 1840. Died in 1879. Glasscock County is named in his honor. (See also Carriage Trade, under Jasper County.)

Twentieth-century descendants include the families of Albert Hor-

---

* There were few churches in those days. Saloons sometimes had to make do, requiring on the part of a saloon keeper a certain degree of introduction: "Oyez, oyez, there's goin to be some hell-fired racket here this mornin', gents, by Fightin' Parson Potter, a reformed gambler, but now a shore-nuff gospel shark . . . the Devil's gonna git ye quicker 'n' Hell kin scorch a feather." Religion generally came late to the Republic. Although the Baptist J. H. Pilgrim founded a Sunday School in Austin's colony, a Catholic mission to the new nation in 1836 found there to be only two priests in the whole of Texas. The Methodists came in the persons of the Reverend Martin Ruter and his assistants Robert Alexander and Littleton Fowler in 1836. The first Lutheran may have been the Reverend Louis C. Ervenberg, a German. The first Protestant Episcopalian, Caleb S. Ives, arrived in 1838.

ton Glasscock, George Washington Glasscock, L. L. Redford, William Samuel Sellers, James M. Keese, W. J. Compton, Seth Darnaby Breeding. (DRT nos. 4684, 4840, 4900, 4954.)

WILLIAM GOYENS (A Carriage Trade Mulatto)

Legends sprouted in Nacogdoches about this mulatto Texan who made a fortune in real estate, despite the efforts to impede his progress on the part of white neighbors and with the help of top lawyers and Texan notables such as Thomas J. Rusk and Charles S. Taylor. His mansion was known as "Goyens' Hill." His father was a free mulatto in North Carolina; his mother a white woman. He married a white woman, Mary Pate Sibley, but had no issue by her. He came to Nacogdoches in 1820 at age twenty-six as an illiterate. There, he combined business skills and legal arbitration, often being deputed to negotiate with the Indians. Seized in Louisiana for slavery, he bargained his way out and later had the agreement he signed annulled. Died in 1856.

PETER WILLIAM GRAYSON (County Namer)

Born in Bardstown, Kentucky, in 1788, Grayson joined Stephen Austin's colony in 1830, bringing with him extensive capital. He became great friends with Austin after succeeding in having him released on bail in Mexico, becoming Austin's aide-de-camp during the Revolution. He and Collinsworth were dispatched to Washington in 1836 in order to obtain recognition of Texan independence and the United States mediation between Texas and Mexico. He was nominated to succeed Houston as president, but committed suicide when in ill health in 1838. Grayson County was named in his honor.

THOMAS GREEN (Adventurer, Artillerist and Princeton Graduate)

The Princeton law graduate fought as a private in Isaac N. Moreland's Company at the Battle of San Jacinto, one of the gun crew of the famous "Twin Sisters." From 1841–1861, as clerk of the Texas Supreme Court, he still found time to soldier in the Vásquez and Somervell episodes, and again in the Mexican War. The Civil War found him a brigadier general. Born in Amelia County, Virginia, in 1814. Married Mary Watson Chalmers. He was killed in action in 1864. Tom Green County is named in his honor.

JARED E. GROCE and *LEONARD WALLER GROCE*
(Firsts in Cotton)

Both Groce brothers were prominent in cotton and were the first to bring a cotton gin to Texas. Jared's Bernardo Plantation was inherited by Leonard in 1835 from father Jared. The "Twin Sisters" cannon were mounted at Bernardo when they arrived in Texas. Sam Houston used the site of the cotton mill where Jared built his mansion to organize a regiment just a week before the Battle of San Jacinto. Leonard supplied corn and beef to the army. The Groce fortune began when father Jared arrived with Stephen Austin's Old Three Hundred complete with 50 covered wagons and all the trappings of a wealthy Georgia planter. By 1838, Leonard was paying taxes on 67,000 acres of Texas. (See the Austin County entry under Carriage Trade of the Republic.) A prominent member of the Texas carriage trade, Leonard was bankrupted by Reconstruction after the War Between the States. Jared was born on a Virginia plantation in 1782; Leonard in Georgia in 1806. Leonard married Courtney Ann Fulton; they had 11 children. Leonard died in 1873.

Twentieth-century descendants include the families of William Wharton Groce, Robert James Calder, George Berlet, Charles Woodbury Salmon, Jared Ellison Groce IV and V, Haddon B. Woods, William M. Bennatt, James Coleman Bennatt, Mabry A. Bouknight, Joseph C. Allen, Charles Courtenay Groce, James B. Mackey, John Wharton Berlet, Charles Gardner Greenwood, Frank Gilson Knapp, Louis Edward Pauls, James McClure Cravens, Edward John Joseph, Louis Edward Livingston. (DRT nos. 471, 472, 1116, 1153, 1440, 2191, 2876, 3130, 3188, 4081, 4608, 6115, 6185.)

JOHN C. HALE (One of the Nine Killed at San Jacinto)

Hale was a junior officer in Captain Benjamin F. Bryant's Company when killed in the Battle of San Jacinto. He settled in Sabine County in 1831. He was born in Maine. Hale County is named in his honor.

JOHN W. ("CAPTAIN JACK") HALL
(Old Three Hundred and Carriage Trade)

Starting out with the Old Three Hundred in comparatively humble circumstances, Captain Jack, as he came to be called, was a bigwig by the time he and Dr. Asa Hoxey founded the Washington Townsite Company to promote the town where the Declaration of Independence was eventually signed. (See entry under Carriage Trade.) Born in South Carolina about 1780. Married Patsy Robinson. Died in 1845.

WARREN D. C. HALL (County Namer)

Born in North Carolina in 1788, Hall fought in the Mexican Republican Army of the North in 1812, and was a captain in the Gutiérrez-Magee Expedition. He resigned in horror at the massacre of prisoners. He located in Brazoria County. Appointed adjutant general by Burnet, he was an obvious candidate for secretary of war in the Republic. He died a lawyer-resident on Galveston Island in 1867. Hall County is named in his honor.

MRS. DILUE (ROSE) HARRIS (Lady Chronicler)

Mrs. Harris arrived in Texas in 1833 and married Ira A. Harris there, mothering nine children. Mrs. Harris was intimately acquainted with the leaders of the Texas Republic. Her impressions published in the quarterly of the Texas State Historical Association and in the Eagle *Headlight* are an important source of early Texas history. She died at Eagle Lake at age eighty-nine in 1914.

Twentieth-century descendants include the families of George Yergler, Christian Joseph Hahn, Hugh F. McKay. (DRT nos. 51, 251.)

JOHN RICHARDSON HARRIS (County Namer)

Harris met Moses Austin in Missouri and arrived in Texas in his own vessel in 1824 to settle. He owned ships on the passage between New Orleans and Texas, including the *Rights of Man.* Born in Cayuga, New York, in 1790. Married Jane Birdsall. Four children. Died in 1829. Harris County is named in his honor.

Twentieth-century descendants include the families of Joseph Milton Howe, Knox Briscoe Howe. (DRT no. 5844.)

JONAS HARRISON ("The Patrick Henry of Texas")

Harrison's resolution at San Augustine proposing immediate independence from Mexico in 1835 earned him his fame as the Patrick Henry of Texas. He was also Houston's divorce lawyer in the case of Eliza Allen, Houston's first wife. Born in Woodbridge Township, New Jersey, in 1777. Died in 1836. Harrison County was named in his honor on its creation in 1839.

CHARLES READY HASKELL (Goliad Martyr and County Namer)

Born in Tennessee in 1817, the young Haskell joined the Texan Revolution straight from school, enlisting in Burr H. Duval's Company under James Fannin. After fighting in the Coleto engagement he was among those who perished in the Goliad Massacre. Haskell County was named in honor of the young hero.

JOHN COFFEE (JACK) HAYS (Texas Ranger)

Jack Hays was one of the more celebrated Indian fighters and Texas Rangers. The defeat of the Comanche from the summit of Enchanted Rock represented one of his more notable actions. He led a caravan to California during the gold rush, where he died in Piedmont in 1883. Born at Little Cedar Lick, Wilson County, Tennessee, in 1817. Married a Miss Calvert of Seguin, Texas. He died rich and made frequent return visits to Texas. Hays County is named in his honor.

JAMES PINCKNEY HENDERSON (County Namer and Diplomat)

Henderson held a number of offices under the Republic, first as attorney general under Houston, then secretary of state, and minister to Britain and France, who were persuaded by him to recognize Texan independence. He negotiated annexation while in Washington. First governor of the new state after it joined the Union, he became a U. S. senator later. Born in Lincolnton, North Carolina. He was numbered among the most able lawyers of the Republic. Married Frances Cox of Philadelphia while in London. Their mansion in San Augustine was modeled after an important Virginian neoclassical example. Died in 1858. Henderson County is named in his honor.

Twentieth-century descendants include the families of J. Pinckney Henderson Adams, Clemens Edward von Preuschen. (DRT nos. 919, 1114.)

GEORGE WASHINGTON HILL (County Namer)

Houston appointed Hill an Indian agent first, and later as secretary of war and navy. He was reappointed by President Anson Jones. In the war he served as a surgeon. He was born in Warren County, Tennessee, in 1814. Married Matilda Slaughter. Died in 1860. Hill County was named in his honor.

WILLIAM G. HILL (A Carriage Trade Veteran)

In Brazoria County's plantation-rich carriage trade (see entry under Carriage Trade of the Republic), Hill ranked as what we would regard today as a two-limousine man. He participated in the Grass Fight, the Battle of Concepción and the siege of Bexar. Living in well-earned luxury, he was in later Republic years to serve on the Supreme Court. Birth and death particulars are not known.

ALBERT CLINTON HORTON (Planter, Carriage Trade, Senator)

One of the wealthiest men in the Republic was Albert C. Horton, who owned extensive sugar and cotton holdings in Matagorda. He represented Matagorda along with other counties in the senate, where he was an active upholder of the code of honor on dueling. An unresolved argument over whether William H. Wharton or Secretary of the Navy Rhoads Fisher had first priority to duel with Horton was a typical example of how many duels were avoided, Fisher being the friend of Horton and obliging him with a convenient challenge! Horton was a leader in the Goliad campaign, and was generally regarded as having done the wise thing in not joining Fannin there, given the odds against his force succeeding. He was born in Georgia in 1798. Married Eliza Holiday in 1829. Died in 1865.

MARGARET MOFFETTE LEA HOUSTON (And Children)

Margaret Moffette Lea met Sam Houston in 1839 at her brother's home in Alabama. A week later they promised to marry, doing so in 1840 before Houston's return to the presidency of the Republic. While managing his farm and other affairs with great competence, she spent much of her time writing poems and love letters to an absent husband, as well as playing the harp and piano. Eight children survived to adult life, although she herself succumbed at age fifty-six to the yellow fever in 1867. Sam, Jr. (a prisoner in the War Between the States), Andrew Jackson (the oldest senator ever to survive in the United States Congress), and Temple Lea Houston (who settled in the Panhandle) were the three most notable sons. A daughter, Nettie Power Bringhurst, was awarded first prize by the *Bohemian,* a Fort Worth magazine, for the best poem on the Alamo. Other poems of hers include "The Lone Star Flag of Texas." She was state historian of The Daughters of the Republic of Texas, and one of its earliest members. Her husband, W. L. Bringhurst, was a professor.

For Twentieth-century descendants, see Sam Houston under Signers of the Declaration of Independence, entry No. 37.

DR. ASA HOXEY (Planter and Bookman)

Dr. Hoxey participated in the siege of Bexar after moving from Alabama to Texas and setting up two large plantations. Houston made him medical censor to the Republic. He owned a fine library and contributed to Baylor University and other educational institutions. He formed a company with others to promote the town of Washington-on-the-Brazos. (See entry under Carriage Trade of the Republic.) Born in Savannah, Georgia, in 1800. Died in 1863.

Twentieth-century descendants include the families of James M. Williams, Thomas Robert Rivers. (DRT no. 399.)

MEMUCAN HUNT (County Namer and Presidential Duelist)

Houston sent General Hunt to Washington to obtain the recognition of Texas by the United States, a task he and fellow agent William H. Wharton successfully accomplished. He then became minister in Washington. Under Lamar he was secretary of the navy. Hunt challenged President Lamar to a duel after being accused of having a "weak and vulgar mind," to which Lamar responded that he could not "allow the call which is made upon my chivalry to go unresponded to," and thereupon agreed to fight. General Albert Sidney Johnson and four other honorable men, however, mediated the dispute. Without such mediations the death toll of Republic notables could have become catastrophic. Compensation for the fortune he spent in the cause of Texas took the form of land, which he sought to improve by promoting a railroad between Galveston Bay and Red River. Born in Vance County, North Carolina, in 1807. Died in 1856. Hunt County is named in his honor.

IRA INGRAM (Old Three Hundred Patriot)

A Vermonter, Ingram came to Texas with his brother, Seth, as members of Stephen Austin's Old Three Hundred at age thirty-eight. The brothers became merchants, Ira achieving prominence as a Mexican alcalde. He and Philip Dimmit drafted the Goliad Declaration of Independence at the Convention of 1835, where Ingram acted as secretary. He died mayor of Matagorda in 1837, leaving $70,000 for the support of Matagorda schools.

ANNA RAGUET IRION (Beloved of Sam Houston)

Houston tried to secure a divorce in order to marry Anna Raguet, who came to Texas in 1833 with her father, Henry Raguet (see Carriage Trade of the Republic), and settled in Nacogdoches. Houston eventually used his influence as president to win a divorce, but not sufficiently to satisfy Anna Raguet, who married Robert Anderson Irion instead. Dr. Irion, Houston's secretary of state, had been acting as go-between for the two. Irion County is supposedly named for Irion. Anna Raguet was born in Philadelphia in 1819. She died in 1883.

Twentieth-century descendants include the families of Lawrence Sterne Taylor, Carl Henry Rulfs. (DRT nos. 3494, 3254.)

WILLIAM HOUSTON JACK and PATRICK CHURCHILL JACK (County Namers)

William Jack fought at San Jacinto in the Columbia Company of William H. Patton. He was Burnet's secretary of state in the ad interim government in 1836. Earlier he fought in the Vásquez action. He is believed by some to have authored the Turtle Bay Resolutions in 1832. He was born in Wilkes County, Georgia, in 1806. Married Laura Harrison. Died in 1844 in Brazoria.

His brother, Patrick Jack, was one of those who were jailed in the Anahuac disturbances that led to the Turtle Bay Resolutions. He was born in 1808. Married Margaret E. Smith. Died in 1844 in the same year as his brother. Jack County is assumed to have been named in their honor.

Twentieth-century descendants include the members of the family of Robert Henry Carmichael. (DRT no. 801.)

GENERAL ALBERT SIDNEY JOHNSON (A Texan Martyr at Shiloh)

One of the great and noble soldiers of the early Confederacy, whose death as Confederate commander at Shiloh may have lost them the battle, Johnson began soldiering in the Black Hawk War and enlisted as a private in the Texas Army in 1836. A rapid career saw him made secretary of war under President Lamar in 1839. Born in Washington, Kentucky, in 1803. Married Eliza Griffin, cousin of his first wife.

FRANCIS WHITE JOHNSON (Stormed the Alamo)

With Ben Milam, Johnson led the attack on San Antonio, and after Milam's death, led the assault on the Alamo in 1835. The next year, leading the Matamoros Expedition, he and four other men were all who escaped. After the Revolution he was in the land business around Austin. He had been alcalde at San Felipe de Austin in 1831, a year later he was a captain in the Anahuac disturbances. Born in Leesburg, Virginia, in 1799. The five-volume work under his name called the *History of Texas and Texans* was edited posthumously from his manuscripts.

ANSON JONES
(Last President of the Republic and the Machiavelli of Annexation)

Anson was elected president in 1844. His canny, reticent "policy of alternatives" earned him his title of "Architect of Independence." He engaged in diplomacy and trade relations with Europe as Houston's minister to the United States, with a view to making Texas either more attractive to United States annexation or strong enough to remain independent, policies he continued persistently to pursue as president of the Republic, despite popular pressures for a more open pursuit of annexation. Protests included his burning in effigy. On January 19, 1846, he was able to announce "the Republic of Texas is no more." He retired to become a prosperous planter. He was one of those who established the first Masonic lodge in Texas in 1835. The future President Jones was an M.D. when he arrived in Nacogdoches in 1833, his practice in Brazoria bringing in $5,000 a year. He joined the army and was surgeon to the 2nd Regiment at San Jacinto where he found Juan Almonte's *Journal and Order Book* (also known as *The Statistical Report of Texas*), a valuable source on the Texas of that time. He challenged James Collinsworth to a duel while expelling him from office in Brazoria. He then took up politics. Born in Great Barrington, Massachusetts, in 1798. Married Mrs. McCrory in Austin in 1840. He was buried in Houston. Jones County is named in his honor.

Twentieth-century descendants include the families of Charles Elliot Ashe, Clayton S. Scott. (DRT nos. 736, 1576.)

DR. LEVI JONES

Jones was one of the organizers and an early agent of the Galveston
City Company. He was also the physician present at Austin's death.
Born in Virginia in 1792. Married. Four children. Died in Galveston in
1879.

DAVID SPANGLER KAUFMAN (County Namer and Princetonian)

The Princeton graduate moved to Texas with a classical education
and honors degree in 1837 from Louisiana, from where he had helped the
colonists. He fought as a major against Cherokees. During a dispute over
a bill in the Texan congress, Kaufman was shot twice in the side by a
fellow legislator, but recovered. He was one of the most prominent of
lawyer-orators in the Republic. After local and state offices, he became
the first Texan seated in the U. S. House of Representatives. He was
born in Pennsylvania in 1813. Married Jane Baxter Richardson. Died in
1851. Kaufman County is named in his honor.

Twentieth-century descendants include the family of Welborn Barton, Jr. (DRT no. 6253.)

GEORGE WILKINS KENDALL
(Newspaperman and County Namer)

A newspaperman of ambition and with a sense of adventure, Kendall was captured on the Santa Fe Expedition in 1841, his account becoming a classic. He was a founder of the *New Orleans Picayune*, but
settled in the county named in his honor in his lifetime. Born in Mount
Vernon, New Hampshire, in 1809. Married Adeline de Valcourt. Four
children. Died in 1862. Kendall County is named in his honor.

Twentieth-century descendants include the family of Eugene J.
Fellowes. (DRT no. 468.)

JAMES KERR (County Namer)

Kerr reputedly was the first to harvest land in the Old Three Hundred colony of Stephen Austin, his close friend. In the Texan congress in

later years, he presented bills to ban dueling and to relocate the capital at Austin. In surveying for the DeWitt colony, he first built his cabin at Kerr's Creek. For Old Three Hundred folk, his house became a place of hospitality pioneer-style for all. Married Sarah Fulton, a foster daughter of John S. Linn. A daughter survived from an earlier marriage. Born in Kentucky, September of 1790. Died in 1850. Kerr County is named in his honor.

Twentieth-century descendants include the families of Courtney Stuart Simons, Thomas Kerr Simons, Joseph Moody Ray, William Henry Crain, Owen Walter Womack, John Milton Canavan, Paul H. Herder, Joseph Augustus Sullivan, Hugh Bourke Lowery, Louis Champ Traylor, James Kerr Crain, Fletcher Stockdale Schleicher, Weldon Steinman, R. H. Wilkin, Joseph Daniel Mitchell. (DRT nos. 584, 762, 1809, 5140, 6213, 6283, 6432, 7069, 8039.)

ROBERT JUSTUS KLEBERG (Of King Ranch Fame)

Kleberg participated at the Battle of San Jacinto in Moseley Baker's Company. He and his family settled near Cat Spring in 1835, where their home was destroyed in the Runaway Scrape. He held various local offices and moved to Corpus Christi as a lawyer, where Richard King became one of his clients. Upon King's death, Kleberg was invited by Mrs. King to take over what became the most famous ranch in all Texas. He married her daughter Alice, and they had five children. He was born in Westphalia, Germany, in 1803. Died in 1888. Kleberg County was named in his honor.

Twentieth-century descendants include the families of Edward Henry Schwab, Edward Allen Palmer, Thomas Edward Swaney, Charles F. Hoff, Otto Ludwig Eckhardt, Col. W. W. Sterling, William Earle Rankin, Robert Lewis Lee Moody, Robert Rufus Lott. (DRT nos. 1726, 2349, 4757, 4976, 6960, 7644.) Richard Mifflin Kleberg.

GEORGE A. LAMB (County Namer and Martyr at San Jacinto)

Lamb was one of the nine killed at San Jacinto on April 21, 1836. He was a 2nd lieutenant in William Ware's Company. Lamb came to Texas in 1834. He married Mrs. Sarah Bankhead, whose family he had been protecting from Indians where they had settled in present Walker

County. He was born in the Laurens District, South Carolina, in 1814. Lamb County was later named in his honor.

Twentieth-century descendants include the families of William Jeptha Fain, Samuel Leslie Anders. (DRT no. 1980.)

THEODORE LEGER (Castigator of Quacks)

Theodore Leger was a French physician who owned a newspaper and who was in Texas from around 1838. Dr. Leger liked to rail against quacks as being "more dangerous than the hostile Indians; and not considerably less numerous. . . . We had rather see a company of armed Mexicans in battle array than a squad of these *grave* gentry." Yellow fever was the other great killer of Texas. Leger described typical treatment of the "self-styled doctors [who] hurry to pour down their incendiary drugs, to administer purgatives, vomitives, bleeding and cupping, and to bring into play all the resources of their pharmaceutick arsenal. Calomel and Blue-pills from their heavy artillery; then advance, in second rank, Jalap and Rhubarb; Epsom-salts and Castor oil bring up the rear." Death was often the cavalry which completed the rout as a result of such multiple assaults on the system.

ASA MILES LEWIS (Carriage Trade)

A landowner in Colorado and Washington counties and a fine lawyer and orator, Lewis represented Colorado County in the important Seventh Congress. His possession of a carriage (see entry under Carriage Trade of the Republic) was no doubt used in his electioneering. He also appears to have been an authority on railroads and a promoter of them.

Twentieth-century descendants include the families of William Gaston Wilkins, Alfred Addison Farley, John Asa Wilkins, Arthur Jackson Eastham, George Samuel Parker. (DRT nos. 239, 408, 2034, 2768, 2790.)

JUDGE ABNER SMITH LIPSCOMB (County Namer)

Secretary of state under President Lamar during 1840, Lipscomb was a lawyer working on the General Land Office report and an associate justice on the Texas Supreme Court later. He was born in the Abbeville

District, South Carolina, in 1789. Married Elizabeth Gains in 1813. Died in 1856. Lipscomb County is named in his honor.

Twentieth-century descendants include the families of J. Sim Foster, Thomas Hunt Lipscomb, B. D. Baugh. (DRT nos. 840, 948, 1989.)

JANE HERBERT WILKINSON LONG ("The Mother of Texas")

Jane Long was the first known woman of English descent to enter Texas and bore the first known child of such parentage in the state. She was the wife of Dr. James Long, who led the Long Expedition across the Sabine in 1819 to Nacogdoches where its citizens organized a "government" declaring the independence of Texas. When the Mexicans retaliated, Long allied himself with Mexican liberals. After her husband's demise, "The Mother of Texas," as she was called, was rescued from a rude fort where only she, her daughter and a slave girl called Kiamatia (descendants living in Richmond in 1900) survived a hard winter. Mrs. Long returned to Texas with the "Old Three Hundred" in 1824, where she made a buckskin suit for Austin, and ran a hotel frequented by notables, who included Benjamin Milam, an admirer. Mirabeau Lamar made his headquarters at another of her hotels in Richmond in 1837, and dedicated to her a poem entitled "Bonnie Jane." She was born in Charles County, Maryland, in 1798. Died in 1880.

Twentieth-century descendants include the family of Jerome Farbar. (DRT no. 1353.)

JAMES LOVE (Carriage Trade and Politician)

A successful planter on the Brazos River, Love was also a partisan politician and jurist. His Galveston home was a rallying point for opponents of Houston. (See entry under Carriage Trade of the Republic.) Born in Bardstown, Kentucky, in 1795. Died in 1874 "an impediment to Reconstruction."

THOMAS S. LUBBOCK (County Namer)

A young lieutenant on the Texan Santa Fe Expedition in 1841, Lubbock jumped from a balcony to escape the Mexicans and in time to join the Somervell Expedition. Later he became a leader of the Texas Rangers under Terry. He came to Texas with the New Orleans Greys to join in the siege of Bexar. Born in Charleston, South Carolina, in 1817. Died in 1862. Lubbock County is named in his honor.

BEN MCCULLOCH (Texas Ranger and County Namer)

One of the leaders of the Texas Rangers, McCulloch was a friend of Davy Crockett before the two came to Texas from Tennessee. He manned one of the famous "Twin Sisters" cannon, which played such a decisive role in the Battle of San Jacinto. He participated in Indian fighting during the Republic, and against the Mexicans; was at the Plum Creek Fight; with Zachary Taylor at the Battle of Buena Vista; and died in battle at Elk Horn during the Civil War in 1862. He was born in 1811 in Rutherford, Tennessee. McCulloch County was named in his honor.

THOMAS F. MCKINNEY and *SAMUEL M. WILLIAMS*
(Bankers of Texas)

Two of the most prominent bankers of early Texas, they helped finance the Texan Revolution, at one time owning a fifth of Galveston and supporting railroads, notably the Brazos and Galveston Railroad. McKinney was one of Austin's "Old Three Hundred," but after the Revolution fell afoul of cotton speculation and died without surviving issue. Williams served in his early Texan years as Austin's indispensable and competent assistant, fluent in French and Spanish, writing all three languages in a fine Spencerian hand. McKinney's pedigreed racehorses were celebrated throughout Central Texas, and he trained them on his own track. Williams married Sarah Scott, daughter of "Old Three Hundred" settler William Scott, who provided the blue silk for one of the first Lone Star flags borne into battle by Volunteers. The firm of McKinney Williams & Co. fell into bad times after Williams' death in 1858 and was closed.

Twentieth-century descendants of Samuel M. Williams include the families of Charles W. Gill, Alexander J. Caldwell, Thomas J. League, John Edward Kaufmann. (DRT nos. 328, 1171, 3063.)

NEIL MCLENNAN (County Namer)

This Scottish Highlander came over the sea from Skye to North Carolina in 1801 and thence to Florida, arriving with brothers John and

Laughlin and their families in an old schooner at upriver Fort Bend. His brothers were both in due course killed by Indians. While Indian fighting, Neil saw and later settled in the land now called McLennan County. Born in Skye, Scotland, in 1787. Died in 1867.

Twentieth-century descendants include the families of Alonzo Seth Bowles, Jr., Victor T. Newman, R. M. Holstead, Duncan McLennan, E. L. McLennan, John L. Alford, Gene Maddin, Henry Forest Clay, William Erath McLennan, Andrew H. Miller. (DRT nos. 1566, 3065, 3189, 3885, 3964, 5847.)

PLEASANT D. MCNEEL
(San Jacinto, Old Three Hundred and Carriage Trade)

McNeel was one of Stephen Austin's Old Three Hundred to fight at San Jacinto. He also fought at the Battle of Gonzales, the Lexington of the Texas Revolution. By 1840, it appears he was part of Brazoria's rich plantation set (see entry under Carriage Trade of the Republic). Born in Kentucky in 1796. Died in 1871 at Gulf Prairie.

PAMELA MANN (Society's Disorderly Hotelier)

One of the most individualist women of the Republic, Pamela Mann opened a famous hotel called the Mansion House in Houston, which won a reputation for constant disorder involving brawls, duels and police raids. She was even condemned to death for forgery at one point, until Sam Houston saved her. Despite all this, she was well regarded and moved in the best of peerage circles, son Flournoy Hunt's wedding being quite an event for notables and heroes of the Republic. Preceding her occupation as hotelier, she supplied the oxen to draw the "Twin Sisters" used at San Jacinto, but withdrew them before the battle because Houston turned toward Harrisburg, Pamela Mann having struck a deal that the cannon and the army would move on Nacogdoches. Married to Marshall Mann, she and her family arrived in Texas in 1834. Died in 1840.

WYLIE MARTIN (County Namer)

As one of Stephen Austin's Old Three Hundred, Wylie Martin was at least one who felt the Declaration of Independence premature. He was a professional soldier. He came to Texas in 1823 after killing a man in a duel. As a member of the Texas Senate, he tried to have his slave, Peter, emancipated for fighting alongside him in the Revolution. Born in Georgia in 1776; died in 1842. Martin County was named in his honor.

MARY ADAMS ("MA") MAVERICK

Mary was the matriarch of the important Texas clan of Maverick and the wife of Samuel Augustus Maverick (see Signers of the Declaration of Independence, entry No. 53). Her charming diary is one of the more delightfully valuable historical documents of the time. She was a leading light of San Antonio, active in philanthropy and Episcopal Church affairs. Born in Tuscaloosa, Alabama, in 1818. Died in 1898.

For twentieth-century decendants, see her husband's entry (as noted above).

BENJAMIN (BEN) RUSH MILAM (Of Siege of Bexar Fame)

Milam was the leader at the siege of Bexar when he and Colonel Francis W. Johnson attacked San Antonio after the success of Milam's appeal ("Who will go with old Ben Milam into San Antonio?") for 300 volunteers to join them. Milam died in the fierce fighting. He was one of the earliest of so-called Anglo-Americans to come to Texas, meeting the future first president of Texas, David G. Burnet, while trading with the Comanches and when Burnet was living with the Indians. A great friendship formed. Milam was active in the settlements and pre-Republic politicking, twice being captured by Mexicans. He was born in Frankfort, Kentucky, in 1788. Milam County is named in his honor, as were the Milam Guards of Houston, who were organized under Houston's administration to act as police, escorts, frontier guards—always useful for processions and as honor guards for affairs of state. When parading in the mud on one occasion they hitched their white pantaloons into their boots giving "each man the appearance of a pair of black boots drawn over his inexpressibles," according to an observer.

ROBERT MILLS ("The Duke of Brazoria")

Robert Mills and the company he formed with his brother became the largest rivals to McKinney and Williams among the entrepreneurage of the Republic. Robert also appears to have been a man of high culture, judging from the fact that he is said to have had an extensive historical library. As a commission merchant and planter, "the duke of Brazoria," as he was known, at one time was producing probably the largest crop of cotton in the Republic. His control extended all the way up the Brazos River to its sources. The Mills brothers acted as bankers, shippers and marine insurers, their own ships eventually transporting sugar and cotton to all parts of the world. They owned more than 200,000 acres of land. In 1865 they were forced to free 800 slaves. Worth between three and five hundred million dollars before the War Between the States, they were bankrupt by 1873. Robert Mills was forced to surrender his carriages, plate and mansions to creditors. The so-called "duke" died childless and dependent upon relatives.

DANIEL MONTAGUE (County Namer)

There were many surveyors in colonist history, and Montague's knowledge in this profession won him acreage as landed gentry on a considerable scale. He arrived in Texas too late for San Jacinto in 1836, but fought in the Mexican War in 1846. Born in South Hadley, Massachusetts, in 1798. Married Mrs. Elizabeth Twitty. One daughter. Died in 1876. Montague County was named in his honor.

JAMES STEEN MONTGOMERY

Montgomery came to Texas in 1838 and immediately served as a Volunteer in the Revolution. A banker and businessman, he represented Colorado County in the Eighth Congress (see entry under Carriage Trade of the Republic). Born in Virginia in 1812. He waited until 1857 before filing a claim against Texas for supply of beef to the Texas Army.

Twentieth-century descendants include the families of George W. Thatcher, Fulton Montgomery, W. E. Davis. (DRT nos. 266, 666.)

EDWIN WARD MOORE (Of the Lieutenant's Navy)

A commander of the Texas Navy in 1839, Moore fell afoul of Houston over the implementation of orders to blockade Mexico. Hampered by inadequate Texan resources, Moore joined forces with Yucatán ships in order to hold the Gulf successfully for Texas. Previously to 1839 he was a lieutenant in the U. S. Navy. Born in Alexandria, Virginia, in

1810. Married Emma (Stockton) Cox of Philadelphia. Died in Virginia in 1865. Moore County was named after him.

DR. FRANCIS MOORE, JR. (Crusader Against Drink and Dueling)

Dr. Francis Moore came to Texas from New England in 1836 and bought Thomas Borden's interest in the *Telegraph and Register*, which he relocated in Houston and edited for 17 years. His best-known campaign was against dueling, which he railed against in his newspaper, particularly after a truculent Mississippian killed a young reporter from the East named Levi Laurens in a duel involving rifles at 20 yards. Shortly after this, the same Goodrich stabbed a gambler in his bed with his bowie knife. Moore finally thought he had been successful when the Texas Congress passed a law against dueling. But it was virtually ignored, death sentence or no. Finally, Editor Moore became a senator and effected the passing of a law which was much weakened by the dueling lobby, who provoked Moore into ranting, "Shall Texas, the youngest Republic in the world, which has sprung into existence, like Minerva from the head of Jupiter, all clad in armor—sir, shall she go back and, regardless of all circumstances, set an example so degraded and so childish?" To the peerage of the Republic, dueling was part of the Code of Honor. More, maybe less, realistically he cautioned ladies not "to permit their snowy fingers or rosy lips to meet the polluting touch of the foul and loathsome wretch whose [duelist] hands have been thus defiled with one of the most horrid of human crimes." Moore also editorialized against drinking, the miscellany of which offered in Texan saloons included such temptations as a Tom and Jerry, a Tip and Ty, a Knickerbocker, the Vox Populi or Moral Suasion, Stone Wall, and various other drops of what was colloquially called "the ardent." It did not assist Moore's efforts that even figures as important as Sam Houston were more than fond on occasion of extended carousal. Moore was born in Massachusetts in 1808. He married Moffat Wood, and they had nine children. He died in 1864 a Union man.

JOHN H. MOORE (Of "Come and Take It" Fame at Gonzales)

John H. Moore took command at the Texan Lexington, as the Battle of Gonzales is called. At Gonzales, settlers had refused to return a cannon to the Mexicans and buried it in a peach orchard. The incident blew up into a fire fight when Moore filled the cannon with scrap iron and old chains and flaunted it at the Mexicans. The battle flag, reputedly invented by Moore, showed a rough sketch of the cannon with the words "Come and Take It." Moore was an Indian fighter and fought as such in the Revolution thereafter. He came to Texas in 1821 and joined the Old Three Hundred. He married Eliza Cummins and built Moore's Fort on the site of the present-day city of LaGrange, where he had a plantation. He was born in Rome, Tennessee, in 1800. He died in 1880.

Twentieth-century descendants include the families of Richard Owen Faires, J. W. McCutcheon, Dr. E. G. Townsend, David Moore Killough, Daniel Fount Wade, Jr., Ernest Eugene Hair, Jr., John Hunter Thompson. (DRT nos. 484, 526, 586, 1148, 3076, 7157.)

JOHN MURCHISON (Carriage Trade Mason)

John Murchison came to Texas shortly before the Revolution and fought in it. After operating a sawmill in Texas, he moved to Fayette County and appears to have prospered (see Carriage Trade of the Republic), representing that county in the Fifth Congress. He was a Mason, like so many Texans in politics. He was killed accidentally on a gold-hunting expedition to California in 1849. Born in South Carolina in the early 1800s.

PHILIP NOLAN
(Horse Trader, Hero, Revolutionary and Early Martyr)

A horse trader in Texas off and on as early as 1790, Nolan is said to be the first Anglo-American to have mapped Texas. A pre-Revolution hero, he was killed by Spanish soldiers dispatched to arrest this early dissident in 1801. Born in Belfast, Northern Ireland, in 1771. Married Frances Lintot. Nolan County was named in his honor.

THOMAS O'CONNOR (From Boy Soldier to Landed Riches)

O'Connor helped raise the Goliad flag of Independence at age seventeen and then fought in the Battle of San Jacinto in Calder's Company. His wife's dowry and his land grants as a colonist were beginnings which led to land holdings of half a million acres and over 100,000 head of cattle in five counties. He was born in County Wexford, Ireland, in

1819. Married Mary Fagan first; Helen Shelly second. Died in 1887.

Twentieth-century descendants include the families of J. Meredith Tatton, John F. Hallinan. (DRT nos. 48, 546.)

CYNTHIA ANN PARKER (Tragic Heroine of *Spirit Bondage*)

At age nine, Cynthia Parker was captured in a Comanche raid on Fort Parker in 1836, and was adopted by an Indian family. The search went on for her for years. Meantime, she had married Peta Nocona, a Comanche chief. Constantly sighted by traders and by soldiers at battles such as Antelope Hill, she was eventually recaptured at the Battle of Pease River in 1860, where her Indian love was reputedly killed. Her son, Quanah Parker, became a great chief of the Comanches, marrying several times and conceiving many children. Noting the fair complexion and blue eyes, her "rescuer" grew convinced of her identity. He summoned her uncle, Isaac Parker, who identified the captive prize upon her immediately recognizing her own name. Yearning for the Indian life, she constantly tried to escape. The most celebrated Indian-adoption case in the United States, her life story was described in Jack Red Hill's play *Spirit Bondage*, presented at the Texas Centennial observance. She died in 1864.

(Note Isaac Parker entry in Carriage Trade of the Republic under Houston County. Parker County was named in his honor.)

EMILY (AUSTIN BRYAN) and *JAMES FRANKLIN PERRY*

Emily Austin was the daughter of Moses Austin. By her first husband, James Bryan, she mothered William Joel, Moses Austin, Guy Morrison Bryan, and a daughter, Mary. Their father died in 1822. She then married James Franklin Perry who fathered Perry, a son born shortly after their arrival in Texas, an event long yearned for by Emily. In the twentieth century, it became the custom among her increasing hundreds of descendants to gather in celebration of her birthday every June 22, when they have been reported as rising up to call her "blessed." Her actual birthdate was June 22, 1795.

For twentieth-century descendants, see the families listed under her father, Moses Austin.

LUCY HOLCOMBE PICKENS
("Lady Lucy, Queen of the Confederacy")

Known as "Lady Lucy, Queen of the Confederacy," Mrs. Pickens was brought up a Texan as a child in Marshall during the days of the Republic. She married Colonel Francis Wilkinson Pickens of South Carolina, who was appointed United States ambassador to Russia, where the Czarina was godmother to her child, whom she called "Douschka." As first lady of South Carolina during the War Between the States, her picture was placed on Confederate money. She was born the daughter of Beverly Holcombe of Tennessee in 1832. She died in 1899 and was buried in the family cemetery in Edgewood, Texas.

REUBEN MARMADUKE POTTER
(Bard Who Wrote the "Hymn of the Alamo")

The best poets of the Republic included the nation's poet-president Mirabeau Buonaparte Lamar, Harry Richardson of San Augustine, and Reuben Marmaduke Potter, who wrote the "Hymn of the Alamo" in the year of 1836. Potter became an authority on the Alamo, advising on the composition of "Dawn at the Alamo" (an epic canvas by a painter called Henry McArdle, which hangs with its sister work in the capitol building in Austin). It is to poets and to dancing that the peerage and folk of a Heroic age turn, rather than to the theater and visual arts usually so popular in consumer societies, life at such times being too romantic and exciting to indulge cultural appetites other than those exercising either the deepest emotions or some participant action. Indeed, in reflection of this, the early newspapers of Texas often delighted in printing large numbers of poems of whatever quality, in preference to moralizings by the religious and by causeworthies. Equally, the accent on news was on national and foreign, local news spreading quicker by word of mouth. In the age of the poet-soldier, Potter made a very effective and popular quartermaster in various army commands, belying the fashionable notion of poets as not being men of action. Born in Woodbridge, New Jersey, in 1802. Married Fidelia Burchard in 1853. Died in 1890. Bearing Potter's name is the monument commemorating the creation of the county named in honor of Ewen Cameron, the chief hero of the Black Bean Episode.

ANDREW RABB (Old Three Hundred and Carriage Trade)

A farmer and stockraiser in the census of 1826, Rabb came with the Old Three Hundred to Texas. He located at Egypt down the Colorado and later petitioned for the creation of Fayette County (see entry under Carriage Trade of the Republic), representing it at the Third Congress. Born in Pennsylvania about 1793. Married Margaret Ragsdale; they had at least three children. He died in 1869.

Twentieth-century descendants include the families of William Farquhar, R. A. McKinney, Joseph Farquhar, W. L. Shaw, F. W. Sternenberg, John P. Compton, George W. Cox, Wade Magruder Hampton, Custer Lee Hampton, Frederic Kevin Conley. (DRT nos. 527, 541, 546, 1142, 1455, 1883, 4698.)

DAVID RANDON (Old Three Hundred and Carriage Trade)

Randon's plantation at Fort Bend grew in value from $33,000 in 1850 to $290,000 in 1860. As an Old Three Hundred member, he started out as a farmer and stockraiser in the late 1820s with a wife and seven slaves. He appears to have been a sporting man (see entry under Carriage Trade of the Republic). He was described as part Indian.

JAMES REILY (Diplomat, Orator, Churchman and Warrior)

Born in Ohio, Reily came into prominence first as an all-round Texan notable in 1839 when President Mirabeau put him in charge of negotiating the sale of a million dollars' worth of Texas bonds. He represented Harris County (see entry under Carriage Trade of the Republic) before taking up his position as chargé d'affaires in Washington, where he signed a trade treaty with Daniel E. Webster. Following a parade in 1840 to celebrate the beginning of construction on a railroad, James Reily is recorded as having proceeded to theatrical producer Henri Corri's theater where he delivered a "bombastic" speech much praised by the local press, they not having heard "so eloquent and powerful an effort" in years. Despite the steam generated there for it in the theater by Houston, Reily and others, the railroad was never built. As a diplomat he was ranked with Ashbel Smith and James Pinckney Henderson, although he opposed annexation to the United States. He was also a soldier prior to that as a captain of the Milam Guards against Indians. An ardent Episcopalian and Mason, he could also preach, and did so on the field of battle. He died defending Texas against the Yankees during the War Between the States at the Battle of Franklin in 1863. He married Ellen Hart, niece of Henry Clay.

JEROME BONAPARTE ROBERTSON
(Leading Founder of the Texas Veterans Association)

Jerome Robertson was born in Kentucky in 1815 the son of Sterling C. Robertson (see entry No. 26 under Signers of the Declaration of Independence). He had studied medicine in Kentucky. There he raised volunteers for the Texas Revolution, arriving with them shortly after San Jacinto. Returning to Texas, he married Mary Elizabeth Cummins, daughter of Old Three Hundred patriarch Moses Cummins. The doctor became an Indian fighter. In the War Between the States he took over Hood's celebrated Texas Brigade after their saving of the Confederacy at Sharpsburg. He was wounded at least three times. In 1873, the Texas Veterans Association formed in response to a call from General Robertson. He died in Waco in 1891.

For twentieth-century descendant families of the Robertsons, see his father's entry as noted above.

JAMES W. ROBINSON
(From Acting Governor to Private Soldier at San Jacinto)

Robinson was elected governor by the executive council of the provisional government after they tried to depose Henry Smith. Robinson was one of many prominent men who then fought as privates at San Jacinto, choosing the cavalry of William H. Smith. While a Mexican prisoner in 1842, he conducted a correspondence with Santa Anna, as a result of which a subsequent armistice may have been facilitated. Later he moved to San Diego. He was born in Hamilton County, Indiana, in 1800. Married Mary Isdell first; Sarah Snider second. Died in 1857.

JOEL WALTER ROBISON
(Capturer of Santa Anna "The Terrible")

The Fayette County private was about twenty years old at the Battle of San Jacinto and could speak Spanish. He was detailed to round up routed Mexicans after the victory, which is how he found the Mexican dictator about nine miles from the American camp. Santa Anna was chivalrously offered a ride behind Robison's horse. His identity was only revealed on arrival at the camp when Mexican prisoners immediately hailed their leader "*¡Viva el Presidente!*" Later Santa Anna gave the lad his own gold brocaded vest. According to tradition, Robison reportedly wore it at weddings. Fancy-designed vests were prized possessions in the Texas of the day. Robison matured to represent Fayette County in the Eighth Legislature. Born in Washington County, Georgia, in 1815. Married. Died in 1889.

Twentieth-century descendants include the families of John W. Teer, Thomas Albert Ledbetter, John Willis Smith, James F. McClatchy, W. E. Odom, Joel Rush Robison. (DRT nos. 493, 538, 547, 808, 848, 856, 867, 1740, 2141.)

WILLIAM PINCKNEY ROSE
("Hell-Roarin' Old Rose" the Regulator and "The Lion of the Lakes")

One of the great characters of East Texas during the Republic, Rose's fame as a force for law and order spread far and wide. Many were the names for "Old Rose" among those who feared him. To his friends he was regarded in less vivid terms as a hero, statesman and patriot. To them nothing was too good to say about him. A lot of the tall talk grew round his leadership of the Regulator faction in the so-called Regulator-Moderator War, which peaked when the Moderators' leader, Robert Potter, was felled by a contingent of Regulators led by the much feared "Lion of the Lakes" himself. They shot Potter as he leaped from a thicket to swim a lake. Born in 1787 in North Carolina, "Old Rose" married Mary Vardaman Smith and died in 1851 in the land over which he ruled.

Twentieth-century descendants include the families of Walter Keeble Rucker, Richard Coke Mills, Sr., Earl M. Lide, William Pinkney McLean. (DRT nos. 4928, 3612, 4164.)

JOHN (DR. JACK) SHACKELFORD (Of "Red Rover" Fame)

At the outbreak of the Texas Revolution, Shackelford personally raised and equipped the company of volunteers called the "Red Rovers" after the red jeans he clothed them in. His son, Fortunatus, also served with them, as well as two nephews. Many were killed at Goliad, Shackelford himself being spared on account of his skill as a physician. He later returned to Alabama. Born in Richmond, Virginia, in 1790. Married Maria Young. Died in 1857. Shackelford County is named in his honor.

DANIEL SHIPMAN (Old Three Hundred and Carriage Trade)

Shipman came to Texas in 1822 and was a late arrival among the Old Three Hundred due to a dispute over land. One of the Anahuac hotheads, he fought at the siege of Bexar. He published his reminiscences under the title *Frontier Life*. Married Margaretta Kelly first; Eliza Hancock second. Died in Goliad in 1881. (See entry under Carriage Trade of the Republic.)

Twentieth-century descendants include the families of Edward Shipman, Thomas Leland Means, Robert Carter Nelson. (DRT nos. 646, 1238, 1568.)

ASHBEL SMITH (Knight of the Order of San Jacinto)

A Yale graduate and a friend of James Fenimore Cooper and the Marquis de Lafayette, Dr. Smith came to Texas in 1837. Houston appointed him a diplomat to Britain and to France, conferring on him one of the three titles of the otherwise abortive order of Texan nobility called Knights of the Order of San Jacinto. Ashbel Smith later negotiated the Smith-Cuevas Treaty with Mexico. In later years the cultivated Texan devoted himself to furthering education. He established the University of Texas. Like so many gentlemen, he loved horse racing, writing: "There is a larger proportion of well-bred geldings about Houston than I have seen in any other part of the world. The days of the races were concluded by a ball given by the Club. It was a large assembly of elegant ladies and high-bred gentlemen; the festivities of the night were unmarred by any adverse incident." Born in Hartford, Connecticut, in 1805. Unmarried. Died on Galveston Bay in 1886.

HENRY SMITH ("First American Governor of Texas")

Smith was the leader of the War (or Independence) Party in 1835. He was made governor of the provisional administration and was in the process of being impeached when the Convention was held and an ad interim government elected. But he came back to prominence under Houston as secretary of the treasury, where he found it as difficult to balance the budget and give value to the currency as earlier he had balancing factions with compromise and diplomacy. He came to Texas in 1827, and fought at Velasco. The Mexicans made him chief of the Brazos area in 1834. Born in Kentucky, in 1788. Married three sisters in turn: Harriet, Elizabeth and Sarah Gillett. Nine children. Died in the California gold rush in 1851.

Twentieth-century descendants include the families of Reuben John Beaman, James Charles Fulton, Albert Louis Bruhl, Charles Gibson. (DRT nos. 3135, 5367.)

JOHN WILLIAM SMITH ("Last Messenger from the Alamo")

Smith was appointed by William B. Travis to bear the last dispatch from the Alamo. He had fought at the Battle of Gonzalez and the storming of Bexar, where he led one of the assault parties alongside Deaf Smith. During the Republic he was mayor of San Antonio and represented Bexar in the Texas Senate from 1842 until his death in 1845. He was born in Virginia in 1792, and moved to Texas in the 1820s.

Twentieth-century descendants include the families of Arthur William Burroughs, Sam C. Bel, A. B. Spencer, James M. Vance, Albert West, Sam T. Newton, John Martyn Newton, Graves N. Fulshear, Joseph Monroe Barnhart, John Travis Walling, Martin Butler, John R. Mooney, Frank Morgan Gillespie, Harry S. Davis, William Herbert Moore, Chalmer Kirk McClelland, Burton Barnes, Albert Washington West, Alexander Herbemont Fraser II, Lloyd Walter Gaedke, Ernest F. Kusener, Edward M. Jacquet, Kenneth Stanley Moss, Taylor Stitt, Anson George Bennett, Oscar Herman Gastring, Christopher Kress Frame, Frank Morgan Gillespie, Jr., John Kenny Matthews, Alfred Edwin McNamee. (DRT nos. 663, 707, 745, 747, 765, 2358, 2895, 3440, 4333, 4449, 4586, 4853, 4936, 6053, 6069, 6788, 6830, 6837, 6838, 7088, 7214, 7712.) Walter Mathis, Alexander Fraser, Tobin Armstrong, Robert Lynn Batts Tobin.

JAMES HARPER STARR
(County Namer and First P. R. Man to Texas)

Lured to Texas by its good press, the honest but persuasive Starr and his wife arrived in 1837. He was quickly put to work on land dues by Houston to the great disgust of dishonest land speculators. President

Lamar made him secretary of the treasury. He and his partner, Nathaniel C. Amory, became land agents who were outstandingly successful in advertising Texas to prospective settlers. Born in New Hartford, Connecticut, in 1809. Married Harriet J. Johnson. Died in 1890. Starr County is named in his honor.

Twentieth-century descendants include the families of Oscar H. Cooper, Arthur John Blake, W. T. Kiely, L. H. Spellings, James Franklin Starr, John H. Niendorff, Harry Webster McGee John Frederic Lentz. (DRT nos. 294, 984, 1004, 1007, 1008, 1027, 2786, 4365.)

PHILIP A. SUBLETT (Partner of Sam Houston)
After the Revolution, Houston and Sublett developed the early town of Sabine. Phil Sublett had nominated Houston for the presidency, as in the earliest stages of the Revolution he had signed the resolution putting his friend in charge of the Nacogdoches forces. Sublett fought in the siege of Bexar but later resigned the offer of the post of commissioned colonel. His base was San Augustine, where he moved in the 1820s from Mexico. Born in Kentucky in 1802. Married Easter Jane Roberts. Died in 1846.

Twentieth-century descendants include the families of Henry W. Sublett, Americus Holman Cartwright, Stephens Charles Kardell. (DRT no. 3695.)

SWEN MAGNUS SWENSON (First Swede of Texan Immigration)
Unlike his fellow Scandinavian Cleng Peerson ("father of Norse immigration to America"), who came too late to Texas to rank as a notable of the Republic, Swenson arrived in Houston as early as 1838, becoming a friend and admirer of Sam Houston and a successful businessman. Operating an unofficial immigration bureau, he attracted hundreds of Swedish immigrants to Texas. His S M S Ranches are well known in Texas and were reported still active under descendants in recent times. Born in Sweden in 1816. Married Mrs. Jeanette Long first; Cora Susan McReady second, by whom he had four children. Died in Brooklyn in 1896.

JOHN S. SYDNOR (Auctioneer and Carriage Trade)
John Sydnor was an efficient, resourceful man who came to Texas

from his native Virginia with a house in prefabricated sections. Later, he applied his administrative skills to setting up schools, fire and police departments and public amenities as mayor of Galveston. He was born in Hanover County, Virginia, in 1812. Died in 1869. (See entry under Carriage Trade of the Republic.)

Twentieth-century descendants include the families of C. C. Oden, John B. Sydnor. (DRT no. 1610.)

GENERAL EDWARD H. TARRANT
(Texas Ranger and County Namer)

A leading Texas Ranger, as brigadier general in 1841 he fought the Battle of Village Creek. Born in North Carolina in 1796, he was a veteran of the War of 1812. He died in 1858 at Fort Belknap. Tarrant County is named in his honor.

FRANCES TRASK THOMPSON (Opened the First Girls' School)

Young girls of elegant breeding like Frances Trask were in short supply in the Republic and were guaranteed quick entree into this world of frontier Southern chivalry. Wrote Sam Houston to her: "Should Miss Trask conclude to ride, Gen. H——— assures her Ladyship that the steed, as well as the carriage, shall be of the first order in appearance and qualities." After her brother was killed in the San Jacinto campaign, Miss Trask had journeyed to the capital in order to claim his headright grant. She came to Texas in 1834 and started a girls' school in Independence, which is believed to be the first in the country. Later she taught in Austin in the old capitol building, and married William Thompson of Michigan. Born in Gloucester, Massachusetts, in 1806. Died in Ashmont, Massachusetts, in 1892.

FROST THORN (The "First Millionaire of Texas")

Thorn's landholdings and other business activities, often in association with Hayden Edwards, encompassed land not only estimated in hundreds of thousands of acres but in much other wealth. Called the first millionaire of Texas, it was said of Thorn that "he accomplished in land acquisitions by legitimate means what many of the land sharks failed to accomplish under questionable circumstances." He came to Texas with the trading company of Samuel Davenport before 1825. During the Revolution he was chairman of the Committee of Safety and Vigilance. Born in Glen Cove, New York, in 1793. Married Susan Wroe Edwards, one of five single women then believed to have been living in Nacogdoches. Died there in 1854.

DR. WILLIAM EDWARD THROCKMORTON
(A First Pioneer of Northern Texas)

Throckmorton County was named "in honor of Dr. William E. Throckmorton, one of the first pioneers of northern Texas," probably as a gesture to his son, James Webb Throckmorton, best known as "Old Leathercoat," a prominent Confederate and an "impediment to Reconstruction" in the view of Yankee General Philip Sheridan, who removed the statesman from the governorship. The father settled near Melissa in Collin County in 1841 after marrying Melina Wilson. He was born in Virginia in 1795. He died in 1843.

Twentieth-century descendants include the families of Zachary M. Shirley, Doc Hill Hart, Jr. (DRT no. 2056.)

JAMES TITUS (Red River Carriage Trade)

Titus moved to Red River County in 1839 (see Carriage Trade of the Republic) and represented that county and Fannin, Bowie and Lamar counties in the later congresses. Born in Pennsylvania during the American Revolutionary War. Son Andrew Jackson Titus was a Royal Arch Mason and Knight Templar, Titus County being named in his honor. The father died in 1843.

Twentieth-century descendants include the families of William Macklyn Benge, William Aubrey Benge, Phineas James Benge, James Tillman Powell. (DRT nos. 2389, 2856, 3205.)

JOHANNA TROUTMAN (Of the Lone Star Flag)

Johanna Troutman's portrait hangs in the Texas Senate Chamber. This eighteen-year-old beauty helped raise the Georgia battalion for the Texan Revolutionary cause in 1835, equipping it with a flag of white silk, bearing a blue five-pointed star inscribed with the words "Liberty or Death." Called the Flag of the Lone Star, it was unfurled above the American Hotel in Velasco and later carried to Goliad where James Fannin proclaimed it the Texan national flag on the news of the signing of the Declaration of Independence. It was torn to shreds in the winds of war during the Goliad campaign. Miss Troutman married a Mr. Pope in Alabama. Her remains were brought to Texas 33 years after her death in 1880.

Earlier flags of Texas and of its Revolution included such designs as the green flag of the Gutiérrez-Magee Expedition; the red and white flag with a lone white star believed to have been the standard of the Long Expedition; the red and white flag inscribed "Independence, Freedom and Justice" raised by the Fredonians; the "Old Cannon Flag" of Gonzales, described as a "breadth of white cotton cloth about six feet long, in the center of which was painted in black a picture of the old cannon, above it a lone star and beneath it the words 'Come and Take It' "; and possibly earlier still, the Sarah Dodson flag (see entry in this section under Sarah Dodson), which was close to the later official flag of the Republic. At the Alamo, Davy Crockett flew a flag of 13 red and white stripes on a blue ground centered with a five-point white star with the letters T E X A S between the points, although there are believed to have been other flags. Various units are reported to have had their own flags, some with the lone star, some without, including even one which included the Union Jack and was used by Moseley Baker's Company at San Jacinto. Preserved but restored is the San Jacinto battle flag made by Mrs. Sidney Sherman. It is of white silk painted with a woman grasping a sword and a streamer with Johanna Troutman's words of "Liberty or Death." The first official flag of the Republic became that adopted by President Burnet for the Texas Navy—a blue union, star central and 13 stripes prolonged, alternate red and white. In 1839, President Lamar enacted the evenly and perpendicularly striped white-blue-white design with the five-point white star central, which became the State flag after annexation.

ISAAC VAN ZANDT (County Namer and One of Three Known Knights of the Order of San Jacinto)

Houston's chargé d'affaires in Washington, Van Zandt originally came to Texas in 1838 a failed store owner. He was born in Franklin County, Tennessee, in 1813. He married Frances Cooke Lipscomb. Died of yellow fever while campaigning for the governor's office in 1847. Van Zandt County is named in his honor. Houston made him a knight of his otherwise abortive nobility called the Knights of the Order of San Jacinto.

Twentieth-century descendants include the families of Elias James Beall, Edgar Doak Capps, Jeremiah M. Clough, James Jones Jarvis, Hyde Jennings, Khleber Miller Van Zandt, Sr. and Jr., Ben F. Allen, Edwin E. Bewley, Leonard Harry Attwell, George B. Hendricks, J. Malcolm Brown, John Innes Burgess, William Alexander DeGress, William Archer Diboll, David Whitney Gray, Jr., Kleber V. Jennings, Leroy A. Smith, Norman Taylor, Isaac Van Zandt, Edmund Pendleton Van Zandt, Sr. and Jr., Emmett Hayne Johnson. (DRT nos. 505, 506, 507, 518, 532, 533, 534, 550, 551, 552, 1324, 1326, 1328, 1333, 1334, 1345, 1346, 1356, 1361, 1369, 1370, 1371, 1374, 1376, 1403, 1406, 1407, 1412, 1421, 1423, 6004, 7317.)

SAMUEL HAMILTON WALKER (Of Colt Revolver Fame)

Regarded as one of the great leaders of Texas Rangers of Republic days and later, Walker suggested modifications to Samuel Colt for a "Texas" pistol, thereafter known as the Walker Colt revolver. He joined Jack Hays' Texas Rangers at San Antonio where he "distinguished himself for courage and coolness." Fought in the Woll, Somervell and Mier episodes. As a captive, he drew a black bean and survived prison to fight later with Zachary Taylor as a Texas Ranger. Born in Maryland about 1810. Killed leading a charge in 1847. Walker County is named in his honor.

W. A. Q. ("BIGFOOT") WALLACE

A folk hero and convivially loquacious soul, "representative of old-timey free days, free ways and free land," is preserved for us through his good ol' boy chat with "Texas John" Duval, a Goliad survivor (see the Duvals of Goliad). Descended from Scottish Highlanders, "Bigfoot" was reputedly descended from those heroes of Scotland, William Wallace and Robert the Bruce. He was described as six foot two inches "in his moccasins" and 240 pounds of firm-knit muscle. He came to Texas to conduct a blood feud with Mexicans in revenge over a brother and cousin massacred at Goliad, participating with well-requited purpose in the Woll, Somervell and Mier fighting. His experiences in Perote Prison are graphically described. In 1840, when he saw the last buffalo of the locality run down Congress Avenue in Austin, he moved to San Antonio for love of adventure and the open spaces. Born in Lexington, Virginia, in 1817. Never married. Died in 1899.

THOMAS WILLIAM WARD (County Namer)

Legend has it that the right leg Colonel Thomas Ward lost at the siege of Bexar lies in the same grave as the body of Ben Milam. The whereabouts of the right arm he lost firing a cannon in celebration of Texas independence, however, have not been hazarded. Rather more of him was fortunately missed altogether when Mrs. Angelina Eberly wildly fired a cannon at the group he had joined in an attempt to remove the archives from Austin, of which he was mayor three times. He was the second commissioner of the Land Office. Called "a passionate man," Ward was almost shot in full view of the senate when he set about Francis Lubbock with a stick "in a sort of brawl," as a result of which Lubbock pulled a derringer and fired at him, although somebody raised a walking stick in time to misdirect Lubbock's deadly aim. Born in Ireland in 1807. Educated as an architect. Married Susan L. Marston. Died of typhoid in 1872. Ward County was named in his honor.

JAMES WEBB (County Namer)

Webb was already an officeholder in the South when he moved to Houston and became a friend and adviser of Lamar, who made him secretary of the treasury, and then secretary of state. A Mason, like so many prominent Texans, he was Grand Master of the Texas Lodge in 1844. Born in Fairfax County, Virginia, in 1792. Married Rachel Elizabeth Lamar in 1813. Died in 1856. Webb County is named in his honor.

Twentieth-century descendants include the families of M. F. Mott, James Spillane, Thomas Herbert Webb, Perryman S. Moore, George J. Trampier. (DRT nos. 167, 180, 2109, 3433.)

WILLIAM HARRIS WHARTON (Revolutionary Statesman)

At the 1832 Convention, Wharton drew up the petition to Mexico asking for statehood, which is an important constitutional document of the history of Texas. He came as a young lawyer to Texas in 1827, where he fell in love with Sarah Ann Groce, the daughter of carriage trade member Jared Ellison Groce. Her father gave them land on which to build their beautiful plantation home, Eagle Island, where a Scottish gardener was employed to tend 500 species of "exotic" plants that were imported by the Whartons. Wharton by 1835 was prominent among those calling for complete independence against the conservatives led by Stephen Austin. The enmity was not allowed to last, and they supported Austin for president against Sam Houston. Wharton was captured at sea by the Mexicans, escaping in time to join the Texas Senate. Born in Virginia in 1802. Killed in a shooting accident in 1839. His brother was adjutant general at the Battle of San Jacinto.

SAMUEL WHITING (The Newspaper Publisher "Pirate" of Texas)

This Connecticut man came to Texas in 1825 to become the Rupert Murdoch of the Lone Star. He published the *National Intelligencer* in Houston in 1838 and 1839, and then started the Austin *City Gazette*, later buying out the *Daily Bulletin*. In 1835 he was granted six blank commissions or letters of marque to outfit privateers at New Orleans (note entry on a Samuel Whiting listed in the Carriage Trade of the Republic under Travis County). Died in New York in 1862.

ROBERT MCALPIN ("THREE-LEGGED WILLIE")
WILLIAMSON (County Namer and Newspaperman)

One of the earliest newspaper editors in Texas, Williamson's crippled right leg was twisted back at the knee, on which he wore a wooden leg. He came to Texas in 1826 from Georgia, establishing a newspaper called *Cotton Plant*. He managed to ride in William H. Smith's cavalry at San Jacinto, after which he served as a representative and as a senator in the Republic's congress. He was born in Georgia in 1804 or 1806. Married Mary Jane Edwards. Seven children. Died in 1859. Williamson County is named in his honor.

JAMES CHARLES WILSON (A British-Born County Namer)

Wilson left Oxford University to go to Texas in 1837. He joined the Somervell Expedition in 1842 and the Mier Expedition as a private soldier. On being captured he refused help from the British, eventually escaping. A lawyer and traveling Methodist minister, he held office as a Texan congress representative. Born in Yorkshire, England, in 1816. Died in 1861. Wilson County was named in his honor.

JOHN HOWLAND WOOD (From Soldier to Great Rancher)

Wood was arrested by the British as a pirate on his way to Texas to fight in the Revolution. He joined the cavalry and was part of the force that pursued the enemy remnants after San Jacinto and buried Fannin and his men there. As a quartermaster to the army, he was forced to accept cattle as pay, a small start to business on his own as a rancher around the Refugio area. He became a community leader early on and partook in operations against the Indians. Born in Hyde Park, New York, in 1816. Married Nancy Clark. Died in 1904.

Twentieth-century descendants include the families of Ephraim Edmund Pickering, Paul Pierre Bertholot, George Watson Kerr, Raymond James Welder, Tobias de Cantillon Wood, Michael Lowery Stoner. (DRT nos. 3057, 4834, 6576, 7237.) Lawrence Wood, Richard Wood.

ANDREW JANEWAY YATES (Phi Beta Kappa and Carriage Trade)

A Phi Beta Kappa of Union College, Yates came to Texas in 1835 as "probably the best-informed and best-trained man in the educational field." Before coming to Texas he had already won a reputation as a college professor, author and lawyer. During the Revolution he was the most qualified man to deal with the business of loans and supplies for the often desperate Texas Army. After 1841 he published the *Daily Advertiser* in Houston. He was already in possession of a fortune on arriving in Texas (see entry under Carriage Trade of the Republic). Born in Hartford, Connecticut, in 1803. Died in California in 1851.

JOHN YORK

York was a member of the Austin County carriage trade in 1840 (see Carriage Trade of the Republic entry), but was elected a commissioner for the new county of DeWitt in 1846, where it is reported he "sold his half interest in a league of land for one dollar in cash," the purchasers agreeing to lay out the town of Yorktown, with York to retain each alternate lot, block and acre lot. He moved to Texas in 1829. Born in Kentucky in 1800. Killed by Indians in 1846.

Twentieth-century descendants include the family of David Brown. (DRT no. 515.)

The Carriage Trade of the Republic

ONE OF THE factors that makes a "First Family" is that they "have style," and are "cutting a dash," visibly a cut above their neighbors. The mark of style in the nineteenth century was a carriage—preferably four- but possibly two-wheeled. Retailers and merchants of the period noted the better class and style of merchandise that such people sought, and called it the "carriage trade." The term lives on. The carriage trade, therefore, is a term which embraces people with class and style, either the leaders of their community, or people with ambitions to be the leaders of their community. If leadership is the mark of the peerage, then so is the carriage trade.

The young Republic of Texas was deeply in debt for the price of winning freedom, and in 1837, the Texas Congress imposed some taxes upon luxuries. Among other things, it imposed taxes on ownership of pleasure carriages and racehorses. The following is a list from the archives of the Treasury of the Republic, extracting the names of those who paid such taxes in 1840. It is not a complete list, for some of the re-

347

*The
Carriage
Trade
of the
Republic*

turns are missing, and others are damaged, but nonetheless, these are many of the prominent men and women of the Republic.

The list classifies these people by the counties in which they were living then. Some moved, of course, and also it must be remembered that county boundaries have been changed, and new counties created since that time. The detail varies, too, according to the detail the county assessor chose to record. In one county there may be a taciturn report of "one carriage," but others identify gigs, barouches, a buggy and a sulky. Mañuel Flores of Gonzales had, surprisingly, what is usually thought of as a London cab driver's vehicle, a Hansom carriage.

In the Texas of the time, with its appalling roads and paucity of bridges, a wheeled vehicle of any sort had limitations, and most traveling was on horseback. Mrs. Mary Austin Holley (whose travels once included coming 60 miles down the Brazos in an Indian dugout canoe) wrote of traveling to Matagorda in a senator's barouche, which was returning without passengers, and once of traveling in a barouche and four, of which the leaders were plow horses in plow harness. But this is not surprising, for one four-wheel carriage listed below was owned by a man who had no horses and but one mule, unless he had hidden his horses from the tax assessor.

These people are the Carriage Trade of the Republic.

Austin County

BRYANT DAUGHTERY: 1 four-wheel carriage
     Twentieth-century descendants include the Eugene Munger Daughtery and William Stockton Nelms families. (DRT no. 1507.)

LEONARD WALLER GROCE: 1 four-wheel carriage
     (See entry for Leonard and Jared Groce in Notables and Heroes of the Republic.)

JARED ELLISON GROCE III: 1 carriage
     (See entry for Leonard and Jared Groce in Notables and Heroes of the Republic.)

JOHN TOWNSEND: 1 carriage

JOHN YORK: 1 carriage
     (See entry under Notables and Heroes of the Republic.)

Bastrop County

JOHN E. O'CONNELL: 1 carriage

Bexar County

JAMES CAMPBELL: 1 carriage

Campbell was born in Belfast, Ireland, in 1810. Married Theresa B. O'Neill in 1840. Died in Aguascalientes, Mexico, in 1860. Twentieth-century descendants include the families of Arlington Andrew Alsbury, Jesse R. Lentz, Richard S. Miller, Frank H. Bushick and G. Malvern Smith. (DRT nos. 288, 1521, 8111.)

Brazoria County

MARTIN ALLEN: 1 racehorse
(See entry under Notables and Heroes of the Republic.)

WILLIAM ASHLEY: 1 two-wheel carriage

JAMES PECAN CALDWELL: 1 four-wheel carriage

J. H. DAVIS: 1 four-wheel carriage

MRS. ELIZA FARRIS: 1 two-wheel carriage

THOMAS JEFFERSON GREEN: racehorses (number not stated)
(See entry under Notables and Heroes of the Republic.)

P. EDWARD HAREY: 1 two-wheel carriage

E. G. AND W. M. HEAD: 1 four-wheel carriage

WILLIAM G. HILL: 1 two-wheel carriage; 1 four-wheel carriage
(See entry under Notables and Heroes of the Republic.)

PLEASANT D. MCNEEL: 1 carriage
(See entry under Notables and Heroes of the Republic.)

EDWIN WALLER: 1 four-wheel carriage
(See under Signers of the Declaration of Independence, entry No. 4.)

Colorado County

WILLIAM B. DEWEES: 1 carriage

ASA MILES LEWIS: 1 carriage
(See entry under Notables and Heroes of the Republic.)

JAMES STEEN MONTGOMERY: 1 carriage
(See entry under Notables and Heroes of the Republic.)

DR. JOEL PONTON: 1 carriage
Ponton was born in 1811; died in 1877. Twentieth-century descendants include the Willie Green Ponton and Frank L. Osteen families. (DRT no. 2788.)

GEORGE WARD THATCHER: 1 carriage
Born in 1808 in Frederick County, Virginia; settled in Colorado County in 1836. Married Sarah, daughter of James Steen Montgomery (see above). Died in Colorado County in 1867. Twentieth-century descendants include the Newton Ford Frazar, Edward Theodore Cubage, John Robert Thatcher and Simon White families. (DRT nos. 3578, 7705.)

GIDEON G. WILLIAMS: 1 carriage
A volunteer in the Texas Army. Twentieth-century descendants include the Claudius Green Rives family. (DRT no. 1211.)

Fannin County

F. SMAWLEY: 1 racehorse

N. K. WOODROW: 1 four-wheel carriage

Fayette County

MYERS FISHER JONES: 1 four-wheel carriage
Jones was a soldier and Indian fighter; born in Missouri. Married Patsy Peery. Died in 1853 in Fayette County. Twentieth-century descendants include the Ira Jones Farriss and William Herman Joekel families. (DRT no. 6059.)

GEORGE ALEXANDER KERR: 1 four-wheel carriage
   Kerr was born in 1810 in Augusta, Georgia. He was the son of Hugh Kerr, born in Sligo, Ireland, in 1777. Married Rebecca McCandliss. Died in Washington County, Texas, in 1843. Twentieth-century descendants include the Charles Preston Johnson family. (DRT no. 7700.)

JOSEPH A. MITCHELL: 1 four-wheel carriage

JOHN MURCHISON: 1 two-wheel carriage
   (See entry under Notables and Heroes of the Republic.)

MARY O'BAR: 1 four-wheel carriage

ANDREW RABB: 1 two-wheel carriage
   (See entry under Notables and Heroes of the Republic.)

WAGER S. SMITH: 1 four-wheel carriage
   Smith was born in 1805 in Dinwiddie County, Virginia. Married Charlotte Mary Claiborne Payne in 1835. Died in 1855 in Fayette County, Texas. Six children. Twentieth-century descendants include the families of James Benjamin Mathis, Andy Renick Alexander, James Frank Lenertz. (DRT no. 7746.)

WILLIAM S. TOWNSEND: 1 four-wheel carriage

E. S. WOOLEY: 1 four-wheel carriage

CHRISTIAN WERTZNER: 1 two-wheel carriage

Fort Bend County

P. P. AND J. P. BORDEN: 1 four-wheel carriage
   (See Bordens entry under Notables and Heroes of the Republic.)

A. C. DODD: 1 four-wheel carriage

T. F. L. PARROTT: 1 carriage

DAVID RANDON: 1 racehorse
   (See entry under Notables and Heroes of the Republic.)

DANIEL SHIPMAN: 1 carriage
   (See entry under Notables and Heroes of the Republic.)

WILLIAM WALKER: 1 carriage

N. F. WILLIAMS: 1 gig

Galveston County

NELSON ARNOLD: 1 two-wheel carriage

DENNIS CAMPION: 1 four-wheel carriage

ANN DARRAH: 1 two-wheel carriage

ALEXANDER EWELL: 1 four-wheel carriage

J. H. FABIR: 1 four-wheel carriage

BENJAMIN CROMWELL FRANKLIN: 1 four-wheel carriage
(See entry under Notables and Heroes of the Republic.)

DAVID S. KELSEY: 1 four-wheel carriage

JAMES LOVE: 1 carriage
(See entry under Notables and Heroes of the Republic.)

CAROLINA NEWLAND: 1 four-wheel carriage

NATHANIEL NORWOOD: 1 carriage
Norwood settled in Texas from Alabama about 1839. Born in 1809 in Abbeville, North Carolina. Married Margarite Adele Ewing in 1832 at Tuscaloosa, Alabama. Twentieth-century descendants include the family of Walter Nathaniel Norwood. (DRT no. 2833.)

FERDINAND PINKARD: 1 carriage

E. A. RHODES: 1 carriage

JAMES SHAW: 1 two-wheel carriage

JOHN SETTLE: 1 buggy

JOHN S. SYDNOR: 1 buggy and sulky
(See entry under Notables and Heroes of the Republic.)

WILLIAMS & MCKINNEY: 1 racetrack and 50 horses
(See entry under Thomas McKinney and Samuel Williams in Notables and Heroes of the Republic.)

351

The
Carriage
Trade
of the
Republic

ANDREW JANEWAY YATES: 1 four-wheel carriage
(See entry under Notables and Heroes of the Republic.)

Goliad County

The taxation records of this county are missing for the entire period of the Republic.

Gonzales County

MAÑUEL FLORES: 1 hansom car
(See entry under Notables and Heroes of the Republic.)

CHARLES LOCKHART: 1 carriage
Lockhart was born in 1790 in Virginia. Married Catharine Wise Barton in 1817. Died in 1844 in Gonzales County, Texas. Twentieth-century descendants include the families of David Hunter Lockhart and Elton Newman Buesing. (DRT no. 7485.)

ELI MITCHELL: 1 carriage
A brother of Asa Mitchell, who helped draft the Declaration of Independence.

JAMES ROBINSON: 1 carriage

Harris County

C. M. ALLEN: 1 carriage

GEORGE ALLEN: 1 carriage
Allen was one of the founders of the City of Houston. Born in 1815 in Canasareaugh, New York. Married Harriet E. Fenley in 1837. Died in 1854 in Houston, Texas. Twentieth-century descendants include the families of John Kirby Allen II, John Kirby Allen III, and John P. Mooney. (DRT no. 6314.)

MOSELEY BAKER: 1 carriage
(See under Senior Officers at the Battle of San Jacinto, entry No. 35.)

353

*The
Carriage
Trade
of the
Republic*

JOHN S. BLACK: 1 carriage

ANDREW BRISCOE: 1 carriage
    (See Signers of the Declaration of Independence, entry No. 57, and Officers at San Jacinto, entry No. 28.)

PARMELIA BROWN: 1 carriage

ELIZA ANN CARRADINE: 1 carriage

LEWIS BIRDSALL HARRIS: 1 carriage

PATRICK CHURCHILL JACK: 1 carriage
    (See entry under William Houston and Patrick Churchill Jack in Notables and Heroes of the Republic.)

ESTHER C. T. LEAGUE: 1 carriage

SAMUEL MILLETT: 1 carriage

JAMES REILY: 1 carriage
    (See entry under Notables and Heroes of the Republic.)

J. W. N. A. SMITH: 1 carriage

Harrison County

The surviving tax list for this county records no owners of carriages or racehorses at all.

Houston County

P. S. BEASON: 1 carriage

ELISHA CLAPP: 1 carriage
    Clapp fought at San Jacinto as a private in William H. Smith's Company.

ISAAC CROOME: 1 carriage

BENJAMIN DAVIS: 1 carriage

J. B. FALKENBERRY: 1 carriage

JOHN A. GOOLSBEY: 1 carriage

GEORGE W. HAILE: 1 carriage

    Haile settled in Houston County in 1836. Married Mary Billingsby in 1822. Died in Houston County in 1841. See Isaac Parker entry below.

JAMES H. HALL: 1 carriage

LUKE JOHNSON: 1 carriage

ROBERT B. LEWIS: 1 carriage

ABEL LOGAN: 1 carriage

HENRY MASTERS: 1 carriage

JACOB OSWALT: 1 carriage

ISAAC PARKER: 1 carriage

    Parker came to Texas with his father, Elder John Parker, in 1833. He was born in 1793 in Baltimore County, Maryland. Married Lucy W. Cheatham in 1816. His daughter, Lucy, married Samuel, the son of George W. Haile (see above). (Also note entry for Cynthia Parker under Notables and Heroes of the Republic.) Twentieth-century descendants of the Haile and Parker families are the families of Samuel C. Haile, John Edwin Reagan and Aubrey E. Orr. (DRT no. 2737.)

J. G. PETTIT: 1 carriage

    Pettit was Justice of the Peace. Born in 1806 in North Carolina. Married Melissa Ann Johnson in 1837. Died in 1852. Twentieth-century descendants include the families of Harrell Hodby Baldwin, Jenner Harvey Chadwick and Olaf Ingvald Carlson. (DRT no. 7087.)

ELIZABETH ROBERTS: 1 carriage

AMASA SMITH: 1 carriage

Jackson County

JAMES KERR: 1 four-wheel carriage
    (See entry under Notables and Heroes of the Republic.)

Jasper County

GEORGE W. GLASSCOCK: 1 pleasure carriage, four wheels
    (See entry under Notables and Heroes of the Republic.)

A. C. PARKER: 1 carriage, four wheels

ISHAM PARMER: 1 racehorse

Isham was one of the sons of Martin Parmer, a signer of the Declaration of Independence (entry No. 40) who was known as the "Ring-tailed Panther."

WILLIAM PARMER: 1 carriage, four wheels

One of the sons of Martin Parmer, a signer of the Declaration of Independence (entry No. 40).

HENRY L. ROER: 1 carriage, four wheels

JAMES F. SEALE: 1 carriage, four wheels

SARAH ANN WILLIAMSON: 1 carriage, four wheels

Jefferson County

RICHARD BALEW: 1 two-wheel carriage

THOMAS M. BRENNAN: 1 carriage

WILLIAM D. SMITH: 1 carriage

Liberty County

JOSEPH B. ELLIS: 1 carriage

R. H. HEBETT: 1 carriage

MATTHEW HUBERT: 1 carriage

Montgomery County

J. E. ANDERSON: 1 two-wheel carriage

ROBERT R. GRAVES: 1 four-wheel carriage

JOHN HIGGINBOTHAM: 2 two-wheel carriages

JOHN RANDOLPH: 1 four-wheel carriage

JOHN SAUL: 1 two-wheel carriage

JAMES SCOTT: 1 four-wheel carriage
   A friend of Davy Crockett, he was born in Georgia and died at sea in 1856. He was a plantation owner.

JAMES M. SMITH: 1 two-wheel carriage

ROBERT SMITHER: 1 four-wheel carriage
   Possibly the Major Robert Goodloe Smither who later in the Republic became a leading merchant at Huntsville.

A. M. WALKER: 1 two-wheel carriage

ROBERT WHITE: 1 two-wheel carriage

A. M. WOMACK: 1 four-wheel carriage

Nacogdoches County

ASA BEALL: 1 carriage

S. B. BROWN: 1 carriage

TAYLOR BROWN: 1 carriage

WILLIAM B. BURDITT: 1 carriage
   A colonist, Burditt was born in Tennessee. Married Caroline Whitaker. He died in 1894 in Leakey, Texas. Twentieth-century descendants include the families of John Steen Billingsley, Dr. William M. Dodson, Rochell B. Gilliam, J. Christian Heinrich Kirchner, Herman Franklin Henry Fleischer, Gus Carl Fleischer. (DRT nos. 2032, 7058, 7434.)

AMBROSE CRAIN: 1 carriage

RODDEN T. CRAIN: 1 carriage

NIMROD DOYLE: 1 carriage

JOHN DURST: 2 carriages
   (See entry under Notables and Heroes of the Republic.)

HADEN H. EDWARDS: 1 carriage
   (See entry under Notables and Heroes of the Republic.)

357

The
Carriage
Trade
of the
Republic

BLACKSTONE HARDIMAN: 1 carriage

THOMAS K. LUCKETT: 1 carriage

WILLIAM MCDANIELL: 2 carriages

A. W. NOBLE: 2 carriages

THOMAS J. RUSK: 1 carriage
    (See Signers of the Declaration of Independence, entry No. 30, and Officers at San Jacinto, entry No. 13.)

ALPHEUS WICKWARE: 1 carriage

HENRY RAGUET: 1 carriage
    (See Anna Raguet Irion entry under Notables and Heroes of the Republic.)

Red River County

W. H. BOYCE: 1 carriage

SAMUEL PRICE CARSON: 1 carriage
    (See under Signers of the Declaration of Independence, entry No. 59.)

JAMES W. GREEN: 1 carriage

JAMES LATIMORE: 1 carriage

ALEXANDER MEBANE: 1 carriage

W. T. MONTGOMERY: 1 carriage

J. C. SHEELE: 1 carriage

JAMES TITUS: 1 carriage
    (See entry under Notables and Heroes of the Republic.)

Robertson County

H. DIXON: 1 carriage

W. D. MOORE: 1 carriage

A. W. NAILON: 1 carriage

L. A. STROUD: 1 carriage

JAMES WARREN: 1 carriage

San Augustine County

JOHN C. BROOKS: 1 four-wheel carriage

JOHN CARTWRIGHT: 1 carriage
    (See entry under Notables and Heroes of the Republic.)

NICHOLAS HENRY DARNELL: 1 four-wheel carriage
    (See entry under Notables and Heroes of the Republic.)

W. W. FRIZZELL: 1 four-wheel carriage

THOMAS H. GARNER: 1 carriage

H. W. GAYNES: 1 four-wheel carriage

ALEXANDER HORTON: 1 four-wheel carriage
    (See under Officers at San Jacinto, entry No. 6.)

DAVID KENDLY: 2 racehorses

SAMUEL NEEDHAM: 1 four-wheel carriage

GEORGE A. NIXON: 1 two-wheel sulky
    Possibly the Major George A. Nixon, land commissioner for the
Galveston Bay and Texas Land Company after 1835, who later is recorded as having settled in Jasper County adjoining San Augustine.

W. B. PATTERSON: 1 four-wheel carriage

C. PAYNE: 1 four-wheel carriage

JAMES ROWE: 1 four-wheel carriage

WILLIAM J. SNEED: 1 four-wheel carriage

SAMUEL STIVERS: 1 beroche (*sic*) and 1 gig

J. D. THOMAS: 1 four-wheel carriage

B. J. THOMPSON: 1 four-wheel carriage

JOHN WOODS: 1 racehorse; 1 four-wheel carriage

359

*The
Carriage
Trade
of the
Republic*

Shelby County

JOHN S. BELL: 1 carriage
   Represented Shelby County in the Fifth Congress.

G. W. LUSK: 1 carriage

H. L. WIGGINS: 1 carriage

Travis County

ASA BINGHAM: 1 carriage

MIRABEAU BUONAPARTE LAMAR: 1 pleasure carriage
   (See under Officers at San Jacinto, entry No. 22.)

JAMES SMITH: 1 carriage

WILLIAM B. SWEENEY: 1 carriage

SAMUEL WHITING: 1 carriage
   (See entry under Notables and Heroes of the Republic.)

Victoria County

WILLIAM C. BLAIR: 1 carriage
   Blair was a Presbyterian noted for establishing Aranama College, which helped fulfill his ambition of bringing better education to Mexicans.

CORNELIUS LANE: 2 carriages

Washington County

R. T. ARMSTEAD: 1 carriage

SAMUEL P. BROWN: 1 carriage

W. CHAMLISS: 1 carriage

HORATIO CHRISMAN: 1 carriage
    Chrisman was surveyor for Stephen Austin's colony from 1823 to 1836, and a member of the Old Three Hundred.

JOHN P. COLES: 1 carriage
    Coles was a member of the Old Three Hundred. Represented Washington County, 1840–1841.

JOSIAH J. CROSBY: 1 carriage

JOHN DIX: 1 carriage

FRANKLIN & GORDEN: 1 carriage

CAPTAIN FULLER: 1 carriage

J. L. FURGERSON: 1 carriage

JOHN W. ("CAPTAIN JACK") HALL: 1 carriage
    (See entry under Notables and Heroes of the Republic.)

J. R. HINDS: 1 carriage

ASA HOXEY: 1 carriage
    (See entry under Notables and Heroes of the Republic.)

J. H. JONES: 1 carriage

JOEL LEE: 1 carriage

R. A. LOTT: 1 carriage

JAMES LYNCH: 1 carriage

JOHN MCNEESE: 1 carriage

IVY MCNESSE: 1 carriage

SHUBAEL MARSH: 1 carriage
    Marsh was a member of the Old Three Hundred. Married Lucinda Pitts. Died in 1865.

MASON MOSELEY: 1 carriage

ROOT & TAYLOR: 1 carriage

VII

The "Old Three Hundred"

Moses Austin was by birth a New Englander, whose business interests became wide-ranging, eventually culminating in a grant from the Spanish Empire to settle 300 families on an area of some 200,000 acres of Texas. This was granted in March 1821, but he died the following June. Completion of the project was left to his son, Stephen Fuller Austin, who had become a judge in Arkansas. Stephen Austin developed the project further with the Spanish authorities, although it became delayed by Mexican independence, and the formal details were not resolved until 1824. He followed this by arrangements to bring in a further 300 in each of the years 1825, 1827, and 1828. By 1832, Austin's colonies numbered some 8,000 people, but nonetheless the "Old Three Hundred" had been the pioneers, although even they were not among the first "Anglo-American" settlements in Texas.

Like so many records of Texas at this time, the records are incomplete, and are debated. The following is based upon the list in the General Land Office in Austin, which is the official record. It includes some

330 names (see Notables and Heroes of the Republic and other sections for the more illustrious members), but some of these were probably members of a single family, and in any event it is well established that Austin regularly exceeded his quotas. Politically, Austin favored a continued existence within Mexico rather than independence, and only one of the "Old Three Hundred" signed the Declaration of Independence. This is perhaps understandable. Most of the chief protagonists of independence were newcomers who had no Mexican land grants to lose if they lost the fight, and everything to gain, whereas Austin's colony owed everything to Mexico.

Allcorn, Elijah	Bloodgood, William	Chance, Samuel
Allen, Martin	Boatwright, Thomas	Chrisman, Horatio
Alley, John	Borden, Thomas H.	Clarke, Anthony R.
Alley, Rawson	Bostick, Caleb R.	Clarke, John C.
Alley, Thomas	Bowman, John	Coats, Merit M.
Alley, William	Bradley, Edward R.	Coles, John P.
Alsbery, Charles G.	Bradley, John	Cooke, James
Alsbery, Harvey	Bradley, Thomas	Cooke, John
Alsbery, Horace A.	Breen, Charles	Cooper, William
Alsbery, Thomas	Bridges, William B.	Crier, John
Anderson, Simon Asa	Bright, David	Crownover, John
Andrews, John	Brooks, Bluford	Cummins, James
Andrews, William	Brotherton, Robert	Cummins, John
Angier, Samuel T.	Brown, George	Cummins, Rebecca
Austin, John	Brown, John	Cummins, William
Austin, Stephen F.	Brown, William S.	Curtis, Hinton
Baily, James B.	Buckner, Aylett C.	Curtis, James
Barrett, William	Bunson, Enoch	Curtis, James, Sr.
Battle, Mills M.	Burnet, Thomas	Davidson, Samuel
Bayless, Daniel E.	Burnham, Jesse	Davis, Thomas
Beard, James	Byrd, Micajah	Deckro, Daniel
Beason, Benjamin	Callahan, Morris	Demos, Peter
Belknap, Charles	Calvit, Alexander	Dewees, Bluford
Bell, Josiah H.	Carpenter, David	Dickenson, John
Bell, Thomas B.	Carson, William C.	Dillard, Nicholas
Berry, Manders	Carter, Samuel	Duke, Thomas
Best, Isaac	Cartwright, Jesse	Duty, Joseph
Betts, Jacob	Cartwright, Thomas	Dyer, Clement C.
Bigham, Francis	Castleman, Sylvanus	Earle, Thomas

Edwards, Gustavus E.
Elam, John
Elder, Robert
Falmash, Charles
Fenton, David
Fields, John T.
Fisher, James
Fitzgerald, David
Flannakin, Isaiah
Flowers, Elisha
Foster, Isaac
Foster, John
Foster, Randolph
Frazier, James
Fulcher, Churchill
Garrett, Charles
Gates, Samuel
Gates, William
George, Freeman
Gilbert, Sarah
Gilleland, Daniel
Gorbet, Chester S.
Gouldrich, Michael
Grey, Thomas
Groce, Jared E.
Guthrie, Robert
Hadden, John
Hady, Samuel C.
Hall, John
Hall, William
Hamilton, David
Hansley, James
Harris, Abner
Harris, David
Harris, John R.
Harris, P.
Harris, William
Harris, William J.
Harrison, George
Harvey, William
Haynes, Thomas B.

Hill, George B.
Hodge, Alexander
Holland, Francis
Holland, William
Holliman, Kirchen
Hope, James
Hudson, Charles S.
Huff, George
Huff, John
Hughes, Isaac
Hunter, Eli
Hunter, Johnson
Ingram, Ira
Ingram, Seth
Irams, John
Irions, John
Isaac, Jackson
Isaacs, Samuel
Jackson, Alexander
Jackson, Humphrey
Jameson, Thomas
Johnson, H. W.
Johnson, Walker
Jones, Henry
Jones, James
Jones, Oliver
Jones, Randall
Keep, Imla
Keller, John
Kelley, John
Kennedy, Samuel
Kennon, Alfred
Kerr, James
Kew, Peter
Kew, William
Kincheloe, William
Kingston, William
Knight, James
Kuykendall, Abner
Kuykendall, Brazilla
Kuykendall, Joseph

Kuykendall, Robert
Lakey, Joel
Leayne, Hosea H.
Linsay, Benjamin
Little, John
Little, William
Long, Jane H.
Lynch, James
Lynch, Nathaniel
Marsh, Shubart
Martin, Wyley
Mathis, William
McCloskey, John
McCormick, Arthur
McCormick, David
McCormick, John
McCoy, Thomas
McFarland, Achilles
McFarland, John
McKensie, Hugh
McKinney, Thomas F.
McLain, A. W.
McNair, James
McNeil, Daniel
McNeil, George W.
McNeil, John
McNeil, Pleasant D.
McNeil, Sterling
McNeill, John G.
McNutt, Elizabeth
McWilliams, William
Milburn, David H.
Miller, Samuel
Miller, Samuel R.
Miller, Simon
Millican, James D.
Millican, Robert
Millican, William
Mims, Joseph
Mitchell, Asa
Monks, John

Moore, John W.
Moore, Luke
Morrison, Moses
Morser, David
Morton, William
Nelson, James
Newman, Joseph
Nidever, Charles Isaac
Nuckels, M. B.
Orrick, James
Osborn, Nathan
Park, William
Parker, Joshua
Parker, William
Pennington, Isaac
Pentecost, George S.
Pettus, Freeman
Pettus, William
Petty, John
Peyton, Jonathan C.
Phelps, James, A. E.
Phillips, Ishan B.
Phillips, Zeno
Picket, Pamela
Polley, Joseph H.
Powell, Peter
Prator, William
Print, Pleasant
Pryor, William
Rabb, Andrew
Rabb, Thomas
Rabb, William
Raleigh, William
Ramey, Lawrence
Randon, David
Randon, John
Rankin, Frederick
Rawls, Amos
Rawls, Benjamin
Rawls, Daniel
Reels, Patrick

Richardson, Stephen
Roark, Elijah
Robbins, Early
Robbins, William
Roberts, Andrew
Roberts, Noel F.
Roberts, William
Robertson, Edward
Robinson, Andrew
Robinson, George
Ross, James
Rubb, John
San Pierre, Joseph
Scobey, Robert
Scott, James
Scott, William
Selkirk, William
Shelley, David
Shipman, Daniel
Shipman, Moses
Sims, Bartlett
Singleton, George W.
Singleton, Phillip
Smith, Christian
Smith, Cornelius
Smith, John
Smithers, William
Sojourner, A. L.
Spencer, Nancy
Stafford, Adam
Stafford, William
Stevens, Thomas
Stout, Owen H.
Strange, James
Strawsnider, Gabriel
Sutherland, Walter
Talley, David
Tayler, John D.
Teel, George
Thomas, Ezekiel
Thomas, Jacob

Thompson, Jesse
Tone, Thomas J.
Tong, James F.
Toy, Samuel
Trobough, John
Tumlinson, Elizabeth
Tumlinson, James
Van Dorn, Isaac
Varner, Martin
Vince, Allen
Vince, Richard
Vince, Robert
Vince, William
Walker, James
Wallace, Caleb
Wells, Francis F.
Westall, Thomas
White, Annie
White, Joseph
White, Reuben
White, Walter C.
White, William C.
Whitesides, Bouldin
Whitesides, Henry
Whitesides, James
Whiting, Nathaniel
Whitlock, William
Wightman, Elias R.
Wilkins, Jane
Williams, George T.
Williams, Henry
Williams, John
Williams, John, Jr.
Williams, John R.
Williams, Robert H.
Williams, Samuel M.
Williams, Solomon
Williams, Thomas
Woods, Zadock

Index of
Texas Family Names